# Black Music in the United States

An Annotated Bibliography
of Selected Reference
and Research Materials

# Black Music in the United States

An Annotated Bibliography
of Selected Reference
and Research Materials

SAMUEL A. FLOYD, JR.
MARSHA J. REISSER

**KRAUS INTERNATIONAL PUBLICATIONS**
Millwood, New York • London, England • Schaan, Liechtenstein
A Division of Kraus-Thomson Organization Limited

First printing 1983
Second printing 1984

94848

Printed in the United States of America

Library of Congress Cataloging in Publication Data

Floyd, Samuel A.
  Black music in the United States.

  Includes indexes.
    1. Afro-Americans—Music—Bibliography.
I. Reisser, Marsha J.   II. Title.
ML128.B45F6 1983     781.7′296073     82-49044
ISBN 0-527-30164-7

# Contents

Contents

Contents

# Introduction

This book is an organized survey of research materials and archives related to black American music. It is designed for research at the undergraduate level, to aid the inexperienced researcher in locating materials and information; it may also serve as a reference tool for mature black music specialists. In addition, this bibliography will be found to be useful for other scholars, teachers at all levels, and interested laymen. The work is not meant to be all-inclusive; rather, it is a basic guide designed to facilitate the selection of appropriate materials from the large number of available sources. Three types of content materials are included: 1) those that are directly related to black music in the United States, i.e., blues, ragtime, jazz, spirituals, concert music, etc.; 2) those that discuss syncretization or fusion processes involving African music and music of the Americas; and 3) those not limited to black music but which are nevertheless important general research tools for scholars of black American music.

Our basic sources for identifying books to be included have been the various appropriate bibliographies, discographies, and bibliographies of bibliographies and discographies; the Subject Guide to Books in Print; and Forthcoming Books. Our basic surces for locating books have been the National Union Catalog, Music, Books on Music and Phonograph Records, and the OCLC Data Base.

We have attempted to include the latest edition or printing of each book. When the most recent versions were not available, we annotated those that were accessible. Readers are urged to secure the latest editions of each work utilized. We have undoubtedly included some sources that will be obsolete, due to the publication of newer and better works by the time this book is released; these newer sources will be included in future editions of this bibliography.

Each bibliographical entry in this volume includes the following information: 1) name(s) of author(s), editor(s), or compiler(s); 2) full title and subtitle; 3) name(s) of author(s) of introduction, preface, or foreword; 4) series title; 5) volume number; 6) edition number; 7) reprint information; 8) place of publication; 9) publisher's name; 10) date; 11) number of both Roman and Arabic pages included; 12) illustrative matter; 13) appendixes; 14) bibliographies; 15) discographies; and 16) indexes. The annotations include statements relating to each item's purpose, organization, presentation of material, usability, and special features.

A selected list of review citations follows the book annotations where appropriate. Each of the citations includes the following information as it is applicable: name of periodical; volume number; page number; and the month, date, and year of publication, or series number and year of publication. Periodical titles are given as they appear in the source index, except that subtitles have been deleted. The basic information contained in the citations is also retained from the source index. The citations were taken from Book Review Index, Current Book Reviews, National Library Service Cumulative Book Review Index, 1950-1974, and Music Index; they cover the year of the entry work's publication and the two years following.

Numbered consecutively throughout the book, the annotations are presented in seventeen sections and, in the case of books, are listed alphabetically by author's last name. Record entries are listed alphabetically by album or set title; each includes the city and name of the company, the label number, the number of records in the album or set, the name of the author of the jacket, liner, or booklet notes, and other available pertinent information. Repository entries are presented alphabetically by state, within each state by city, and within each city by the name of the archive.

Generally, we have refrained from commenting on the quality of the annotated items, except when such comment has been directly related to an item's use. As an aid to judging the quality of any of the books listed in this volume, users may consult the reviews cited at the end of each annotation.

The information contained in our repository descriptions is essentially that which was provided by the repository respondents themselves, on a form designed and provided by the authors. Their completeness, therefore, has been determined both by the effectiveness of the form and by the thoroughness of the respondents' replies. In the descriptions, all numbers that describe the contents of collections are approximate.

Users seeking particular resources may find them by four different routes: the direct route (by way of the various chapters themselves) and the three indexes. When seeking sources related to particular areas of study, the Subject Index is the appropriate route. It lists the names of musical genres, styles, events, and movements contained in the citations and in the annotations. For example, by consulting this index for sources appropriate to concert music, the user will be referred to items in several chapters of the book, achieving access to specific sources of bibliography, discography, history, survey, photo collections, pedagogy, printed music, and recorded music of, on, or related to black "classical" music in the United States. The Author Index can be consulted when the name of an author, editor, or compiler of a source is known. The Title Index may be used to determine the exact locations of the specific titles annotated in the book. The book's indexes, then, are not simply convenient appendages. Designed to give quick and efficient entry to a wide variety of specific items of need and interest, they are meant to be integral to the work and vital to its use.

Currently available are four bibliographies devoted exclusively to the general study of black American music. Bibliographic Guide to the Study of Afro-American Music (Washington, D.C.: Howard University Libraries, 1973) by James Peter Johnson is an excellent source; however, it is limited to "primarily the 'folk' and 'popular' music of black people" (p. [3]). The book does not contain annotations, although the author indicates that annotations and other explanatory notes will be included in a future edition.

JoAnn Skowronski's Black Music in America: A Bibliography will be useful to researchers seeking bibliographical sources for the study of certain specific individual musicians and for those who wish to explore general research topics in a broad way. Its lack of annotations and selectivity limit its usefulness beyond such basic studies. Dominique René de Lerma's multi-volume Bibliography of Black Music catalogues more than 90,000 sources of information. It includes books, journal articles, theses, dissertations, journals, and other source materials. It is not selective and does not contain annotations; it may therefore be a formidable tool for the beginning researcher. In our opinion, however, de Lerma's set will be an excellent complement to our annotated work, and, vice versa.

David Horn's The Literature of American Music in Books and Folk Collections: A Fully Annotated Bibliography (Metuchen, N.J.: Scarecrow Press, 1977) is one of several general American music bibliographies that contain sections devoted exclusively to black American music. Horn's book is cited here because its listing of books on black American music is one of the most extensive available. The main limitation of the work is that it does not list periodicals, archives, anthologies, or records; another weakness is that it contains entries that are only peripheral to the subject. For example, under his "Black Music" rubric, there are 250 entries, but among the first thirty-three there is not a single book about music. The annotations are excellent, but in its attempt to be all-inclusive, the section tends to be self-defeating. The listings on jazz and blues, for example, are too extensive to be useful to an inexperienced researcher.

The need for the present book became clear when work began on a project, conducted by one of the authors, to develop an anthology of printed music entitled "Music by Black American Composers: An Anthology." The amount of research necessary to locate materials for the anthology was inordinate and, as the project progressed, the necessity for a basic reference guide became more and more apparent. The discovered information about research materials and archives related to black American music, and the desirability of a tool to facilitate their use, necessitated the preparation and publication of the present volume.

The hospitality and services of a number of libraries were graciously offered during the preparation of this book. The Fisk University Library, the music library at Vanderbilt University, the library of the Country Music Foundation, all in Nashville, Tennessee; and Mills Music Library at the University of Wisconsin and the library of the State Historical Society of Wisconsin in Madison were our primary sources of books and records. Next in importance, where access to sources is concerned, were the Library of Congress in Washington, D.C., and the Institute of Jazz Studies at Rutgers University in Newark, New Jersey. Many other libraries assisted by allowing the use of items either on-location or via interlibrary loan. We extend our thanks to all.

Individuals representing the repositories listed in our final chapter graciously responded to our requests for information describing their archives. Without their help, Part XVII would not be a part of this book. We are grateful for their cooperation and assistance.

The assistance of the following graduate students at the University of Wisconsin-Madison was invaluable in the preparation of the review citations: Mike Allsen, Ruth Mack, Beth Robin, Patricia Ann Severt, Jean Marie Staral, and Bruce C. Stark. We are grateful for the expert and inestimable assistance of our proofreader, Jean Bonin.

Several publishers graciously provided us with books, easing our task considerably. Although upon later reflection a small number of these books were not included in this edition, we thank all of the publishers sincerely, and list them here alphabetically: AMS Press, American Library Association, Cassell, Da Capo Press, Dover Publications, Free Press, Garland Publishers, Greenwood Press, International Publishers Co., Jazzmedia, Robert E. Krieger Publishing Co., Libraries Unlimited, Louisiana State University Press, Macmillan Publishing Co., Reese Markowich, W. W. Norton & Co., Prentice-Hall, Scarecrow Press, Seabury Press, Shoe String Press, Temple University Press, University of Iowa Press, and University of Massachusetts Press.

Some of the works annotated in this volume are currently out-of-print, although they do remain accessible. Perhaps this publication, and whatever research may be generated by it, will cause them to be reprinted.

It is our hope that Black Music in the United States will provide guidance that has previously been unavailable, stimulate additional research, and contribute to the advancement of black music scholarship.

## Of Omissions and Auxiliary Sources

Auxiliary sources—works that will serve the researcher in an adjunct capacity—have not been included in this work. We have chosen to treat them separately as follows: 1) to comment on the more closely related sources in this foreword and reconsider their inclusion after this book has been tested in the field, and 2) to provide an annotated listing of the more general, but equally important, sources in an appendix to the work.

Introduction

We realize that much valuable and crucial information can be found in sources that are devoted primarily to fields other than music. Such works as Lawrence Levine's Black Culture and Black Consciousness (Oxford University Press, 1977), Eugene Genovese's Roll, Jordan, Roll (Random House, 1976), Monroe N. Work's Negro Year Book (Sunday School Union Print and Negro Year Book, 1912-1952), Norman E. Whitten and John F. Szwed's Afro-American Anthropology (Free Press, 1970), as well as many others, are indispensable to thorough and comprehensive research in Afro-American music. However, they have all been omitted in the interest of time and focus because they more properly belong in other sources, and because of the constraints of long-distance collaboration. Researchers will be able to identify and locate such sources by consulting Walter Schatz's Directory of Afro-American Resources (which we have included in our section on "General Guides and Directories"), and other appropriate finding aids.

Scholars will want to consult books on general American music history, if only to see how black music is treated in such sources. Among the few of these books that give more than token treatment to the subject are: Edith Borroff's Music in Europe and the United States (Prentice-Hall, 1971), Gilbert Chase's America's Music: From the Pilgrims to the Present (McGraw-Hill, 1966), William Austin's Music in the 20th Century (W. W. Norton, 1966), and John Tasker Howard's Our American Music: A Comprehensive History from 1620 to the Present (T. Y. Crowell, 1965). Information on the early black composers and bandsmen of Philadelphia such as Frank Johnson, James Hemmenway, and others, can be found in the following works: A History of Philadelphia, 1609-1885 by Thomas J. Scharf and Thompson Wescott (H. Everts & Co., 1884), Music in Philadelphia by Robert A. Gerson (1940, reprinted by Greenwood Press, 1970), and William Carter White's A History of Military Music in America (1944, reprinted by Greenwood Press, 1975). Important early black musicians of New Orleans are discussed in Henry A. Kmen's Music in New Orleans: The Formative Years, 1791-1841 (Louisiana State University Press, 1966).

Books on African music have been omitted since information about such works more properly belongs in a bibliography devoted to African music or arts. Researchers seeking introductory materials on African music might start with a survey such as The Music of Africa by J. H. Kwabena Nketia (W. W. Norton & Co., 1974), a finding aid such as Douglas Varley's African Native Music: An Annotated Bibliography (Humanities Press, 1970), a discography such as Alan Merriam's African Music on LP: An Annotated Discography (Northwestern University Press, 1970), and other works that can be found by consulting appropriate bibliographies, discographies, and other works. Users will note, however, that several of the books included in the present volume do treat African music as it relates to Afro-American music; a case in point is Paul Oliver's Savannah Syncopators: African Retentions in the Blues (entry no. 185). For Latin American connections, researchers will want to begin with surveys such as Music in Latin America: An Introduction (Prentice-Hall, 1979) by Gerard Béhague, Music in the Americas (Indiana University, 1967) by George List and Juan Orrego-Salas, and Folk and Traditional Music of the Western Continents by Bruno Nettl (Prentice-Hall, 1973), and finding sources such as Ralph Boggs' Bibliography of Latin American Folklore (H. W. Wilson,

1940). John Storm Roberts' Black Music of Two Worlds (Praeger, 1972), which treats music in all of the Americas, is annotated in the present volume (entry no. 147).

The question of whether to include works of individual biography was a difficult one. Books such as W. C. Handy's Father of the Blues (1941, reprinted in paperback by Collier Books, 1970), Geneva Southall's series on Blind Tom (Challenge Productions, 1979), Willie "The Lion" Smith's Music on My Mind: The Memoirs of an American Pianist (1965, reprinted by Da Capo Press, 1975), are valuable sources of information. In the end, however, we found it necessary to limit the number of books in our "Biographies" section to collective sources, omitting those that are devoted to fewer than three individuals. Researchers seeking biographical information can easily identify individual biographies by consulting sources listed in Part III.

Works of jazz discography are rather numerous, and their contents redundant. Only the primary and necessary ones are annotated in the present work.

Eileen Southern's new book, Biographical Dictionary of Afro-American and African Musicians, will have a large impact on biographical and other research. Such previously valuable sources as Thomas Yenser's Who's Who in Colored America (Who's Who in Colored America Corp., 1927) and William J. Simmon's Men of Mark (1887, reprinted by Arno Press, 1968) have been made virtually obsolete by the publication of Southern's work. These older and more general sources have not been included in the present work.

The "how to" books of jazz have been left out also, although they sometimes will be useful to researchers. Examples are David N. Baker's Jazz Improvisation: A Comprehensive Method for All Players (Maher, 1969), George Russell's The Lydian Chromatic Concept of Tonal Organization for Improvisation (Russ-Hix Music Co., 1959), Jamey Aebersold's A New Approach to Jazz Improvisation (Aebersold, 1969), Russell Garcia's The Professional Arranger-Composer (Criterion, 1968), and William Russo's Composing for the Jazz Orchestra (University of Chicago Press, 1961). Other such guides can be identified by consulting Eddie Meadows' Jazz Reference and Research Materials (entry no. 49).

Scholars studying art songs by black composers will sometimes find it necessary to consult and investigate the writings of poets whose works have been set to music. Useful in this regard are Daniel Hoffman's Harvard Guide to Contemporary American Writing (Harvard, 1979) and Dorothy Chapman's Index to Black Poetry (G. K. Hall, 1974). Some researchers will also require sources of oral history; Alan M. Meckler's Oral History Collections (Bowker, 1975) is a major source for such information.

A wide variety of trade and scholarly periodicals carry articles on or related to black American music. These range from general publications such as Melody Maker (trade) and Ethnomusicology (scholarly) to Blues and Soul and The Journal of Negro History. Nearly all of these publications carry only occasional pieces useful to most researchers of black American music, while others will carry many. We have chosen to limit our selections to currently published scholarly journals and newsletters that devote all or significant portions of their space to black music. Researchers will want to consult Joan Meggett's Music Periodical Literature: An Annotated Bibliography of Indexes and Bibliographies (entry no. 26) and other sources for the identity of additional journals of potential use.

Theses and dissertations have also been excluded. The sheer number and nature of such works suggest that they warrant a separate volume of their own. Researchers can identify and locate dissertations by consulting Dissertation Abstracts International, Cecil Adkins' International Index of Disssertations, Rita Meade's Doctoral Dissertations in American Music, and two sources published by University Microfilms International: Music: A Dissertation Bibliography and Black Studies: A Bibliography.

Musical recordings and their accompanying notes are valuable research sources. Only the most general of these resources are included here. Listed in Part XVI, therefore, are collections and albums that are of general application in the several categories listed. Researchers seeking more specific items should consult Part V for sources for appropriate recordings. But let us note that CRI's (Composers Recordings, Inc.) "Music of the Twentieth Century" recordings include concert music by at least eight black composers. The CRI catalogue indexes them separately for the convenience of its users. Cespico Records' Black Artists Series (CR-77001—CR-77006) unfortunately could not be obtained in time for its inclusion in Part XVI; its six albums feature six nationally acclaimed black performers presenting works by both black and white composers.

With regard to repository collections, we felt that some of those considered were too specialized for our purposes. The repositories selected for description in our book are those that are more comprehensive in scope. Researchers seeking repositories housing collections on specific individuals, or on particular black colleges, will find it profitable to consult the index to Resources in American Music History (University of Illinois Press, 1981) by D. W. Krummel, Jean Geil, Doris Dyen, and Deane L. Root.

The quest for certainty about black music will lead the researcher to additional sources and into uncharted regions. This quest and the knowledge resulting from it are the real and ultimate fruits of scholarship. Perhaps this book can enhance them both.

# Annotated
# Bibliography

# I

# General Guides

## *DIRECTORIES*

1. Briegleb, Ann, ed. <u>Directory of Ethnomusicological Sound Recording Collections in the U.S. and Canada.</u> Special Series, no. 2. Ann Arbor, Mich.: Society for Ethnomusicology, 1971. 46 pp. bibliography. index.

>    This guide to sound-recording collections is arranged alphabetically by state or province, then by city, and by name of the collection or collector. Each entry contains the following information where appropriate: collection name, address, telephone number, name of the librarian, hours open to the public, a list of the number and types of playback equipment available, and a brief description of the holdings of the collection. Among the collections listed are the John D. Reid Collection, Arhoolie Records, the John Edwards Memorial Foundation, the Institute of Jazz Studies, and the Schomberg Collection, all of which are pertinent to black music research. The index is a guide to the "Geographical Content of the Collections."

2. De Lerma, Dominique-René. <u>A Name List of Black Composers.</u> AAMOA Resource Papers. Minneapolis: AAMOA Press, 1973. iv, 76 pp.

>    This is a collection of 1,813 names of black composers of concert music, jazz, blues, gospel and spiritual songs, and other musical genres. Arranged alphabetically by composer's last name, each entry carries the individual's full name, with any alternate version in parentheses, and date of birth and/or death. Including the names of figures from Africa and South America, as well as from the

3

2. De Lerma (<u>continued</u>)

United States, this provisional list is a useful tool for scholars of black music, especially for verifying the racial identities of composers.

3. Felton, Gary S.  <u>The Record Collector's International Directory</u>.  New York: Crown Publishers, 1980.  xviii, 365 pp.  indexes.

This guide is the best source for researchers seeking sound-recordings that are not available through the usual outlets.  The work lists the names and addresses of more than one thousand record dealers and stores that carry rare, discontinued, or hard-to-locate recordings of jazz, blues, gospel, rock, country and western, and other musical performances.  Each entry carries all pertinent information, including the dealer's name, address, and telephone number; days and hours of operation; services available (i.e., walk-in, mail order, search, lending library); specialties; stock volume; and ordering information.  The book's "Index of Record Dealers Listed by Category of Recording" lists among its 110 categories at least fifteen that are particularly pertinent to black music research, including Boogie Woogie, Folk, Motown, Ragtime, Reggae, Soul, and Vocal Jazz.
Reviews:  American Reference Books Annual 12:454 '81; Library Journal 105:1721 S 1 '80; Reference Services Review 9:44 Ap '81; Wilson Library Bulletin 55:300 D '80

4. Mapp, Edward.  <u>Directory of Blacks in the Performing Arts</u>.  Metuchen, N.J.:  Scarecrow Press, 1978.  xv, 428 pp.  appendix.  bibliography.  index.

Consisting of biographical information on more than "850 black individuals, living and deceased, who have earned a degree of recognition for their work in the performing arts" (p. x), the volume is arranged in alphabetical order by the last names of the performers.  The information in each entry is presented under as many as eighteen rubrics:  name; category of career, such as actor, composer, concert singer, jazz musician, etc.; dates of birth and death; education; special interests; address; honors; career data; clubs; films; memberships; musical compositions; publications; radio; records; television; theater; and "relationships."  The appendix is a "Directory of Organizations."  The index lists the performers included in the book; it is organized into twenty-six career categories.
Reviews:  American Reference Books Annual 10:498 '79; Booklist 76:572 D 1 '79; Choice 16:205 Ap '79; Library Journal 103:1730 S 15 '78; Library Journal 104:885 Ap 15 '79; Wilson Library Bulletin 53:344 D '78

5. National Alliance of Businessmen.  <u>Directory of Predominantly Black Colleges and Universities in the United States of America</u>.  Washington D.C.:  National Alliance of Businessmen, [1971].  91 pp.

4

5. National Alliance (<u>continued</u>)

      Researchers concerned with the musical activities of historically black colleges will find this book a valuable source of the names of such schools and their addresses. Entries of eighty-seven colleges and universities, are arranged in alphabetical order by the name of the institution. The information contained in each entry includes the school's address and telephone number; the names of the officers at the time of publication; enrollment information; a summary of the degrees offered and the numbers of the various degrees granted ca. 1966-1971; a brief description of the school; and a list of the association(s) with whom the institution is affiliated. Also included in the book are a list of four-year schools arranged by geographical location, and a list of those schools that are supported and controlled by city or state government. The book will be useful as a source of information for scholars who are investigating topics such as the presence and activities of gospel choirs on black campuses, biographical information about a composer or artists who may have attended a predominantly black college or university, the activities of alumni of such institutions, comparison of the musical activities of historically black and white institutions in a given location, or other subjects related to higher education.

      Reviews: Wilson Library Bulletin 47:416 Ja '73

6. Schatz, Walter, ed.  <u>Directory of Afro-American Resources</u>.  New York: R. R. Bowker Co., 1970. xv, 485 pp. bibliography. index.

      Collections of primary source materials related to black history and the black experience are listed in this volume. Included are holdings of libraries, civil rights groups, radical organizations, and government or private agencies. The listings are arranged alphabetically by state, city, institution, and name of the collections themselves. Each entry includes the address, telephone number, the name of the director or librarian in charge of the collection, services offered, and sometimes a brief description of the archive. This information is accompanied by a description of the archive holdings. When appropriate, each entry carries a list of publications issued by the institution. Although much of the work describes collections whose holdings do not relate directly to black American music and musicians, this book is a useful tool for pinpointing the locations of pertinent collections in particular locales.

      Reviews:  American Archivist 34:385 O '71; Bibliographical Society of America—Papers 65:432 O '71; English Journal 62:153 Ja '73; Journal of Negro History 56:300 O '71; Library Journal 95:821 Mr 1 '71; Wilson Library Journal 45:783 Ap '71

## *RESEARCH TOOLS*

7. Irvine, Demar.  <u>Writing About Music: A Style Book for Reports and Theses</u>.  2nd ed.  Seattle:  University of Washington Press, 1956.  xiii,

7. Irvine (continued)

211 pp. musical examples. appendix. bibliography. index.

This style manual is a valuable aid to anyone who is writing about
music. The book is divided into two sections: "Style in the Typescript" and "Writing Skills." In addition to the topics treated by
other style manuals (proper spacing, punctuation, footnotes, and
bibliographies), the first section contains guidelines for the
treatment of the special bibliographic problems of music
scholarship—the documentation of musical editions, manuscripts,
facsimilies, sound recordings and iconographic material in
footnotes; the use of foreign words in English text; and the proper
treatment of music examples. This first section also contains
guidelines for the styling of titles of various kinds of musical works,
as well as definitions of English, Latin, French, and German
abbreviations commonly found in discussions of music. Writing
About Music is al-so unique among style manuals in the depth of
detail contained in its second section. Not only does the section
contain instructions for handling direct quotations of information
and in organizing a re-search paper, but also includes guidelines for
sentence and para-graph structure; discussion of the functions of
individual words; dis-cussion of the "Control of Literary Style;" and
suggestions on writing for various purposes, including the
publication of program notes, reviews, articles, and books. To
illustrate the rules and guides given in the book, the appendix
contains sample pages of a research paper.

Reviews: Journal of Research in Music Education 5:59 Spring
'57

## RESEARCH METHODOLOGY

8. Hood, Mantle. The Ethnomusicologist. Foreword by Charles Seeger.
McGraw-Hill Series in Music. New York: McGraw-Hill Book Co., 1971.
xii, 386 pp. drawings, photographs, musical examples. index.
phonograph records.

Although much of The Ethnomusicologist is devoted to matters that
will not concern the researcher of black American music, the author's statement that "The attitudes of different societies and of
different groups within society toward the arts vary widely" (p. 9) is
sufficient to qualify this title as a candidate for inclusion in the
present volume. On the other hand, in spite of Hood's statement
that ". . . it was the American Negro's contribution to jazz that produced the blues" (p. 14), his book is useful because it describes the
responsibilities, procedures, and the techniques of the scholar of
ethnomusicology and discusses possible solutions to the problems of
transcribing music which deviates from the strict practices of
European concert music. Although the author devotes his attention
to the researching of Eastern cultures, he presents his material in a
manner which makes obvious its potential value for the beginning
field researcher of black folk music. Particularly useful is the

8. Hood (continued)

> Introduction and the chapters on "Field Methods and the Human
> Equation", "Field Methods and the Technical Equation", and
> "Scientific Methods and the Laboratory."
>> Reviews:  AB Bookman's Weekly 48:516 S 6 '71; American
>> Anthropologist 75:1062 Au '73; Choice 8:1517 Ja '72; Music
>> Educators Journal 59:145 O '72; Musical Quarterly 58:136 Ja
>> '72; Musical Times 113:863 S '72; Yearbook for Inter-American
>> Musical Research 7:161 '71; Yearbook of the International Folk
>> Music Council 3:146 '71

9. Krummel, D. W., comp.  Guide for Dating Early Music:  A Manual of
   Bibliographical Practices.  Hackensack, N.J.:  Joseph Boonin; Kassel:
   Barenreiter Verlag, 1974.  267 pp.  facsimilies.  index.

> While much of the information contained in this book is not
> pertinent to black American music, a researcher working with pre-
> Civil War sheet music will find it a valuable tool for determining
> dates of publication. The book has three parts: the Preface, which
> discusses the need for dating and general information about early
> editions; the Synopsis, which discusses such topics as plate numbers,
> publisher's addresses, copyright and registration, and house
> practices; and National Reports, which makes up more than one-
> half of the book and contains specific information about early
> publishers and publications in eighteen nations. The section about
> the United States contains the following subsections: Summaries
> and Bibliographies, Directories, Important Names, Plate Numbers,
> Catalogues, Copyright, Announcements, Design & Printing Practice,
> and Important Collections.
>> Reviews:  Brio 12:18-19 '75; Choice 11:1716 F '75; Fontes Artis
>> Musicae 22:158-159 '75; Journal of the American Musicological
>> Society 29:138-140 '76; Library 5th series 32:75 Mr '77; Library
>> Journal 100:746 Ap 15 '75; Library Quarterly 45:317 Jy '75;
>> Music and Letters 57:175-176 '76; Musikhandel 26:154 '75;
>> Notes 32:533-555 Mr '76

10. Metfessel, Milton.  Phonophotography in Folk Music.  Introduction by
    Carl E. Seashore.  Chapel Hill:  University of North Carolina Press,
    1928.  x, 181 pp.  bibliography.  index for meanings of terms.

> In spite of some unreliable generalizations and dated information
> owing to its early publication, this book is useful for the researcher
> of black American folk songs. As a research-preparation guide, it
> contains discussions of workaday religious songs, spirituals, work
> songs, blues, and other secular songs; the discussions focus on topics
> such as ornamentation, falsetto, dialect, voice patterns, and other
> techniques employed in Afro-American vocal music. The book will
> aid the beginning field-researcher in preparing and developing
> viable research designs.
>> Reviews:  American Journal of Psychology 41:659 O '29; St.
>> Louis 27:20 Ja '29; Times Literary Supplement p235 Mr 21 '29

11. Rose, James, and Alice Eichholz. <u>Black Genesis</u>. Gale Genealogy and
    Local History Series. Detroit: Gale Research Co., 1978. xiv, 325 pp.
    indexes.

> Designed especially for researchers interested in black family
> history, this source book will offer significant guidance to
> researchers who wish to trace the origins of little-known black
> musicians. It presents many genealogical guides that will prove
> useful—directories; indexes; bibliographies; articles on black
> genealogy; reference works on black genealogy; histories, name
> books, and manuscript collections; lists of slaves and black freemen;
> checklists of black newspapers; war records; appropriate research
> libraries and archives; and surveys of most of the United States, the
> West Indies, and Canada. The book's three indexes—author, title,
> and subject—facilitate its use.
>> Reviews: American Notes and Queries 17:178 Jy '79; American
>> Reference Books Annual 11:213 '80; Booklist 75:1647 Jy 15 '79;
>> RQ 19:83 Fall '79; Wilson Library Bulletin 53:723 Ju '79

# II

# Dictionary Catalogues and Related Sources

12. Boston Public Library. <u>Dictionary Catalog of the Music Collection,</u> <u>Boston Public Library.</u> 20 vols. Boston: G. K. Hall & Co., 1972. each vol. approx. 800 pp. supplements [published by G. K. Hall & Co.]

   Although not available through interlibrary loan, books and periodicals about music, as well as musical scores, held in the Boston Public Library are catalogued in these volumes. Sheet music and phonorecords are not included. Access to materials pertinent to black music research may be gained not only through the author's name, book title, or specific subject (such as "Minstrels") but also through headings such as "Negro Musicians," "Negro Songs," and "Music—Negroes."

13. Brown, Rae Linda. <u>Music, Printed and Manuscript, in the James Weldon</u> <u>Johnson Memorial Collection of Negro Arts and Letters: An Annotated</u> <u>Catalog.</u> New York: Garland Publishing, 1982. xxiii, 322 pp. addendum. index.

   This volume is a guide to the 1,067 items of sheet music, music manuscripts, and anthologies that can be found in the Johnson Memorial Collection. Housed at Yale University, the collection includes materials from 1850 to the present, but is especially rich in Harlem Renaissance holdings, containing works of major literary and musical figures of the movement. The collection contains a large number of photographs of Afro-Americans, original paintings, papers and books, and approximately 1,200 78-rpm recordings of early black blues, lieder, and opera singers. The printed and manu-script music listed in the catalogue comprises 148 manuscripts, 848

13. Brown (continued)

> published individual works, and fifty-nine anthologies. Included are
> sheet music; scores for ballets, operas, and broadway musicals; and
> collections of compositions and arrangements by 156 black
> composers, including W. C. Handy, William Grant Still, Harry T.
> Burleigh, Clarence Cameron White, Will Vodery, Hall Johnson,
> Howard Swanson, Ulysses Kay, Hale Smith, and J. Rosamund
> Johnson. The addendum lists miscellaneous materials and minstrel
> books. Each entry carries the following information: entry number;
> composer; title; lyricist; publication imprint; description;
> performing medium; miscellaneous comments; and call number.

14. Detroit Public Library. Catalog of the E. Azalia Hackley Memorial
Collection of Negro Music, Dance, and Drama. Boston:  G. K. Hall &
Co., 1979. iv, 510 pp.

> This dictionary catalogue consists of photocopies of the catalogue
> cards for the Hackley Collection. The work is arranged into four
> parts. Part I, "Catalog of Books and Musical Scores," makes up
> approximately two-thirds of the catalogue and is organized as a
> single alphabetical list of authors, titles, and subjects. Part II,
> "Book Shelf List," is a chronological list of the Dewey Decimal
> System numbers of the volumes contained in the collection. Part
> III, "Broadsides and Posters," is organized alphabetically by the
> name of the performing artist(s), the title of the performance, or
> the organization sponsoring the advertised performance. Part IV,
> "Index of Photographs," catalogues the photographs held in the
> Hackley collection, providing an alphabetical listing of the people
> and productions photographed.

15. Fisk University Library. Dictionary Catalog of the Negro Collection of
Fisk University Library, Nashville, Tennessee. 6 vols. Boston: G. K.
Hall & Co., 1974. each vol. approx. 450 pp.

> Included are more than thirty-five thousand titles of books,
> pamphlets, and some printed music, collected between the library's
> founding and 1974. Essentially, these volumes reflect the holdings
> described in entry 385 of the present book. All of the items listed
> in the catalogue either have black authors or they are concerned
> with the black heritage. Although the majority of the holdings
> pertain to Afro-Americans, listings by and about West Indian
> individuals are also present.
>
> Reviews: American Reference Books Annual 7:211 '76

16. Howard University Library. Dictionary Catalog of the Arthur B.
Spingarn Collection of Negro Authors. 2 vols. Boston: G. K. Hall &
Co., 1970. iv, 676; 684 pp. appendix.

> An important feature of this catalogue is the appended listing of
> music by Negro composers held in the Spingarn Collection, many
> pieces of which are unobtainable from any other source. All the
> works contained in the collection were written or composed by

16. Howard University (continued)

    black persons. References to books, pamphlets, and other primary
    source material in many languages, including various African
    vernaculars, form the contents of the set.
    Reviews: Journal of Negro History 56:312 O '71

17. Howard University Library. Dictionary Catalog of the Jesse E.
    Moorland Collection of Negro Life and History. 9 vols. Boston: G. K.
    Hall & Co., 1970. each vol. approx. 750 pp. indexes.

    Extensive listings found under the subjects "Music" and "Musicians"
    are particularly relevant for the black music researcher. The
    catalogue contains entries for books and periodicals that are either
    written by black persons or are concerned with the heritage of
    persons of African descent in many nations. Three indexes are
    provided:   guides  to  African  periodicals,  American  Negro
    periodicals, and biographies contained in the volumes.
    Reviews: Journal of Negro History 56:312 O '71

18. Library of Congress. Music, Books on Music and Sound Recordings:
    Cumulative List of Works Represented by Library of Congress Printed
    Cards. Washington, D.C.: Library of Congress, 1953-.

In its several compilations, the catalogue appears with varying subtitles
and has been published by a number of different firms:

Music and Phonorecords, 1953-1957. Ann Arbor, Mich.: J. W. Edwards
    Publishers, 1958. (Originally published as vol. 27 of a now-discarded
    Library of Congress series.) iv, 1049 pp. index.
Music and Phonorecords, 1958-1963. Totowa, N.J.: Rowman and
    Littlefield, 1963. (Originally published as vols. 51 and 52 of Author
    List.) [iv], 1094; [iii], 514 pp. index.
Music and Phonorecords, 1963-1967. Ann Arbor, Mich.: J. W. Edwards
    Publishers, 1969. 900 pp. index.
Music and Phonorecords, 1968-1972. Ann Arbor, Mich.: J. W. Edwards
    Publishers, 1973. each vol. approx. 750 pp. index.
Music, Books on Music and Sound Recordings, 1973-1977. Totowa, N.J.:
    Rowman and Littlefield, 1978. each. vol. approx. 600 pp. index.
Music, Books on Music and Sound Recordings. Washington, D.C.:
    Library of Congress, 1978-. each vol. approx. 600 pp.

This work consists of photocopied catalogue cards for the scores
and sheet music, books, and sound recordings held by the Library of
Congress. The catalogue is organized by title and author or
performer.   Entries  for  books  and  printed  music  contain
bibliographic information, a list of other subject headings under
which the item appears, the Library of Congress call number, and
the Dewey Decimal System classification number. Each sound-
recording entry contains discographic information, a list of the
performers who made the recording, a list of the other works that
may be heard on the recording, a brief statement regarding the
presence of program notes on the record jacket, a list of other

18. Library of Congress (continued)

>    subject headings under which it may be found, and the Library of
>    Congress and Dewey Decimal System numbers.

19. Matfield, Julius, comp.  Variety Music Cavalcade, 1620-1969:  A
    Chronology of Vocal and Instrumental Music Popular in the United
    States.  Preface by Abel Green.  3rd ed.  Englewood Cliffs, N.J.:
    Prentice-Hall, 1971. xx, 766 pp. appendix. index.

>    Each section of this work presents a list of the titles of songs that
>    "enjoyed a degree of popularity in the United States" (p. v) during a
>    particular year; the heading for each section is the date with which
>    the section is concerned.    Within each category, songs are
>    alphabetized by title; each entry is accompanied by the names of
>    the author, composer, and publisher, as well as the copyright date.
>    Descriptions of prominent events of the year are also contained
>    under each heading; included are historical events, musical events,
>    sports events, names of popular books and plays, and notable motion
>    pictures.    The appendix includes titles of "Some Late-Blooming
>    Perennials."  The index is an alphabetical list of titles only; access
>    is not provided through the name of composer or lyricist. The book
>    includes citations of tunes by such composers as James A. Bland
>    ("Carry Me Back to Old Virginny" and "Oh! Dem Golden Slippers"),
>    Fats Waller ("Squeeze Me"), and Duke Ellington ("It Don't Mean a
>    Thing" and "Sophisticated Lady").
>    Reviews:  Musical Times 113:47-48 Ja '72

20. New York Public Library.  Dictionary Catalog of the Music Collection,
    New York Public Library.  33 vols.  Boston:  G. K. Hall & Co., 1964.
    each vol. approx. 800 pp.  supplement [published by G. K. Hall & Co.].

>    Catalogued listings include books, periodicals and articles within
>    periodicals concerned with music, as well as many musical scores.
>    In addition to the entries found under specific authors, titles, and
>    subjects, information pertinent to black music researchers may be
>    found  under  rubrics  such  as  "Negroes,"  "Negroes—U.S.,"  and
>    "Negroes—Music."

21. New York Public Library.   Dictionary Catalog of the Schomburg
    Collection of Negro Literature and History.  9 vols.  Boston: G. K. Hall
    & Co., 1962.  v, 8473 pp.  supplements [published by G. K. Hall & Co.].

>    Books, periodicals, printed music, and sound recordings, including
>    approximately sixty thousand bound volumes, held in the Schomburg
>    Collection are the subjects of the entries in this dictionary
>    catalogue; references to manuscripts, photographs, sheet music, and
>    vertical file materials are excluded.  All of the materials in the
>    collection are written by or about black persons throughout the
>    world, a substantial amount of material being concerned with native
>    Africans.  The catalogue contains extensive subject entries, many
>    of which refer to only a portion of a book; this feature of the

21. New York Public (continued)

    catalogue is a valuable aid to research on many topics for which
    sources of information are limited.

22. Olmsted, Elizabeth H., ed. Music Library Association Catalog of Cards
    for Printed Music, 1953-1972: A Supplement to the Library of Congress
    Catalogs. Totowa, N.J.: Rowman and Littlefield, 1974. vii, 575; iii,
    563 pp.

    This book contains photocopied catalogue cards for music scores
    held in selected libraries in the United States and Canada that do
    not appear in the Library of Congress Catalog: Music and
    Phonorecords. Entries are alphabetized by title and name of
    composer; no subject entries are included. Included are citations of
    compositions by such black composers as W. C. Handy, Scott Joplin,
    Hall Johnson, William Grant Still, Howard Swanson, J. J. Johnson,
    Duke Ellington, and David Baker.
        Reviews: Choice 11:914 S '74; Library Journal 99:1928 Au '74;
    Library Quarterly 45:109 Ja '75; Reference Services Review
    2:34 Jy '74; RQ 14:265 Spring '75

23. University of Rochester, Eastman School of Music, Rochester, New
    York. Sibley Music Library Catalog of Sound Recordings. 14 vols.
    Boston: G. K. Hall & Co., 1977. each vol. approx. 450-700 pp.

    These volumes are a dictionary catalogue of the contents of the
    phonorecord collection at the Eastman School of Music.
    Photocopies of the library cards are arranged alphabetically and
    include as their keywords the names of performers, the names of
    composers, the titles of the recorded works, and the titles of
    phonorecord series. Included are artists such as Grace Bumbry,
    Marian Anderson, Paul Robeson, Ornette Coleman, and Louis
    Armstrong. Among the composers whose works are represented are
    William Grant Still, Duke Ellington, Ulysses Kay, and Olly Wilson.

# III

# Bibliographies of Bibliographies, Biographies and Discographies

## *BIBLIOGRAPHIES OF BIBLIOGRAPHIES*

24. Jackson, Richard. United States Music: Sources of Bibliography and Collective Biography. I. S. A. M. Monographs, no. 1. Brooklyn, N.Y.: Institute for Studies in American Music, 1973. vii, 80 pp. index.

> This book is an annotated bibliography of selected works that deal with the subject of American music. It includes listings of reference works as well as historical, regional, and topical studies. The works under each heading are arranged alphabetically by author. Of the approximately one hundred entries in this volume, most of the references of interest to a black music researcher are concentrated in twenty-six entries under the rubrics "Black Music as a Genre" and "Blues, Ragtime, Jazz"; a few others are scattered throughout the remainder of the book.
> Reviews: Journal of Research in Music Education 22:331-332 n4 '74; Library Journal 98:2843 O 1 '73; Musical Times 116:796 S '75; Pan Pipes 67:38 n2 '75; Stereo Review 31:10 Au '73

25. Library of Congress, Archive of Folk Song. An Inventory of the Bibliographies and Other Reference and Finding Aids Prepared by the Archive of Folk Song, Library of Congress. Washington, D.C.: Library of Congress, n.d. 11 pp.

> This pamphlet contains lists of bibliographies in the fields of folk music, ethnomusicology, and folk lore. Published by the Archive of Folk Song, many of these lists were compiled by Joseph Hickerson,

25. Library of Congress (continued)

> Head of the Archive. The bibliographies are unannotated and are contained under two headings, "Bibliographies, Directories and Other Reference Aids" and "Finding Aids and Other Descriptions of the Archive of Folk Song." Under each rubric, titles are listed alphabetically by the key word in the title which indicates its subject. Among the publications of interest to a black music researcher are "Blues," "Bibliographies in the Field of Ethnomusicology," "Freedom Songs of the Civil Rights Movements," "Huddie (Leadbelly) Ledbetter," and "The Negro Spiritual."

26. Meggett, Joan M. Music Periodical Literature:  An Annotated Bibliography of Indexes and Bibliographies. Metuchen, N.J.: Scarecrow Press, 1978. ix, 116 pp. bibliography. indexes.

> This bibliography is designed to facilitate research "through music periodical literature" and to assist researchers in locating "periodical articles on music through the fields of the humanities and of the social sciences" (p. iii). It is an annotated list of 335 finding sources for music periodical literature in general and for special nonmusic indexes, as well as for articles in music indexes and bibliographies; it also includes a "Bibliography of Lists of Music Periodicals." This tool is indispensable for thorough and complete research, since it lists items that are not included in other music finding sources. For example, it lists articles published before 1949, the point at which the Music Index begins its listings. Quick references to specific research areas are possible with the book's three indexes—author, editor, compiler; subject; and title.
> Reviews:    American Reference Books Annual 10:468 '79; Booklist 75:1394 My 1 '79; Choice 15:1350 D '78; Fontes Artis Musicae 25:417-418 O '78; Library Journal 103:1050-1051 My 15 '78; Library Journal 103:2321 N 15 '78; Notes 35:37-38 n3 '79; Notes 35:637 Mr '79; RQ 18:406 Summer '79; Triangle 72:15 n4 '78

## BIBLIOGRAPHIES OF BIOGRAPHIES

27. Bull, Storm. Index to Biographies of Contemporary Composers. Vol. 1. New York: Scarecrow Press, 1964. Vol. 2. Metuchen, N.J.: Scarecrow Press, 1974. 405 pp. and 567 pp. respectively.

> These two volumes contain separate alphabetical listings of contemporary composers. The second volume contains entries for composers whose importance became apparent during the decade after Volume 1 was published; it also contains entries for some composers cited in the first volume, but with enlarged biographical source listings. The first volume, however, has not been superseded because it contains entries which were not included in the newer edition. Each entry contains the name of the composer, date of birth and death, the country with which the composer is commonly

27. Bull (continued)

associated, the country of birth if it is different from country of
association, and a list of abbreviations that indicates sources of
biographical information.  Composers were included in the volumes
if they were alive at the date of publication, if they were born after
1900, or if they died after 1950.  There are usually five or fewer
biographical sources for any entry on a black composer.
Reviews: Dansk Musiktidsskrift 40:168 n5 '65; Instrument 18:16
Ju '64

28. District of Columbia Historical Survey.  Bio-Bibliographical Index of
Musicians  in  the  United  States  of  America  Since  Colonial  Times.
Foreword  by  Harold  Spivacke.    2nd  ed.    Washington,  D.C.:    Pan
American Union, 1956. xxiii, 439 pp. appendix. bibliography.

Treating musicians and other figures who contributed to American
musical activity from colonial times till ca. 1930, this volume
provides data about sources of biographical information found
primarily in seventy-eight volumes, many of which do not contain
an individual index.  The entries are arranged alphabetically and
contain birth and death dates, a brief description of the entrant's
musical activity (e.g., singer, composer, organmaker), his/her
country of birth if foreign-born, and a list of the sources of
information; the latter are comprised of a siglum and page
number.    Among  the  black  musicians  represented  are  James  A.
Bland, Thomas (Blind Tom) Bethune, and Will Marion Cook.

## BIBLIOGRAPHIES OF DISCOGRAPHIES

29. Cooper, David Edwin.   International Bibliography of Discographies:
Classical Music and Jazz and Blues, 1962-1972.   Preface by Guy A.
Marco.  Keys to Music Bibliography, no. 2.  Littleton, Colo.: Libraries
Unlimited, 1975. 272 pp. index.

This bibliography is a list of sources for identifying sound
recordings, arranged in an easily usable form.  The book is divided
into three parts:  Part I, "Classical Music"; Part II, "Jazz & Blues";
and Part III, "Summary of National Discographies, Catalogs, and
Major Review Sources."  For the black music reseacher, the primary
usefulness of the work lies in the seventy-five pages of information
about blues and jazz discographies; cited are discographies
contained in books, articles, and sections of books.  In the second
part, Cooper separates blues discographies, jazz discographies and
discographies devoted entirely to the recordings of a single
performer or group.  The blues and jazz categories are each further
divided into general discographies, discographies that list recordings
of a specific time period, discographies of reissued recordings,
discographies  devoted  to  a  particular  record  label,  and
discographies concerned with a specific subject, such as free jazz or
the tenor saxophone.  Materials published between 1962 and 1972
form the majority of the listings, others being included on the basis

29. Cooper (continued)

    of their importance.
        Reviews: American Recorder 16:147-148 n4 '76; American Reference Books Annual 7:471 '76; Association for Recorded Sound Collectors 7:58-63 n3 '76; Brio 12:48-49 n2 '75; Catholic Library World 48:220 D '76; Choice 12:1288 D '75; Fontes Artis Musicae 22:155-157 n3 '75; Instrument 30:22 N '75; Notes 32:554 Mr '76; Recorded Sound n61:512 Ja '76; RQ 15:268 Spring '76; Wilson Library Bulletin 50:122 O '75

30. Gray, Michael H., and Gerald D. Gibson. Bibliography of Discographies. Foreword by J. F. Weber. New York: R. R. Bowker Co., 1977. xi, 164 pp. index.

    This volume contains bibliographic information on discographies of works by contemporary composers of "classical" music arranged under an alphabetical listing of the names of the composers; a few subject headings, such as "Negro music," are also included in the listing. Each entry contains standard bibliographic information as well as an indication of the contents of the discography with which it is concerned, such as the inclusion of matrix numbers, release dates, take numbers, and date and place of recording. Although few discographies of music by black composers are contained in this volume, later volumes should be more helpful to black music researchers; the topics of the proposed volumes are "jazz," "popular music," "ethnic and folk music," and "general discographies of music" (p. ix).
        Reviews: American Record Guide 42:56 D '78; American Reference Books Annual 10:473 '79; Association for Recorded Sound Journal 10:297+ n2/3 '79; Booklist 76:60 S 1 '79; Brio 15:22 n1 '78; Choice 15:700 Jy '78; Fontes Artis Musicae 25:418-419 n4 '78; High Fidelity 28:29 O '78; Library Association Record 80:191 Ap '78; Library Journal 103:737 Ap 1 '78; Library Review 27:188 Autumn '78; Musical Times 120:309 Ap '79; Music Teacher 58:35 F '79; Notes 35:876-877 Ju '79; Reference Services Review 6:28 Ap '78; Wilson Library Bulletin 52:588 Mr '78

31. Moon, Pete, comp. A Bibliography of Jazz Discographies Published Since 1960. Edited by Barry Witherden. 2nd ed. South Harrow, Middlesex, England: British Institute of Jazz Studies, 1972. unpaged. appendixes.

    This is a compilation of jazz discographies issued between 1960 and 1972. The book contains primarily single-artist listings presented alphabetically, with each entry giving the name of the artist, the name of the compiler of the listed discography, the format (whether in book form, in a journal, etc.), and the publication's date of release. Listings of new releases of previously out-of-print records and first-time releases of previously recorded performances by older musicians, as well as new releases of contemporary artists,

31. Moon (continued)

are included.   Appendixes give details of selected collective jazz discographies.
Reviews:  Reference Services Review 6:6 Jy '78

# IV

# Bibliographies

## *GENERAL*

32. Hatch, James V. Black Image on the American Stage: A Bibliography of Plays and Musicals, 1770-1970. New York: DRS Publications, 1970. xiii, 162 pp. bibliography. indexes. addenda.

> This is a listing of more than two-thousand plays, musicals, revues, and operas written by black playwrights or containing "at least one Black character" (p. ix). The contents span the years 1767-1970 and are limited to works "written or produced in America" (p. ix) between those years. In the body of the book, the entries are presented by decades (e.g., 1900-1909, 1910-1919 etc.) and are alphabetical by authors' last names, with each including the title of the play, genre, date, publisher, and the name of the library in which the script may be found. The indexes list titles and authors, respectively. Since the compiler often was unable to credit authorship in cases of collaboration, "the names of composers are listed only when there was an indication that they had written either part of the book and/or the lyrics" (p. ix). For this reason, the work is woefully incomplete, especially as far as opera is concerned, listing only one of fourteen operas by Harry Lawrence Freeman, one of nine works by William Grant Still, and none by Ulysses Kay. The listings do include, however, titles of musicals and revues by Edward Boatner, Perry Bradford, Oscar Brown, Bob Cole, [Will] Marion Cook, Henry Creamer, Maude Cuney-Hare, Donald Heywood, J. Leubrie Hill, Ernest Hogan, J. C. Johnson, J. Rosamund Johnson, Scott Joplin, John Layton, Cecil Mack, Maceo Pinkard, Alex Rogers, Noble Sissle, and others.

33 IV. Bibliographies

32. Hatch (continued)

Reviews: American Literature 43:315 My '71; Library Journal 95:4243 D 15 '70; Quarterly Journal of Speech 57:473 D '71

33. McPherson, James M., Laurence B. Holland, James M. Banner, Jr., Nancy J. Weiss, and Michael D. Bell. Blacks in America: Bibliographical Essays. Garden City, N.Y.: Doubleday & Co., 1971. xxii, 430 pp. index.

Serving as an introduction not only to black music, but to every aspect of the black American experience, this volume is arranged chronologically, ranging from slavery and the Civil War through the Civil Rights Movement of the twentieth century. Many of the references to black American music are contained in the section titled "Soul Music: Blues, Jazz, and Variations," and "Blacks in Opera and Symphonic Music"; information about the spiritual is found integrated in the chapters that treat the nineteenth century and is cross-referenced in the "Soul Music" chapter. Written in prose form, each chapter contains a brief discussion of the topic with which it is concerned; the bibliographic citations are given in the text and include only the name of the author, the title, and the place and date of publication.
Review: Biographical Society of America—Papers 67:220 Ap '73; Booklist 68:470 F 15 '72; Choice 9:492 Ju '72; Journal of American History 59:117 Ju '72; Kirkus Reviews 39:1056 S 15 '71; Library Journal 96:3591 N 1 '71; Negro History Bulletin 35:144 O '72

34. Spradling, Mary Mace, ed. In Black and White: A Guide to Magazine Articles, Newspaper Articles, and Books Concerning More Than 15,000 Black Individuals and Groups. Foreword by Albert P. Marshall. 3rd ed. Detroit: Gale Research Co., 1980. xiii, 1282 pp. bibliography. index.

Organized alphabetically, this valuable bibliographical tool contains citations of information sources from books, newspapers, and periodicals; "much of this information is not found in the traditional reference sources" (p. xiii). Each entry includes a brief description of the achievements of the person(s) treated and a list of citations; the number of references varies from one or two to a complete column. The guide has a broad scope, treating persons and groups from the early eighteenth century to the present, including composers, concert artists, critics, historians, teachers, popular music stars, jazz and blues musicians, folk and gospel singers, conductors, and composers and performers of musical theater. The handy and convenient "Occupational Index" provides quick access to the people treated in the guide.
Reviews: American Reference Books Annual 12:218 '81; Booklist 77:1211 My 1 '81; Choice 18:780 F '81; Journal of Academic Librarianship 6:375 Ja '81; Library Journal 106:1041 My 15 '81; Wilson Library Bulletin 55:382 Ja '81

35. Szwed, John F., and Roger D. Abrahams. Afro-American Folk Culture: An Annotated Bibliography of Materials From North, Central, and South America and the West Indies. Bibliographical and Special Series, no. 31. Philadelphia: Institute for the Study of Human Issues, 1978. xvii, 814 pp. general index. locale index.

This bibliography offers material descriptive of black folk culture in North America, the Caribbean, Central America and South America, citing works published before 1974. Part I consists of titles of general works, bibliographies, and materials relating to North American culture, while titles of works concerned with black culture in the Caribbean and Central and South America are contained in Part II. The entries include books and articles in six languages. Excluded are unpublished materials, as well as materials concerned with black culture as it has been assimilated into the culture of the majority within which it exists. Entries under each heading are organized into an alphabetical list of authors' last names and include one- or two-sentence annotations. Among the topics listed in the index are autobiographies and biographies, bands and orchestras, jazz, blues, musical instruments, composers, ragtime, and other topics pertinent to black music research.
Reviews: American Reference Books Annual 10:228 '79; Choice 16:60 Mr '79; College and Research Libraries 40:350 Jy '79; Library Journal 103:2506 D 15 '78

36. West, Earle H., comp. A Bibliography of Doctoral Research on the Negro, 1933-1966. Ann Arbor, Mich.: University Microfilms, 1969. vii, 134 pp. index.

Using Dissertation Abstracts International and American Doctoral Dissertations as its sources of information, this volume "lists 1,452 dissertations arranged in seven major categories covering every aspect of study relating to the Negro in the United States" (p. vii). The humanities category contains two sections related to music research: "Drama, Theater, Movies," and "Music." The musical topics treated by the dissertations cited include folk and popular music, curriculum, bibliography, jazz, spirituals, gospel music, and composers of concert and recital music. The sections are arranged alphabetically by author. Each entry includes the following information: author, title, degree-granting institution, date the degree was awarded, a one-sentence description of the dissertation, and the University Microfilms order number. The index is organized alphabetically by author, each entry accompanied by its Dissertation Abstracts citation and its University Microfilms order number.

## WRITINGS ON MUSIC

37. Carl Gregor Herzog zu Mecklenburg. International Jazz Bibliography: Jazz Books from 1919 to 1968. Collection d'Etudes Musicologiques/ Sammlung Musikwissenschaftlicher Abhandlungen. Strasbourg: Editions P. H. Heitz; Baden-Baden: Verlag Heitz GMBH, 1969. xx, 198 pp.

37.  Carl Gregor (continued)

indexes.  supplements.

This bibliography represents an attempt to gather under one cover
all publications on the subject of jazz that appeared during the
fifty-year period indicated.  In additon to general articles and
books, the work includes listings of jazz literature, ragtime
literature, "symphonic jazz," and other topics.  Arranged
alphabetically by author, the location of specific items among its
1,562 entries is facilitated by the book's several indexes:
I. Collections and Series, II. Persons, III. Country Index, and
IV. Subject Index.  Each entry is a full bibliographical citation;
multiple entries by the same author are listed chronologically.
Reviews: Ethnomusicology 14:177-178 n1 '70; Instrumentenbau-
Zeitschrift 24:399 Ju '70; Jazz Hot n256:21 D '69; Jazz Journal
22:12 S '69; Musikforschung 24:330-331 n3 '71; Orkester
Journalen 37:2+ S '69; Reference Services Review 6:15 Jy '78

38.  De Lerma, Dominique-René.  Bibliography of Black Music.  Foreword to
Vol. 1 by Jessie Carney Smith; to Vol. 2 by Georgia Ryder; to Vol. 3 by
Samuel A. Floyd, Jr. (12 volumes projected).  Greenwood Encyclopedia
of Black Music.  Westport, Conn.: Greenwood Press, 1981-.  each vol.
approx. 200 pp.  indexes.

When completed, this monumental set will provide the most
complete bibliographic listing available for all topical areas
pertinent to black music research; although unannotated, it is a
first effort at a bibliography that covers the whole field.  The
twelve volumes will treat the following topics:  Reference
Materials; Histories; Geographical Studies; Musical Instruments and
Performance; Music Theory; Pedagogy; Related Arts; Psychology,
Physiology, Politics, and Sociology; Liturgy and Religion;
Biographies; A Bibliography of the Music; A Discography of the
Concert Music, Spirituals, and Performers.  The entries in Volumes
1 to 3, the only parts of the series available at this writing, are
arranged in alphabetical order by author, under each of the headings
and subheadings that comprise the book; multiple entries by the
same author are alphabetical by title.  Volume 3 has an index, as
will all future volumes.  The wide scope of Volume 1 is indicated by
the selection of titles below (taken from that volume's bibliography
of dissertations):  Adkins, Aldrich Wendell.  The development of
Black art songs.; Akpabot, Samuel Ekpe.  Functional music of the
Ibibio people of Nigeria.; Alexander, Jo Helen.  The history of music
instruction at Howard University from the beginning to 1942.; and
Alkire, Stephen Robert.  The development and treatment of the
Negro character as presented in American musical theatre, 1927-
1968.  The set will be an invaluable tool to anyone involved in black
music research.
Reviews:  American Reference Books Annual 13:504 '82;
Cadence 7:25-26 Jy '81; Choice 19:1045 Ap '82; Choice 19:354
N '81; Library Journal 106:1063 My 15 '81

39. Duckles, Vincent.  Music Reference and Research Materials:  An Annotated Bibliography.  3rd ed.  New York:  Free Press; London: Collier Macmillan Publishers, 1974. xvi, 526 pp. indexes.

One of the standard bibliographic tools for music research, Duckles' work contains annotated citations of books applicable to black music research, even though most of the book is devoted to music in the European tradition.  The chapters that contain references to black music research sources are:  "Dictionaries and Encyclopedias," with fifteen entries in the subsection "Biography, Jazz, Popular and Folk Musicians"; "Bibliographies of Music Literature," with five entries under "Jazz"; "Bibliographies of Music," with eight entries under "Jazz and Popular Music"; and "Discographies," with fourteen entries under "Ethnic and Folk Music on Records."  Each entry presents the standard bibliographic data, a brief annotation, and a list of reviews of the subject of the entry. The indexes consist of authors, subjects, and titles listed separately.
Reviews: American Recorder 15:102 n3 '74; Booklist 71:384 D 1 '74; Choice 11:1108 O '74; College and Research Libraries 36:69 Ja '75; Reference Services Review 3:14 Ap '75; Wilson Library Bulletin 49:87 S '74

40. Gillis, Frank, and Alan P. Merriam, comps.  Ethnomusicology and Folk Music:  An International Bibliography of Dissertations and Theses. Special Series in Ethnomusicology, no. 1.  Middletown, Conn.: Wesleyan University Press, 1966. [viii], 148 pp. indexes.

Although not devoted to the topic of black music, this volume contains listings of many dissertations that directly and indirectly relate to black music research.  Being both international and multilingual in scope, the work contains entries for dissertations completed before 1966, as well as some works-in-progress.  Entries are organized alphabetically by author and contain standard bibliographic information for dissertations, the Dissertation Abstracts International order number, and publication information if the work has been published.  Some entries also include a brief annotation.  The indexes consist of an index of granting institutions and a subject index.  The latter, through its detailed headings and subheadings, serves as an excellent point of access to the dissertations.
Reviews: American Anthropologist 70:180 F '68; Antiquarian Bookman 39:2205 My 29 '67; Ethnomusicology 12:453-454 n3 '68; Journal of Research in Music Education 15:240 n3 '67; Journal of the International Folk Music Council 20:96-97 '68; Library Journal 91:4958 O 15 '66; Notes 24:499-500 n3 '68; Recorded Sound n25:161 Ja '67; Second Line 17:160 N/D '66; Wilson Library Bulletin 41:229 O '66

41. Haywood, Charles.  A Bibliography of North American Folklore and Folksongs. The American People North of Mexico, vol. 1. 2nd ed., rev. New York: Dover Publications, 1961. xxx, 748 pp.

This rather general work on the American folk tradition is divided

41. Haywood (continued)

> into four large sections: General Bibliography; Regional
> Bibliography; Ethnic Bibliography; Occupational Bibliography; and
> Miscellaneous Bibliography. While items on Afro-American music
> can be found in each of these sections, the portion of the Ethnic
> Bibliography titled "The Negro," spanning 132 pages, stands as a
> somewhat extensive "tool-within-a-tool" for the black music
> researcher. In this portion of the book, seventy-eight pages are
> devoted to folk song; this section includes citations of works about
> and related to spirituals, work songs, lyric songs, social songs,
> dance, children's rhymes and games, blues, minstrelsy, "Creole," and
> "West Indies." Also included is a list of some six hundred published
> spirituals, in alphabetical order, each title accompanied by the
> appropriate bibliographical information. A list of sound recordings
> is also included—records in collections and as singles—showing
> titles, performers, and labels/numbers. The "Blues" listings contain,
> in an individual titles list, approximately 420 recorded blues songs.
> These conveniences alone make this work indispensable to black
> music researchers.
>
> Reviews: Tennessee Folklore Society Bulletin 28:100-102 n4
> '62

42. Hefele, Bernhard. Jazz Bibliography: International Literature on Jazz,
    Blues, Spirituals, Gospel and Ragtime Music with a Selected List of
    Works on the Social and Cultural Background from the Beginning to the
    Present. Munich: K. G. Saur, 1981. viii, 368 pp. index.

> This is a near-comprehensive bibliography of books on Afro-
> American music, containing titles in several jazz-related areas.
> The work "lists international literature on jazz, blues, spirituals,
> and gospel music, as well as selected literature on the background
> and origins of this music" (p. 7), containing more than 6,600 books,
> articles, theses, and dissertations ranging from 1836 to 1980. The
> book lists publications in twenty-eight independent subject areas,
> including reference works; topical studies (e.g., blues, ragtime,
> etc.); sociological works (criticism, politics, ideology, etc.); didactic
> treatises; jazz clubs, people, organizations, communications (radio,
> TV, and film); phonograph records; and descriptive works on musical
> instruments, dance, and photographs. The work is international in
> scope, with each listing being presented in the language of its
> publication. The book's "Index of Persons" contains the names of
> more than 450 black and nonblack jazz musicians and writers,
> ranging from Buddy Bolden and Walter Kingsley (writer, 1917) to
> Anthony Braxton and Albert Murray.
>
> Reviews: American Reference Books Annual 13:525 '82; Jazz
> Podium 30:59 S '81; Journal of Academic Librarianship 8:54 Mr
> '82

43. Horn, David. The Literature of American Music in Books and Folk Music
    Collections: A Fully Annotated Bibliography. Metuchen, N.J.:
    Scarecrow Press, 1977. xiv, 556 pp. appendix. index.

43. Horn (continued)

A comprehensive research tool for the study of American music,
this valuable and well-annotated work is divided into seven main
sections as follows: A. General Works; B. The Musical Tradition to
1800; C. The Tradition in the 20th Century; D. The Music of the
American Indian; E. Folk Music; F. Black Music; G. Jazz; and
H. Popular Currents. The author's extensive sections on "Black
Music" (250 entries) and "Jazz" (243 entries) are extremely
valuable; the well-written annotations on the nonmusic books on
black culture are particularly valuable because they are designed to
guide the researcher to sections of these books that contain black
music or are relevant to the field. This volume is highly
recommended.

Reviews: Booklist 74:707 D 15 '77; Choice 14:1024 O '77; Notes
34:89 S '77; Wilson Library Journal 52:188 O '77; Stereo Review
39:14 Jy '77

44. Jackson, Irene V., comp. Afro-American Religious Music: A
Bibliography and a Catalog of Gospel Music. Westport, Conn.:
Greenwood Press, 1979. xiv, 210 pp. indexes.

As its subtitle suggests, this item contains a list of scholarly
sources that treat black gospel music, as well as a list of black
gospel compositions. Also included is information on the
classification of black gospel songs which are listed in the Library
of Congress Catalog. The introductory statement to the "Key to
the Catalog" section contains instructions for visually identifying
black gospel songs, distinguishing them from those of white
composers. This work is a useful tool for researchers seeking black
gospel music and the writings pertaining to it.

Reviews: American Reference Books Annual 11:425 '80;
Choice 17:364 My '80; Ethnomusicology 25:147-148 n1 '80;
Hymn 31:214-215 n3 '80; JEMF Quarterly 16:165-166 n59 '80;
Journal of American Folklore 94:242+ n372 '81; Journal of
Church Music 22:11 F '80; Journal of Negro History 65:89-90
Winter '80; Library Journal 104:1130 My 15 '79; RQ 19:175
Winter '79; Wilson Library Bulletin 54:255 D '79

45. Kennington, Donald, and Danny L. Read. The Literature of Jazz: A
Critical Guide. 2nd ed., rev. Chicago: American Library Association,
1980. xi, 236 pp. indexes.

The primary value of this book lies in the bibliographies which
constitute approximately two-thirds of each of its nine chapters.
The topics addressed by the several chapters include such subjects
as the blues, jazz history, biography, "Analysis, Theory and
Criticism," "Reference Sources," "Jazz Education," "Jazz in Novels,
Poetry, Plays, and Films," and "Jazz Periodicals." Although the
work is quite selective, the author feels "that all significant books
published in the English language up to the end of 1979 have been
listed" (p. x). The entries consist of references to books and
dissertations written in or translated into English. The entries are

27

45. Kennington (continued)

        not restricted to those concerned with the origins and development of jazz in the United States, although such works constitute the majority of the entry subjects. The contents include information about periodical literature, and about anthologies of music. Each entry provides information concerning the author, the title, and the publication of all of the editions of the work with which it is concerned; many include brief annotations. Each chapter begins with a discussion of its topic and a brief narrative relating to important sources of information. The indexes consist of separate listings of names and of titles.

            Reviews: American Reference Books Annual 13:527 '82; Brio 18:36-37 n1 '81; Jazz Journal International 34:30 Ju '81; Jazz Podium 30:55 N '81; Library Journal 106:1210 Ju 1 '81; Library Review 30:196 Autumn '81; Times Educational Supplement p27 Ju 19 '81

46. Lawrenz, Marguerite Martha. Bibliography and Index of Negro Music. Detroit: Board of Education of the City of Detroit, 1968. vi, 52 pp. index.

        Although containing a relatively small number of entries, many of which can be found in other sources, this bibliography includes an invaluable aid to researchers in the list of performers and composers about whom information is held in the vertical file of the E. Azalia Hackley Collection at the Detroit Public Library. The book is organized under five rubrics: 1) "General Negro Music— Books," containing entries for fifty-eight books and seventeen theses in the areas of jazz, curricula, minstrelsy, African music and instruments, popular and folk music, spirituals, and composers of concert and recital music; 2) "Books on Jazz," containing entries for forty-nine books or portions of books and two theses about jazz, ragtime, and the blues; 3) "Periodical Articles," containing eighty-nine citations of articles published between 1915 and 1967 which treat jazz, the blues, composers of concert and recital music, folk music, and African music; 4) "Negro Musicians," containing 208 entries from books and articles about ninety performers and composers; and 5) "Vertical File of the E. Azalia Hackley Collection." The fourth chapter is arranged alphabetically by the names of the musicians and includes folk and popular singers, blues and jazz musicians, and composers and performers of concert and recital music, among whom are Marian Anderson, Louis Armstrong, Nat Cole, Dean Dixon, Mattiwilda Dobbs, Dizzy Gillespie, Odetta, and Bessie Smith. The volume is not without errors, e.g., the names William Levi Davis and Henry T. Burleigh are substituted for William Levi Dawson and Harry T. Burleigh. Each entry presents only bibliographical information; no annotations are given. Listed in the final chapter are 449 artists whose specialties include jazz, concert and recital music, folk and popular music, blues, and musical theater. Since the index is less than adequate, containing only subjects, the user must search each chapter for relevant

46. Lawrenz (continued)

   entries; this task is not difficult, since there are relatively few
   entries present.

47. Markewich, Reese.  Jazz Publicity II:  Newly Revised and Expanded
   Bibliography of Names and Addresses of Hundreds of International Jazz
   Critics and Magazines. New York:  Reese Markewich, 1974. 25 pp.

   Arranged alphabetically by author or periodical title, this
   monograph lists the addresses of jazz critics in many countries.
   The majority of the critics reside in Europe and North America; a
   few are in South America, the Middle East, India, Japan, and the
   U.S.S.R. Absent are the names of persons from Africa and Central
   America.
       Reviews:  Coda 12:28 n6 '75; Jazz and Blues 3:10 D '73; Jazz
       Forum n34:23 Ap '75; Orkester Journalen 42:2 Ja '74

48. Markewich, Reese.   The New Expanded Bibliography of Jazz
   Compositions Based on the Chord Progressions of Standard Tunes.
   Pleasantville, N.Y.: Maurice Markewich, 1974. 45 pp.

   An "expanded revision of Bibliography of Jazz and Pop Tunes,
   Sharing the Chord Progressions of Other Compositions" (title page),
   this monograph is a simple but effective and useful compendium
   designed to inform users of the titles of recorded jazz compositions
   that are based on the standard chord progressions of other
   particular standard jazz tunes.   Arranged alphabetically by the
   titles of the standard tunes, the book is basically a simple, quick,
   and easy-to-use research guide to "groups of compositions that
   share the same chord progressions" (title page). Each of the more
   than 150 standard tune entries includes title, author, publisher,
   selected recordings, and the names of movies or shows in which the
   composition was performed. The number of compositions derived
   from the main entry titles ranges from one (1) (e.g., "Hanid" from
   "Dinah") to twenty-one from "Sweet Georgia Brown." For black
   music researchers, the latter song is particularly interesting; its
   derivatives include performances ranging from Coleman Hawkins's
   "Bay-U-Bah" on the Prestige, Vogue, and Milestone labels, to Kenny
   Dorham's "Windmill" on Blue Notes, with intervening performances
   by such figures as Lucky Thompson, Clifford Brown, Horace Silver,
   Wardell Gray, Thelonius Monk, and others.
       Reviews:  Coda 12:28 n6 '75; Jazz Forum n34:23 Ap '75; Jazz
       Forum n35:64-65 Ju '75; Jazz Journal 28:31 F '75; Jazz
       Magazine n242:10 Mr '76

49. Meadows, Eddie S.   Jazz Reference and Research Materials:  A
   Bibliography. New York: Garland Publishing, 1981. xii, 300 pp. indexes.

   This is a partially annotated, comprehensive, and selected list of
   books, articles, theses, and dissertations "written on or about
   specific jazz styles and jazz musicians from the turn of the century

49. Meadows (continued)

through 1978" (p. ix). Organized into two major sections, the work lists materials related to: 1) jazz styles, appreciation, criticism, and sociology, with musicians being treated within the various categories (i.e., pre-swing, bop, etc.) as appropriate; and 2) reference materials, including bibliographies, discographies, dictionaries, and other research tools. In addition to printed items (articles, books, and theses), the work also lists thirty-seven record anthologies and twelve "Jazz Research Libraries," all of which will be useful to the researcher. The book's more than 2,563 print entries are numbered consecutively throughout. Each of the book's two main sections has its own index, simplifying the user's search for items applicable to specific research needs.
Reviews: American Reference Books Annual 13:529 '82; Choice 19:892 Mr '82; Journal of Academic Librarianship 8:54 Mr '82; Library Journal 106:2382 D 15 '81

50. Meadows, Eddie S. Theses and Dissertations on Black American Music. Beverly Hills, Calif.: Theodore Front Musical Literature, 1980. ii, 19 pp.

This bibliography is the only published monograph that is devoted exclusively to theses and dissertations in the field of black American music. Although some titles have been inadvertently omitted, this bibliography, current to January 1978, lists its entries in thirteen different categories, ranging from "Practices Before 1900" and "Origins and Acculturation," through several areas devoted to varieties of Afro-American music (i.e., blues, jazz, R&B, gospel), to "Classical." Full bibliographical citations are given for each entry. The more than 260 items included in this monograph were taken from eleven different bibliographical sources, seven of which are devoted entirely to doctoral dissertations, the other four being more general sources.

51. Merriam, Alan P., and Robert J. Benford. A Bibliography of Jazz. Bibliographical Series, no. 4. Philadelphia: American Folklore Society, 1954. xiii, 145 pp. appendix. indexes.

Providing citations of periodicals and newspaper articles and some portions of books, this bibliography contains entries arranged alphabetically by author. They are composed of standard bibliographical information and include abbreviations that indicate the subject classifications of the articles. The latter consist of one or more of thirty-two classifications that describe the main topics of the articles, e.g., jazz, bibliography, blues, criticism, history, "Jazz and the Classics," New Orleans, and biography. The book's subject index consists of an alphabetic list of the subject classification abbreviations. The second index consists of an alphabetical listing of the periodicals from which entries were taken. The book contains "a listing of magazines that have been devoted wholly or in considerable part to jazz music" (p. xi). This

51. Merriam (continued)

> work is a good source for the location of information on jazz
> published before the mid-1950s.
>
> Reviews: Downbeat 22:30 My 18 '55; Etude 73:8 Ju '55; High
> Fidelity 5:94 Au '55; Jazz Journal 8:10 My '55; Notes 12:436-
> 437 Ju '55

52. Nettl, Bruno. Reference Materials in Ethnomusicology: A Bibliographic
Essay. Detroit Studies in Music Bibliography, no. 1. 2nd ed., rev.
Detroit: Information Coordinators, 1967. xv, 40 pp.

> Nettl's small and concise work is a bibliographic summary of
> surveys and compendia. It emphasizes primary source materials
> pertinent to Eastern cultures, although some American folk music
> references are included. The work surveys books and articles
> specifically related to ethnomusicology and is arranged by the
> following topics: definitions, surveys, research techniques, musical
> elements, instruments, special approaches to the study, collections,
> periodicals, directories, and bibliographies. Although the
> monograph is primarily focused upon researching non-Western
> music, some items may be helpful to black music researchers,
> including works by Charles Seeger, Alan P. Merriam, Alan Lomax,
> and A. M. Jones.
>
> Reviews: American Music Teacher 13:30 n1 '63; Choice 5:182
> '68; Dansk Musiktidsskrift 37:274 n8 '62; Instrument 16:26 Mr
> '62; Journal of American Folklore 76:270 n301 '63; Journal of
> the International Folk Music Council 15:113 '63; Library
> Journal 87:1593 '62

53. Reisner, Robert George, comp. The Literature of Jazz: A Selective
Bibliography. Introduction by Marshall W. Stearns. New York: New
York Public Library, 1959. 59 pp.

> Arranged alphabetically by author, with no subject index, this
> booklet is basically a checklist of books, articles, and magazines
> devoted to jazz music. The literature is presented in four
> sections: "Books," "Background Books," "Selective List of Magazine
> References," and "Magazines Devoted Wholly or Principally to
> Jazz." Each entry carries full imprint information, where
> appropriate, and bibliographical citations. The selectivity of the
> work presumably is due to the ready availability and convenience of
> the collections the author used for the compilation.
>
> Reviews: Notes 16:398 Ju '59

54. Skowronski, JoAnn. Black Music in America: A Bibliography.
Metuchen, N.J.: Scarecrow Press, 1981. ix, 723 pp. index.

> This finding source is designed to assist users in identifying writings
> on, about, and pertinent to black American music. Its 14,319
> entries are organized into three sections: "Selected Musicians and
> Singers," "General References," and "Reference Works." The
> entries include books and articles that are listed chronologically

31

54. Skowronski (continued)

within each category. The work's value is limited due to the
omission of significant works and the lack of useful annotations;
however, its primary value lies in its potential use for students and
other researchers seeking secondary source materials on well-known
musicians such as, for example, Louis Armstrong, Johnny Mathis,
Grace Bumbry, John Coltrane, Roberta Flack, Scott Joplin, or
Stevie Wonder. The entries for each musician are copious, e.g.,
eighty-nine citations for Andre Watts, 195 for B. B. King, and 1,242
for Duke Ellington.
    Reviews:    Choice 19:1050 Ap '82; Journal of Academic
Librarianship 8:54 Mr '82; Library Journal 106:2228 N 15 '81;
Wilson Library Bulletin 56:541 Mr '82

# MUSIC TITLES

55. Lewine, Richard, and Alfred Simon. Songs of the American Theater: A
Comprehensive Listing of More Than 12,000 Songs, Including Selected
Titles from Film and Television Productions. Introduction by Stephen
Sondheim. New York: Dodd, Mead & Co., 1973. x, 820 pp. index.

This book is concerned with musical theatrical productions that
were staged between 1925 and 1971. It is organized into three
parts: "Theater Songs," "Productions," and "Chronological List of
Productions." The first part constitutes approximately two-thirds
of the book and is arranged alphabetically by song title; each entry
includes the name of the song, the composer, and the lyricist,
together with the song's date. The second part is arranged
alphabetically by production title; each entry contains the year of
the production, the number of performances, the names of the
composer(s) and lyricist(s), and the titles of the songs in the show.
The last part of the book lists the shows produced during each year
between 1925 and 1971 and is arranged alphabetically by show title
under each year. Although information in the book is not limited to
black musicians and productions, it includes many black composers
and lyricists, among whom are Eubie Blake, Perry Bradford, Will
Marion Cook, Ford Dabney, Duke Ellington, James P. Johnson,
Rosamund Johnson, Andy Razaf, Noble Sissle, Fats Waller, Clarence
Williams, and Will Vodery.
    Reviews:    Booklist 69:1030 Jy 15 '73; Canadian Composer
n88:34 F '74; Choice 10:1168 O '73; Christian Science Monitor
65:15 S 5 '73; High Fidelity/Musical America 23:MA32 S '73;
Library Journal 98:2423 S 1 '73; Library Journal 99:1096 Ap 15
'74; Wilson Library Bulletin 48:167 O '73

56. Rosenburg, Bruce A. The Folksongs of Virginia: A Checklist of the
WPA    Holdings,    Alderman    Library,    University    of    Virginia.
Charlottesville: University Press of Virginia, 1969.    xx, 145 pp.
bibliography.

Consisting of a list of folk songs collected in Virginia between 1938

56. Rosenburg (continued)

and 1942, this book contains 1,604 entries arranged alphabetically by title; some include two or more variants of a single title. Each entry or subentry provides information about the number of stanzas of the song, the name and address of the informant, the "date of collection or the date reported to the Richmond headquarters" (p. xiv), and an identification of the collector. Many of the folksongs had never before been published. Others are variants of songs contained in collections such as Slave Songs of the United States (Allen, Ware, and Garrison), American Ballads and Folk-Songs (Lomax and Lomax), and On the Trail of Negro Folk-Songs (Scarborough); this information is noted in the entry.
Reviews: Journal of American Folklore 83:96 n327 '70

57. White, Evelyn Davidson, comp.   Choral Music of Afro-American Composers:   A Selected Annotated Bibliography.   Metuchen, N.J.: Scarecrow Press, 1981. vi, 167 pp. appendixes. index.

Previous title:   Selected Bibliography of Published Choral Music by Black Composers.  Washington, D.C.: Howard University, 1975.

This work is essentially a list of more than one thousand published choral compositions by more than eighty-five black American composers. Arranged alphabetically, first by composer's last name, then by title, each title entry carries the following information: copyright date, number of pages, voicing, vocal range, level of difficulty, type of accompaniment, publisher, and catalog number. This primary list is supplemented by an unannotated list of "Selected Collections of Negro Spirituals."   Each entry in this supplementary list carries the title of the collection, the names of the collection's arranger/editor/compiler, and a list of the spirituals contained in the collection.   Also included in the work are biographical sketches of the composers whose compositions are listed; a selected bibliography of articles, books, and dissertations; and a list of publishers' addresses. A title index is included in the supplement and complements the composer lists.  In addition to such well-known names as Robert Nathaniel Dett, Noah Ryder, Mark Fax, William L. Dawson, and Undine Moore, the list also includes names of relative newcomers to the world of choral composition, such as Leslie Adams, Noel Da Costa, James Furman, Adolphus Hailstork, Eugene Hancock, Wendell Logan, and others. The compositions included in the work date from 1913 (Harry T. Burleigh's Deep River); the collections date from 1872 (Jubilee Songs as sung by the Jubilee Singers of Fisk University). This work is a good initial source with which to begin research relating to choral music by black American composers.
Reviews:   American Reference Books Annual 13:518 '82; Choice 19:612 Ja '82

33

# V

# Discographies and Catalogues of Sound Recordings

## GENERAL

58. Library of Congress, Copyright Office. Catalog of Copyright Entries: Sound Recordings. 3rd series. Washington, D.C.: Library of Congress, 1975-. each vol. approx. 800 pp.

> Each volume of this catalog is a list of all sound recordings copyrighted during the year covered. The entries are arranged by copyright registration number in numerical order. Each entry includes the title of the composition, the record label number, a description of the disc itself, the names of the composer and the performer, the name of the person or firm holding the copyright, the date of copyright and other pertinent information. The comprehensive index precedes the main entry list and is organized in alphabetical order by song title, record company, performer, and composer. The catalogue begins with the 1973 issue of the Catalog of Copyright Entries.

59. Library of Congress, Music Division. Check-List of Recorded Songs in the English Language in the Library of Congress Archive of American Folk Song to July, 1940: Alphabetical List with Geographical Index. New York: Arno Press and The New York Times, 1971. 456 pp. geographical index, 138 pp.

> Originally published in three volumes: A-K, L-Z, and Geographical Index. Washington, D.C.: The Library of Congress: Music Division, 1942.

59. Library of Congress (continued)

The main body of this work lists recorded folk songs contained in the Folk Song Archive of the Library of Congress, in alphabetical order by title. Each entry contains the name of the person or persons performing the song, the name of the person who recorded the song, the place and date of the recording, and the call number. Folk songs from thirty-six states, the District of Columbia, and the Bahamas are included in this checklist.

## *FOLK*

60. Library of Congress, Music Division. Folk Music: A Catalog of Folk Songs, Ballads, Dances, Instrumental Pieces, and Folk Tales of the United States and Latin America on Phonograph Records. Washington, D.C.: U.S. Government Printing Office, [1964]. iv, 107 pp. indexes.

Title varies: 1943--Catalog of Phonograph Records: Selected Titles from the Archive of American Folk Songs; 1945--Folk Music of the United States: Catalog of Phonograph Records, No. 2; 1948—Folk Music of the United States and Latin America.

Consisting of a listing of the contents of the phonorecord albums of field recordings produced by the Archive of Folk Song, this volume contains information about fifty-nine 33 1/3-rpm discs, many of which are rereleases of the material originally contained on 107 78-rpm discs. The listings are arranged sequentially by record label number. Each entry presents the following information: name of the album; name of the editor; record label number; a brief description of the disc(s), e.g., "LP 33 1/3 rpm," or "Five 78 rpm records"; price; titles of the songs; name(s) of the performer(s); place and date of recording; name(s) of those who collected the song. Included among the albums are: "Afro-American Spirituals, Work Songs, and Ballads," "Afro-American Blues and Game Songs," "Negro Work Songs and Calls," "Negro Religious Songs and Services," and "Afro-Bahian Religious Songs from Brazil." The indexes provide access to the songs through an "Alphabetical List of Album and Long-Playing Titles," an "Alphabetical List of Titles," and a "Geographical Index."

## *JAZZ AND RAGTIME*

61. Peek, Philip M., comp. Catalog of Afro-American Music and Oral Data Holdings. Bloomington, Ind.: Folklore Institute, Archives of Traditional Music, 1970. 28 pp.

This is a listing of sound recordings of black American music, as well as materials relating to the field, which are among the holdings of Indiana University's Archives of Traditional Music as of March 1970. The approximately seven hundred listed items include musical and oral data recordings collected from North, Central, and

61. Peek (continued)

South America, as well as the Caribbean. The music listings are limited, primarily, to folk music: "Shouts, Hollers, Work Songs;" "General Folk;" "Topical;" children's songs; blues; religious music; rhythm & blues; jug, washboard, and miscellaneous bands; and jazz. Oral data listings include "Sermons and Services," folk tales, jokes, poetry, lectures on the sociology and politics of race, and other items. Appearing in most listings are the names of the performer(s), collection(s), and editor(s); year of acquisition or publication; size of the item (in number of tape reels, cylinders, or discs); and the repository's Archives Accession Number.

62. Blackstone, Orin. Index to Jazz: Jazz Recordings 1917-1944. 1945, 1947, 1948. Reprint. Westport, Conn.: Greenwood Press, 1978. 444 pp.

Included in this work are all of the "hot" items issued between 1917 and 1944. Designed for record collectors, the work contains the recorded output of the obscure and well-known individuals and groups in the field of "hot jazz." The Index, compiled from early Record Changer issues, was originally published in four sections; this 1978 reprint is in one volume. The discs are arranged alphabetically by performer(s), and are listed in the order of their issue, together with the following information: name of performer or group; personnel; catalog number(s); titles of sides; master number; and reissue number.
Reviews:   American Reference Books Annual 11:440 '80; Reference Services Review 6:7 Jy '78

63. Bruyninckx, Walter, comp. Fifty Years of Recorded Jazz, 1917-1967. 40 vols. Mechelen, Belgium: Walter Bruyninckx, 1967-1975. irregular pagination.

Probably the most complete of all jazz discographies, extending into the closely related areas of rhythm & blues, the spiritual, and the blues, this monumental work is organized alphabetically by artist, with each entry carrying matrix numbers, titles of cuts, label numbers, and dates of the recording sessions. Included are all the important and lesser known figures in jazz who recorded during the fifty year period covered by the work.
Reviews:   Cadence 4:26 Jy '78; Cadence 5:29 Ap '79; Jazz Journal International 33:16 Au '80; Jazz Podium 28:50 My '79; Orkester Journalen 46:2 S '78; Reference Services Review 6:5 Jy '78; Reference Services Review 6:8 Jy '78

64. Evensmo, Jan, comp. The Jazz Solography Series. 11 vols. Hosle, Norway: Jan Evensmo, n.d. each vol. approx. 40 pp. photographs.

This series of monographs lists and treats the recorded solos of selected jazz musicians—primarily tenor saxophonists, but also alto saxophonists, trumpeters, guitarists, and vocalists—who figured importantly in the development of jazz in the 1930s and the early 1940s. Among the performers treated are Chu Berry, Herschel

64. Evensmo (continued)

Evans, Coleman Hawkins, Lester Young, Charlie Christian, and Roy Eldridge. Volume 7, The Tenor Saxophones of Budd Johnson, Cecil Scott, Elmer Williams, Dick Wilson, 1927-1942, is typical of the monographs in the series; it contains complete listings of commercially recorded performances that feature solos by the four musicians listed, containing the compiler's critical assessments of the recordings included. Each entry provides the following information: matrix number, take number, label, record number, length of solo in measures, and tempo. The author also provides his rationale for jazz criticism, supplementing it with a critical assessment of each of the works included in the volume.

65. Fox, Charles, Peter Gammond, Alun Morgan, and Alex Korner. Jazz On Record: A Critical Guide. London: Hutchinson of London, 1960. 352 pp. appendixes. index.

This is a guide to selected mainstream and modern jazz records, with critical sketches on a wide range of jazz and blues musicians such as Blind Boy Fuller, Cannonball Adderly, Mildred Bailey, Louis Armstrong, Ornette Coleman, and many others. The authors discuss the subjects' influences and their associates, give critical assessments of the performers listed, provide overviews of the performers' styles, and recommend a highly selective list of recordings for each musician. This book is a good source with which to begin critical studies on any of the performers listed.
Reviews: Gramophone 38:507 Mr '61; Jazz Hot 167:41 Jy/Au '61; Jazz Monthly 6:30 Ja '61

66. Jasen, David A. Recorded Ragtime, 1897-1958. Hamden, Conn.: Shoe String Press, 1973. viii, 115 pp. bibliography. index.

This discography is a listing of all 78-rpm flat-disc recordings which were released on thirty-one different labels from 1897 to 1958. It is organized by title of composition with each entry identifying the composer, performer(s), record company and number, and the year and month in which the particular recording was made.
Reviews: AB Bookman's Weekly 52:344 Jy 30 '73; Choice 10:1358 N '73; Coda 11:7 '74; Jazz Digest 2:44 N/D '73; Jazz Journal 27:3 My '74; Jazz Report 8:32 '73; Journal of Popular Culture 7:356 '73; Library Journal 98:3005 O 15 '73; Notes 31:63 S '74; Ragtimer p9 S/O '70

67. Jepsen, Jorgen Grunnet. Jazz Records, 1942-1969. 8 vols. Copenhagen: Knudson, 1963-1970. each vol. approx. 400 pp.

These volumes, used together with Brian Rust's Jazz Records, 1897-1942, cover the history of recorded jazz to 1969. The entries appear alphabetically by artist, giving instrumentations, matrix numbers, titles, session dates, labels, and record numbers. This work is an essential tool for jazz researchers.

67. Jepsen (continued)

> Reviews: Blues Unlimited 85:22 O '71; Coda 9:7 '71; Coda 10:14 '71; Jazz Hot 266:33 N '70; Jazz Hot 275:32 S '71; Jazz Monthly 189:28 N '70; Orkester Journalen 38:18 Jy/Au '70

68. Lyons, Len. The 101 Best Jazz Albums: A History of Jazz Records. New York: William Morrow and Co., 1980. 476 pp. photographs. appendixes. bibliography. index.

> Intended as a consumer's guide, this compendium of long-playing disc recordings of ragtime, New Orleans jazz, swing, bebop, modern jazz, fusion, and free jazz is an excellent handbook for the beginning jazz researcher. The book focuses on music of the most important figures in jazz history and chronicles their contributions to its evolution and substance. The author has sought to document these artists' "peak periods of creativity" and to present the progress of jazz by offering a selection of what he considers to be the 101 most important records to be made over the past sixty years. The book is divided into three main sections: "Traditional Jazz," "Modern Jazz," and "Contemporary Jazz," each of which is broken into a number of chapters. The chapters cover the various genres of jazz-oriented black music, not only treating the selected recordings, but also listing general discographies of "Available Recommended Albums." Each of the three main sections ends with several photographs of the principal musicians of the period under treatment. Two valuable appendixes are included: "The 101 Best Jazz Albums" and a list of the "Names and Addresses of Record Labels and Companies."
>
> Reviews: Booklist 77:496 D 1 '80; Cadence 7:25 Mr '81; Contemporary Keyboard 7:59 Mr '81; Downbeat 48:69 N '81; Library Journal 105:2415 N 15 '80; Reference Services Review 9:35 Ap '81

69. McCarthy, Albert, Alun Morgan, Paul Oliver, and Max Harrison. Jazz on Record; A Critical Guide to the First Fifty Years: 1917-1967. Foreword by John Hammond. London: Hanover Books, 1968. vi, 416 pp. index.

> The guide is a selective discography of what the authors consider to be the best, most significant, or the most typical commercially recorded performances of the most important jazz artists of the designated fifty year period. The volume lists numerous recordings by approximately two thousand jazz musicians who were chosen for inclusion on the basis of their "historical or musical significance" (p. v). This superbly organized work has two main parts, the first of which treats "Individual Jazz and Blues Artists," while the second goes somewhat beyond jazz to include collective headings such as "Arrangers and Composers," "Blues Festivals and Concerts," "Field Calls and Hollers," "Post-War Brass," and several others. In addition to basic discographical information, each entry includes a discussion of the individual artist or group. The discographical

69.  McCarthy (continued)

listings include British- and American-released 78-rpm and microgroove discs.
Reviews: AB Bookman's Weekly 44:316 Au 4 '69; Billboard 81:12 Ap 12 '69; Blues Unlimited 60:30 Mr '69; Jazz and Pop 8:13 S '69; Jazz Monthly 167:29 Ja '69; Matrix 81:12 F '69; Melody Maker 44:16 Ja 11 '69; Musical Times 110:634 Ju '69; Notes 26:756 Ju '70; Pieces of Jazz 6:2 '69; Recorded Sound 38:627 Ap '70

70.  McCoy, Meredith, and Barbara Parker, comps. Catalog of the John D. Reid Collection of Early American Jazz. Little Rock: Arkansas Art Center, 1975. 112 pp. photographs.

This monograph contains entries for "4,000 records taken from 10,000 discs" (p. [7]) collected primarily between 1935 and 1945 and currently held by the Arkansas Art Center. The entries are organized into five chapters: 1) "Original Recordings," containing references to sound recordings of performances, by nine groups or soloists, collected between 1939 and 1949, more than one-half featuring Sidney Bechet; 2) "Blues," containing references to sound recordings by 230 blues performers, including Mamie Smith, Alberta Hunter, Bessie Smith, Leadbelly, and Blind Lemon Jefferson; 3) "Bands," containing listings for 656 ensembles ranging from the early bands of King Oliver, Louis Armstrong and Jelly Roll Morton, through the big bands of Jimmie Lunceford, Fletcher Henderson, and Duke Ellington, to bands led by such figures as Fats Waller; Willie "The Lion" Smith, Clarence Williams, and Mary Lou Williams; 4) "Piano and Organ Solos," containing references to recordings by fifty-three performers, including Earl Hines, James P. Johnson, Jelly Roll Morton, Pinetop Smith, Art Tatum, and Fats Waller; and 5) "Gospel and Spirituals," containing entries for seventeen individuals and groups such as the Fisk Jubilee Singers, the Golden Gate Jubilee Quartet, and Sister Rosetta Tharpe. Each entry presents the following information: title, record label number, and the collection identification number; the latter has importance because a cassette recording of any of the recordings listed in the catalogue may be ordered from the Arkansas Art Center.

71.  Raben, Erik, comp. A Discography of Free Jazz: Albert Ayler, Don Cherry, Ornette Coleman, Pharoh Sanders, Archie Shepp, Cecil Taylor. Copenhagen: Karl Emil Knudsen, 1969. 38 pp.

This volume lists the phonorecords on which performances by each of the six artists are featured. The book is organized alphabetically by artist, and the listings for each artist are organized alphabetically by the names of the groups under which the recordings were made. Where appropriate, the information provided about each individual recording includes the name(s) of the personnel, the title of the album, the titles of the individual cuts, the place and date of recording, and the record label number. Since the artists frequently collaborated, the listing of the recordings on

71. Raben (continued)

which each artist is featured necessitates the repetition of some information in each of the six sections of the book.

72. Rust, Brian. Jazz Records, 1897-1942. 2 vols. 4th ed., rev. and enl. New Rochelle, N.Y.: Arlington House Publishers, 1978. each vol. approx. 1000 pp. indexes.

This is the "basic" two-volume discography of jazz records issued prior to 1943. The use of this set in conjunction with Jorgen Jepsen's Jazz Records, 1942-1969 gives the researcher complete discographical coverage of the jazz field from 1897 to 1969. The entries in this work appear alphabetically by artist, giving instrumentations, matrix numbers, titles, session dates, labels, and record numbers. In addition, an Artists' Index and a Title Index are included, making this tool eminently useful, handy, and effective.

Reviews: American Reference Books Annual 10:488 '79; Billboard 90:47 My 13 '78; Cadence 4:15 My '78; Catholic Library World 50:310 F '79; Choice 15:1196 N '78; Downbeat 45:63-64 O 5 '78; Hobbies 83:133 D '78; Jazz Journal International 31:32 D '79; Journal of Jazz Studies 5:91 '79; Journal of Popular Culture 12:761 Spring '79; Library Journal 103:1970 O 1 '78; Music Journal 36:39-40 S '78; Museums Journal 36:39-40 S '78; Notes 35:638 Mr '79; Radio Free Jazz 20:14 Ju '79; Reference Services Review 6:5 Jy '78; Reference Services Review 6:8 Jy '78

73. Stagg, Tom, and Charlie Crump, comps. New Orleans, the Revival: A Tape and Discography of Negro Traditional Jazz Recorded in New Orleans or by New Orleans Bands, 1937-1972. n.p.: Bashall Eaves, 1973. 332 pp. photographs. index.

This book serves as a finding aid to recordings, both issued and unissued, made by black New Orleans jazz bands between 1937 and 1972. Arranged alphabetically by the principal artist, each entry gives the following information: name of the band; place and date of recording; name of the performers together with an indication of their instruments; song title(s); and record label number. Among those whose recordings are cited are Bunk Johnson, Papa Celestin, Papa French, George Lewis, the Onward Brass Band, Kid Ory, and the Eureka Brass Band. A smaller section contains similar information for "The Religious Recordings of New Orleans" performed by persons and groups such as Sister Elizabeth Eustis, the Holy Family Spiritual Church of Christ, the New Orleans Street Gospel Singers, and the New Orleans Humming Four. Eighteen photographs of individuals and groups conclude the main body of the work. The index is divided into four sections to give access to 1) black New Orleans musicians, 2) white New Orleans musicians, 3) non-New Orleans musicians, and 4) miscellaneous persons.

Reviews: Footnote 5:24 '73/'74; Jazz Journal 27:14 Ja '74; Melody Maker 49:24 Au 31 '74; Orkester Journalen 43:2 F '75

74. Tudor, Dean, and Nancy Tudor.  Jazz.  American Music on Elpee.
Littleton, Colo.: Libraries Unlimited, 1979. 302 pp. index.

This companion to the author's Black Music is a "survey [of] and
buying guide" to approximately 1,300 long-playing "pre-selected and
annotated" jazz recordings (p. 5). The record titles are grouped into
broad sections as follows:  Anthologies; Ragtime; Geographic
Origins and Stylings; Mainstream Swing and Big Bands; Bop, Cool,
Modern; and Diverse Themes. These categories are broken down
into further divisions. Each record entry includes the name of the
"artist, title, last known serial number, and country of origin"
(p. 5). The annotations average three hundred words each. Each
discographic section is preceded by a narrative essay that discusses
definitions, history and development, hybrid forms, criteria for
selection, and other pertinent matters.  Although the historical
narrative is filled with errors of fact, this is a good record guide for
the novice researcher, especially since it identifies the innovators
in each style.
Reviews:  American Reference Books Annual 11:444 '80;
Cadence 5:28 Ap '79; Choice 16:651 Jy '79; Coda 169:15 O 1
'79; JEMF Quarterly 15:186 '79; Library Journal 104:940 Ap 15
'79; Notes 36:648 Mr '80; Reference Services Review 9:32 Ap
'81; Wilson Library Bulletin 53:655 My '79

## BLUES, GOSPEL, AND POPULAR

75. Godrich, John, and Robert M. W. Dixon, comps.  Blues and Gospel
Records. Rev. ed. London: Storyville Publications and Co., 1969. 912
pp.

The authors of this discography have attempted to list every
recording of black folk music made prior to 1943. Consequently, it
is essentially a comprehensive "race record" catalogue that includes
the black-oriented issues of such labels as Victor and Bluebird,
Columbia and Okeh, Brunswick, Vocalion, A.R.C., Gennett and
Champion, Paramount, QRS, Ajax, and Decca. Not listed are the
black-owned "race" labels of Black Swan and Black Patti. This
source book provides researchers with information on the entire
recorded output of gospel singers and groups such as the Dinwiddie
Colored Quartet, the Heavenly Gospel Singers, Mitchell's Christian
Singers, the Gospeleers, the Golden Gate Quartet, and Mahalia
Jackson, and of blues groups and singers such as Georgia White,
Peetie Wheatstraw, Roosevelt Sykes, the Sparks Brothers, Huddie
Ledbetter, The Five Breezes, Ethel Waters, the Memphis Jug Band,
and many other artists of the approximately forty year period,
1902-1942.  The work is arranged alphabetically by artist's or
group's last name, with their recorded tunes listed in chronological
order.  The entries provide session credits, accompaniment
information, recording dates, matrix numbers, "take" numbers,
Library of Congress numbers, and issue numbers.  This is an
indispensable source for researchers of early blues and gospel
music.

75. Godrich (continued)

> Reviews: Blues Unlimited 65:20 S '69; Ethnomusicology 14:499 '70; Jazz Journal 22:24 D '69; Jazz Monthly 175:26 S '69; JEMF Quarterly 6:40 '70; Melody Maker 44:12 Jy 12 '69; Orkester Journalen 38:2 Ja '70; Record Research 106:9 Jy '70; Saturday Review of Literature p62 My 15 '65

76. Gonzales, Fernando L. Disco-File: The Discographical Catalog of American Rock & Roll and Rhythm & Blues, 1902–1976. Foreword by Marv Goldberg. Introduction by Rick Whitesell. Flushing, N.Y.: Fernando L. Gonzales, 1977. viii, 447 pp. appendixes.

> Containing more than thirty-one thousand titles, this book lists the recorded output of rock & roll and rhythm & blues vocal groups from 1902 to 1976. It also includes titles and information on groups that are peripheral to those styles, i.e., spiritual and gospel groups such as the Dinwiddie Quartet, Southern Negro Quartet, Golden Gate Quartet, Mills Brothers, Ink Spots, and others. But the bulk of the book's contents comprise R&B groups from the 1950s and 1960s—groups such as the Five Red Caps, Ravens, Robins, Orioles, Flamingoes, Five Satins, Supremes, Temptations, and hundreds of other similar groups. The contents appear alphabetically by the names of the groups, each entry including label and number, title of cut, recording date, and master number. The appendixes include lists of "Bootleg and Private Releases" and "Unissued Recordings." This work is an indispensable tool for researchers of R&B and soul music.
> Reviews: Melody Maker 54:54 Ju 16 '75; Reference Services Review 6:5 Jy '78; Reference Services Review 6:9 Jy '78

77. Hayes, Cedric J., comp. A Discography of Gospel Records, 1937–1971. Copenhagen: Karl Emil Knudsen, 1973. 116 pp.

> This compilation of commercial recordings of fourteen black American gospel singers is a convenient and important source for researchers of Afro-American gospel music. Although the various listings are incomplete, the book contains numerous citations of recordings by the Caravans, Dixie Hummingbirds, Original Five Blind Boys, Gospelaires, Mahalia Jackson, Mighty Clouds of Joy, Soul Stirrers, Spirit of Memphis Quartet, Staple Singers, Stars of Faith, Swan Silvertone Singers, Sister Rosetta Tharpe, Ward Singers, and Marion Williams. Appearing alphabetically, the entries include the following information: personnel (in the cases of groups, each member is named), instrumentation, location of session, date of session, matrix number, titles of sides, lead singer, label, and record number.

78. Hounsome, Terry, and Tim Chambre. Rock Record. New York: Facts on File, 1981. x, 526 pp. index.

Original title: Rockmaster, published in 1978. The present edition is a

78.  Hounsome (continued)

revised   and   expanded   version,  published  in  Great  Britain  as  New
Rock Record (1981).

This discography "contains some 4,500 entries, 30,000 LP records
and  25,000  different  musicians"  (p.  vii).   The  book  is  organized
alphabetically by artist or group.  Each entry contains a list of the
names of the record albums made by the entry subject; each album
title is  accompanied  by  the  name  of  the  record  company  that
produced it, the catalogue number, and, in most cases, the year the
album was issued.  Also included in each entry are a list of the
musicians  who  participated  in  one  or  more  of  the  albums  and
indications  of  their  instruments.    Although  the  book  is  not
absolutely  all-inclusive,  it  includes  groups  and  individuals  that
recorded  in  the  field  of  rock  &  roll  from  the  mid-1950s  to  1981;
some examples are Little Richard, Little Walter, the Platters, Sam
Cooke, the Drifters, Ray Charles, Wilson Pickett, the Supremes, the
Commodores, Jimi Hendrix, Chaka Khan, and Gladys Knight and the
Pips.  The scope of the book also extends beyond a strict definition
of  "rock"  and  includes  "much  information  on  pop,  soul,  reggae,
jazz/rock, blues, country and folk music as well . . ." (p. vii).
Reviews:  American Reference Books Annual 13:527 '82; Book
World 11:12 O 18 '81; Choice 19:1380 Ju '82; Library Journal
107:248 F 1 '82; Library Journal 107:960 My 15 '82; Melody
Maker 56:4 N 7 '81; Reference Services Review 9:26 Ap '81;
Stereo Review 47:94 Mr '82

79.  Leadbitter, Mike, and Neil Slaven.  Blues Records, January 1943 to
December 1966.  New York: Oak Publications, 1968.  381 pp.

This discography takes up where Godrich and Dixon's Blues and
Gospel Records leaves off with its blues items.  The work is
intended to include all blues artists who may be of interest to
collectors of blues records.  The entries appear alphabetically by
author's name or nickname, ranging from J. T. Adams to Muddy
Waters, and including such artists as Sonny Boy Williamson, Sonny
Terry and Brownie McGhee, Little Walter, Albert King, Howlin'
Wolf, Peg Leg Howell, Son House, John Lee Hooker, Cecil Gant,
Lowell Fulson, and all the other great, and the unknown, blues
artists.    Each  entry  includes  vital  data  (if  available);
instrumentation; matrix number; title; city and date of recording
session; and record number.
Reviews:  Billboard 81:12 Ap 12 '69; Jazz and Pop 8:54 Jy '69;
Jazz and Pop 8:13 S '69; Jazz Hot 247:5 F '69; Jazz Monthly
167:27 Ja '69; Library Journal 94:2456 '69; Matrix 81:13 F '69;
Melody Maker 44:11 Mr 8 '69; Orkester Journalen 37:27 Ja '69;
Recorded Sound 38:628 Ap '70

80.  Propes, Steve.  Golden Oldies:  A Guide to 60s Record Collecting.
Radnor, Penn.: Chilton Book Co., 1974.  xii, 240 pp.

This book covers the rhythm & blues and rock & roll 45-rpm singles
of the 1960s.  Comprising "the representative best of 60s popular

80. Propes (continued)

music" (p. vii), the records are listed in fourteen sections ranging from "Early Rhythm and Blues Artists" to "British Hard Rock," the latter featuring The Jimi Hendrix Experience. The other sections feature recordings by more than one hundred other individuals and groups, including Sam Cooke, The Four Seasons, The Isley Brothers, "Notable Do-Wop Vocal Groups," The Shirelles, "Notable Female Vocal Groups," Marvin Gaye, Stevie Wonder, The Dells, Wilson Pickett, and Sly and the Family Stone. The opening chapter, titled "Record Collecting," discusses "The Long Play versus the 45 RPM Record," bootlegs, sources for original records, collectors' magazines, and other matters pertinent to record collecting. The second chapter, which precedes the discography, discusses the "Dominant Themes in 60s Music"--dance records, implied sex/drugs, rebellion, and civil rights.

    Reviews: AB Bookman's Weekly 54:1936 N 4 '74; Booklist 71:366 D 1 '74; Choice 11:1112 O '74; Hobbies 79:158 O '74; Library Journal 99:1956 Au '74; Reference Services Review 2:144 O '74; Reference Services Review 3:16 Ap '75

81. Schleman, Hilton R. Rhythm On Record. 1936. Reprint. Westport, Conn.: Greenwood Press, 1978. 333 pp. photographs. index.

This book is devoted to the "rhythm" or "sweet" performing groups—bands and vocal ensembles—active between the years 1906-1936, a thirty year period during which dancing was one of the primary means of popular social intercourse. It is a discographical listing of the important dance music recordings of the period that it treats. Alphabetically arranged by author/group, each entry contains a short biographical sketch; in the case of a group, a listing of personnel; and a list of recorded works by label and number. The primary value of the book lies in its inclusion of bands and vocal groups that are not usually listed in other sources, e.g., Handy's Orchestra, Jones Jazz Wizards, The Versatile Four, The Dixie Rhythm Kings, The Three Keys, and other all-black groups.

    Reviews: Music Journal 36:51 D '78

82. Tudor, Dean, and Nancy Tudor. Black Music. American Popular Music on Elpee. Littleton, Colo.: Libraries Unlimited, 1979. 262 pp. book citations. directories. artists index.

This buying guide to black popular music on discs and tapes is also a valuable research tool. It contains a well-organized compilation of 1,300 selected and annotated recordings of blues, rhythm & blues, gospel, soul, and reggae music. Included are "roots anthologies," general anthologies, field recordings, and albums of such blues types as vocal blues, topical blues, rural blues, acoustic and electric blues, and "classic" and jump blues made by male and female individuals and groups. In each category, the performers are grouped as "innovators" or "standards." This work is not simply a selective discography, however. It briefly discusses the various stylings, and it reviews the printed literature that pertains to each

82. Tudor (continued)

genre. The annotations are quite informative and serve as reliable guides to acquisition, research, and teaching.
Reviews: American Reference Books Annual 11:443 '80; Cadence 5:28 Ap '79; Library Journal 104:940 Ap 15 '79; Notes 36:648 Mr '80; Reference Services Review 9:32 Ap '81; Wilson Library Bulletin 53:655 My '79

83. Whitburn, Joel, comp. Top Pop Records, 1955-1970: Facts About 9800 Recordings Listed in Billboard's "Hot 100" Charts, Grouped Under the Names of 2500 Recording Artists. Detroit: Gale Research Co., Book Tower, 1972. 662 pp. photographs. indexes.

Included here are all the records that reached every Billboard chart between late October of 1955 and late December of 1970. Each particular entry includes the following information: the date the record first hit the chart, the highest position reached by the record, the total number of weeks on the chart, record title, and label and record number. Peaches and Herb, The Mills Brothers, B. B. King, Eddie Heywood, Marvin Gaye, Count Basie, and James Brown are among the wide variety of black artists listed.
Reviews: Billboard 86:3 Ja 5 '74; Reference Services Review 6:6 Jy '78; School Musician 44:36 Ap '73

## CONCERT MUSIC

84. De Lerma, Dominique-René. Concert Music and Spirituals: A Selective Discography. Occasional Papers, no. 1. Nashville, Tenn.: Fisk University Institute for Research in Black American Music, 1981. 14, 43 pp. index.

Based on the compiler's personal record collection, this reference tool contains listings of commercially available disc recordings of over five hundred works by ninety-four black composers of concert music and of spirituals that have been composed or arranged by black writers. Arranged alphabetically by composer and, under composer, by title, each title entry includes the following information: record number, date of issue (when available), duration and recording date (when applicable). A convenient feature of this provisional list is its "media index," which contains thirty performance categories, including, for example, "Voice and Chorus," "String Ensemble," "Orchestra," "Opera," "Flute," and "Band."

85. De Lerma, Dominique-René. Discography of Concert Music by Black Composers. Afro-American Music Opportunities Association Resource Papers, no. 1. Minneapolis: AAMOA Press, 1973. 29 pp. index.

This monograph lists recorded works by black composers including American composers, organized by phonorecord label number. It contains 203 entries, many of which are no longer in print; only

## 85. De Lerma (continued)

those works which the author has identified as "concert music"--art songs, chamber and symphonic compositions, and formal solo instrumental literature—are included. The index is organized by composer.

Reviews: Choice 12:510 Ju '75

## 86. Turner, Patricia. Afro-American Singers: An Index and Preliminary Discography of Opera, Choral Music and Song. Minneapolis: Challenge Productions, 1977. xvi, 255 pp. bibliography. appendix. addenda. index.

This discography contains listings of the recorded performances of approximately ninety black American singers and eight choral groups singing the music of more than 150 composers, fourteen of whom are black. Divided into five main sections—"Singers and Recordings," "Choral Groups," "Composers and Recordings," "Arias," and "Songs"—the entries are alphabetized by singers' last names, and include brief biographical sketches, quotations from record reviews, listings of records, and selected biographical sources. Out-of-print items are noted, black composers are identified, and release dates are indicated.

Reviews: American Reference Books Annual 10:476 '79; Association for Recorded Sound Collections, Journal 9:114-116 n1 '77; Fontes Artis Musicae 25:416-417 n4 '78; Notes 35:94 S '78

# VI

# Indexes and Guides
to Periodical Literature

## GENERAL

87. Hallie Q. Brown Memorial Library, Central State University, Wilberforce, Ohio. Index to Periodical Articles By and About Blacks. Boston: G. K. Hall & Co., 1974-. each vol. approx. 500 pp. published annually.

Published between 1950 and 1970 as Index to Selected Periodicals Received in the Hallie Q. Brown Memorial Library. Boston: G. K. Hall & Co. decennial cumulations. Published between 1971 and 1973 as Index to Periodical Articles By and About Negroes. Boston: G. K. Hall & Co. annual cumulations.

Articles contained in approximately twenty-two black periodicals are indexed in this series of books; among them are such scholarly publications as Phylon, Crisis, Black Scholar, Journal of Black Studies, Journal of Negro History, Negro History Bulletin, Journal of Negro Education, Journal of Religious Thought, and Negro Educational Review. Also indexed are popular magazines—Jet, Ebony, Essence—in which useful information might be found. The entries in the work are arranged in alphabetical order by subject and by author. The Index is useful as a finding tool for periodical articles which are not as readily accessible in other sources. For example, the Reader's Guide to Periodical Literature indexes only five of the periodicals found in the present work.
Reviews: Wilson Library Bulletin 47:529 F '73

88. Jacobs, Donald M., ed. Antebellum Black Newspapers: Indices to New York Freedom's Journal (1827-1829), The Rights of All (1829), The Weekly Advocate (1837), and The Colored American (1837-1841). Westport Conn.: Greenwood Press, 1976. 587 pp.

For scholars investigating aspects of black musical culture during the period 1827-1841, this is a potentially valuable tool. Although all the newspapers indexed here were published in New York, they contain information about the conditions and activities of black people throughout the United States. In four sections, each devoted to one newspaper, authors and subjects are listed under one alphabet in each section. While the entries under "Music" are severely limited, pertinent information can be accessed through other subjects and via the names of individuals.
   Reviews:     American Archivist 40:94 Ja '77; American Historical Review 82:1068 O '77; American Reference Books Annual 8:222 '77; Booklist 73:562 D 1 '76; Choice 14:180 Ap '77; Reference Services Review 6:8 Ap/Ju '78; RQ 16:348-349 Summer '77

89. LaBrie, Henry G., III. The Black Newspaper in America: A Guide. Iowa City:     Institute for Communication Studies, School of Journalism, University of Iowa, 1970. 64 pp.

This guide presents information about 219 black newspapers, 178 of which are published weekly or daily (forty-one of which have ceased publication) and eleven journals that publish biweekly or monthly. Entries are arranged alphabetically by state, by city, and by name of newspaper. For those newspapers or journals still being published, each entry provides the following information where appropriate:     name of newspaper, address, telephone number, circulation, editor, method of printing, day of publication, year of founding, number of staff, number of white persons on staff. Two other books with a similar purpose are worth investigating for those needing information about black newspapers; they are:     Negro Newspapers in the United States, 1964 (Jefferson City, Missouri: Department of Journalism, Lincoln University, 1964); and Directory of U.S. Negro Newspapers, Magazines and Periodicals, 1966, Frank B. Sawyer, ed. (n.p.: U.S. Negro World, n.d.).

90. Library of Congress. Negro Newspapers on Microfilm: A Selected List. Washington, D.C.: Library of Congress Photoduplication Service, 1953. [iv], 8 pp.

In this booklet, more than two hundred black newspapers of 103 cities in twenty-seven states are listed as having been microfilmed and on file at the Library of Congress as of 1953. Arranged alphabetically by state, from Alabama to Wisconsin, each entry carries the title of the paper, reel number, and title number.

91. Strache, Neil E., Maureen E. Hady, James P. Danky, Susan Bryl, and Erwin K. Welsch, comps. Black Periodicals and Newspapers: A Union List of Holdings in the Libraries of the University of Wisconsin and the

91. Strache (continued)

Library of the State Historical Society of Wisconsin. 2nd ed. Madison:
State Historical Society of Wisconsin, 1979. xiii, 83 pp. indexes.

Listed alphabetically in this monograph are the titles of "more than
600 periodicals and newspapers relating to black Americans which
were received before February, 1979" (p. iii) in the named
libraries. Many of the newspapers and periodicals began publication
or were published in the late 1800s; others are more recent and are
still being published. Each title is accompanied by the place and
date(s) of publication, the name of the library in which it is held, a
list of the holdings in that library, and the location in the library (if
known). A geographical index and a subject index conclude the
volume. This monograph would prove a valuable finding guide to
those searching for copies of black newspapers and periodicals.
Reviews: American Reference Books Annual 12:219 '81

# MUSIC

92. Brook, Barry S., ed. RILM Abstracts. Flushing, N.Y.: International
Repertory of Music Literature, 1967-. published quarterly with annual
cumulations.

Organized by subject heading, these volumes contain the following
major divisions: reference and research materials; historical
musicology; ethnomusicology; instruments and voice; performance
practice and notation; theory, analysis, and composition; pedagogy;
music and other arts; music and related disciplines; and music and
liturgy. The index covers periodical articles, books, dissertations,
reviews, and commentaries about programs, recordings, or
editions. Each entry includes standard bibliographic data plus a
brief annotation. Access to entries may be found either directly
through the various classifications into which the volume is
organized, or through the cumulative subject index contained in the
fourth issue of each year (or the quinquennial subject index).

93. Kretzschmar, Florence, ed. The Music Index. Detroit: Information
Coordinators, 1950-. each vol. approx. 850 pp. published monthly with
annual cumulations.

An indispensable tool for research, this series is a finding guide for
periodical literature in the field of music. Authors of articles,
subjects, and proper names are all listed in a single alphabet. Each
entry gives the title of the article; name(s) of its author(s); and the
title, volume, and page numbers of the periodicals in which it may
be found. During the years the series has been published, the
number of journals indexed has varied from approximately eighty to
approximately 380; many of these are of particular interest to the
researcher of black American music, including The Black
Perspective in Music, Jazz Journal, Jazz Hot, Living Blues, Melody
Maker, and The Ragtimer.

94. Maleady, Antoinette O., comp.  Index to Record and Tape Reviews:  A
    Classical Music Buying Guide.  San Anselmo, Calif.:  Chulainn Press,
    1976-. pp. per vol. varies.

    Previously published as Record and Tape Reviews Index.  Metuchen,
    N.J.:  Scarecrow Press, 1972-1975.  covering reviews written between
    1971 and 1974.

    A guide to reviews of classical music recorded on phonorecords and
    tapes, this series is comprised of several volumes, each of which
    treat reviews published in a single year beginning in 1971.  Each
    volume is organized under four section rubrics:  "Composers,"
    "Music in Collections," "Anonymous Works," and "Performer
    Index."  The first section constitutes the main portion and is
    arranged in alphabetical order by the name of the composer.  Each
    entry contains discographical information, together with a series of
    abbreviations that indicate the bibliographical source for review(s)
    of that recording.  The entries of the second section of each volume
    contain the same information and are organized under the name of
    the record label and chronologically under the record label
    number.  The last two sections consist of indexes to aid the user in
    finding reviews of works by anonymous composers and works
    performed by artists.
        Reviews:   American Music Teacher 26:47 n6 '77; American
        Recorder 17:41 n1 '76; Musical Times 118:306 Ap '77; Notes
        32:178 n4 '76

95. Music Article Guide.  Ann Arbor, Mich.:  Music Article Guide, 1965-.
    each vol. approx. 35 pp. published quarterly.

    This is an annotated listing of articles that have been printed in
    some current American music periodicals since 1965.  Each issue
    contains titles of articles appearing in journals received by the
    editors during the three-month period prior to its publication.  The
    listings are alphabetical by subject heading and include complete,
    although abbreviated, reference information.  The fact that the
    subject headings change with each issue is an unattractive feature
    of the Guide, being both inconvenient and irritating.  Aside from
    listing articles from such well-known journals as Musical Quarterly
    and Music Journal, the Guide also includes titles from participating
    bulletins particularly relevant to black music research, such as
    American Folklore Newsletter, The Black Perspective in Music, and
    Jazz Report.  Conspicuously absent are journals such as Living
    Blues and Journal of Jazz Studies.

96. Ruecker, Norbert, and Christa Reggentin-Scheidt, comps.  The Jazz
    Index:  Bibliography of Jazz Literature in Periodicals and Collections.
    Frankfurt, West Germany: Norbert Ruecker, 1977-. each vol. approx.
    500 pp. published quarterly with annual cumulations. index.

    Indexed in this series are periodicals that publish articles related to
    jazz, including The Grackle, Blues Unlimited, Down Beat, Jazz
    Research, Journal of Jazz Studies, Rag Times, The Second Line, and

96. Ruecker (continued)

Storyville. The volumes contain both English and German text; the subject entries are alphabetized according to the German term. Entry keywords consist of subjects and proper names. Each entry contains the name of the article; the name(s) of the author(s); and the title, volume, and page number of the periodical in which it may be found. Supplements contain a list of the periodicals indexed and an author index.

97. Tudor, Dean, and Linda Biesenthal, comps. Annual Index to Popular Music Record Reviews. Metuchen, N.J.: Scarecrow Press, 1973-. each vol. approx. 500-600 pp. indexes.

A guide to reviews of popular music on phonorecords and tape recordings, this series was intended as an aid to libraries in collecting popular music recordings. Critiques from both American and European periodicals are indexed in the series. Each volume of the series compiles reviews published during the previous year, beginning with 1972. The chapters of each volume are organized under topical headings; among the pertinent rubrics are "Jazz," "Blues," and "Rhythm and Blues [and Soul]." The entries in each chapter are arranged in alphabetical order by name of performer and contain discographical information, together with bibliographical information about the pertinent review(s). For listings of reviews by subject and author, see the Popular Music Periodicals Index annotated below.

98. Tudor, Dean, and Linda Biesenthal, comps. Popular Music Periodicals Index. Metuchen, N.J.: Scarecrow Press, 1974-. each vol. approx. 250-350 pp.

This index is intended to be used in conjunction with Tudor and Biesenthal's Annual Index to Popular Music Record Reviews. The reviews in the latter volume are listed under the name of the performer of a certain category of music. Each volume of the Popular Music Periodicals Index compiles reviews published during the previous year, beginning with 1973, and is organized into two sections—a subject index and an author index. The entries in each section are arranged in alphabetical order and contain discographical information together with bibliographical information about the pertinent review(s).

Reviews: Fontes Artis Musicae 23:147 n3 '76; Library Journal 101:2360 N 15 '76; Living Blues 23:44 S/O '75

# VII

# Indexes and Catalogues of Printed and Recorded Music

99. Board of Music Trade of the United States of America. Complete Catalogue of Sheet Music and Musical Works, 1870. Introduction by Dena J. Epstein. New York: Da Capo, 1973. xxvi, 575 pp.

This volume "can be regarded as a cross-section of what was published in mid-nineteenth century United States" (p. xx). It presents an indexing of the entire list of compositions published in 1870 by the twenty firms that were members of the Board of Music Trade at that time. The titles are grouped according to "categories that were . . . familiar to the trade" (p. xx) in 1870, e.g., "Duetts," "Rondos, Fantasies, Variations, &c.," "Overtures, Battle Pieces, &c." "Redowas and Polka Redowas," "Four Hands," or "Flute Solo." Within each category, the titles are arranged alphabetically (with initial articles included) and are accompanied by a numeral representing the publisher, the name of the composer, and the price of the sheet. Use of the volume is hindered by the lack of a composer index, making it necessary for a user to search entire lists of compositions when information about a particular person's works is needed.
Reviews: Choice 11:733 Jy '74

100. Cleveland Public Library. Index to Negro Spirituals. Cleveland: Cleveland Public Library, 1937. 149 pp.

This research tool lists more than one thousand spirituals found in thirty anthologies that were widely held and frequently used in branches of the Cleveland Public Library at the time that this work was produced. The work takes note of identical songs that have

100. Cleveland Library (continued)

> different titles (e.g., "Lay This Body Down" aka "O Graveyard" and "My Soul is a Witness" aka "Witness for My Lord"), different songs that have identical titles, and songs having similar titles but having no other relationships. Each entry gives the title of the song; any cross-listings; the compiler(s) and title(s) of the collection(s) in which the song can be found, together with the page reference; and the library catalogue number of the collection(s). This is an indispensable source for comprehensive research on the Afro-American spiritual.

101. Davis, Elizabeth A., comp. Index to the New World Recorded Anthology of American Music: A Users Guide to the Initial One Hundred Records. New York: W. W. Norton & Co., 1981. ix, 235 pp.

> This is a comprehensive guidebook to the repertoire and narrative text of the title collection. Although designed as a guide to the Recorded Anthology, the book is also useful as a more independent research tool for the investigation of more than two hundred years of American music, including that of Afro-Americans. In five parts, this work consists of a "Master Index," an "Index to Recorded Material," an "Index to Printed Material," an "Index to Genres and Performing Media," and a "Chronological Index." Each of these indexes is preceded by a short introductory paragraph that explains the functions and structure of the index and makes recommendations for its use. The following information is included in the Master Index: record title; liner note author; composer, title, and performers for each individual selection; and information on the cover art. The remaining four subsidiary indexes are keyed and refer back to the Master Index. A quick perusal of the A—C entries of the "Index to Recorded Materials" reveals dozens of black music entries including, the following: Alton A. Adams, "Ain't Misbehavin'," David Baker, Bandana Days, Blackbirds of 1928, Blind Blake, James A. Bland, Clifford Brown, Harry T. Burleigh, "Castle House Rag," Buck Clayton, and Clouds of Joy. The Index to Printed Material will lead the user to liner notes on a variety of topics; the jazz entry, for example, will refer the user directly to eight such narrative writings, and through cross-references to fifteen others. The Index to Genres and Performing Media is broken into numerous categories and subcategories; among those pertaining directly to black music are Blues, Boogie Woogie, Jazz, Ragtime, Rhythm & Blues, and Spirituals. Titles of cries, hollers, folksongs, show music, and other black music genres can be found in other, more comprehensive, categories. The Chronological Index lists the recorded selections alphabetically, from the earliest to the latest, beginning with those composed in the 1770s and ending with works completed in 1977.

102. De Charms, Desiree, and Paul F. Breed. Songs in Collections: An Index. Detroit: Information Service, 1966. xxxix, 588 pp. indexes.

> At least eleven collections of black songs are indexed in this book—

102. De Charms (continued)

including anthologies of spirituals and of art songs by Harry
Burleigh, Edgar Clark, Hall Johnson, William Grant Still, and John
Work. The book is convenient to use, being organized for easy
reference. The indexed collections are listed at the front of the
book; this section is followed by the various lists of composed songs,
anonymous songs and folk songs, carols, and sea chanties. The
indexes of titles/first lines and of authors are additional
conveniences.

Reviews: American Organist 49:8 S '66; Antiquarian Bookman
37:2132 My 16 '66; Choice 3:891 D '66; Journal of Research in
Music Education 15:169-170 n2 '67; Library Journal 91:3188 Ju
15 '66; Library Quarterly 37:135 Ja '67; Library Review 20:489
Au '66; Musical Events 21:33 D '66; Musical Opinion 89:737 S
'66; Musikhendel 17:401 n8 '66; Musikrevy 21:311-312 n7/8 '66;
Musik und Gesellschaft 17:496-497 Jy '67; Notes 23:269-270 n2
'66; Österreichische Musikzeitschrift 22:683 N '67; Recorded
Sound 27:230 Jy '67; Sing Out 16:63 n4 '66; Wilson Library
Bulletin 4:427 D '66

103. Eagon, Angelo. Catalog of Published Concert Music by American
Composers. 2nd ed. Metuchen, N.J.: Scarecrow Press, 1969. viii, 348
pp. supplements [published by Scarecrow Press]. indexes.

The published music listed in these volumes is organized into the
following categories according to medium: 1) Vocal—solo; chorus,
both a cappella and accompanied; and chorus with instrumental
ensemble accompaniment; 2) Instrumental Solo—keyboard, strings,
woodwind, and brass; 3) Instrumental Ensemble—strings, woodwind,
and brass; 4) Concert Jazz; 5) Percussion; 6) Orchestra; 7) Opera;
and 8) Band. Each entry includes the title of the work, the name of
the composer, the name of the publisher of the work, as well as
other information appropriate to the individual entry, i.e., range,
the author of the text, duration, the voice range(s) of solo(s) used,
the type of instruments needed for the accompaniment,
instrumentation, and the names of the movements of the work.
Each of the volumes provides a list of publishers with their
addresses. Subsequent supplements are planned for biennial issue.

Reviews: American Music Teacher 20:32 n6 '71; Library
Journal 94:3039 S 15 '69; Music Educators Journal 58:14 D '71;
Notes 26:759-760 n4 '70; Pan Pipes 63:25 n2 '71; RQ 9:265
Spring '70; Wilson Library Bulletin 44:329 N '69

104. Finding List of Vocal Music. Rochester, N.H.: J. B. Cook & Co., 1969.
xvi, 260 pp.

The individual song titles contained in more than one thousand song
books are listed here in alphabetical order. Some titles are
followed by the name of the composer; all titles are accompanied
by the title of the song album in which it may be found, and an
indication of the album's publisher. Many titles may be found in
several song books. The songs that are indexed here cover a wide

104. Finding List (continued)

range of musical styles and include popular songs by black American composers such as "Ain't Misbehavin'," "Sophisticated Lady," "Strange Fruit," "Beat Me, Daddy, Eight to the Bar," and "In the Baggage Coach Ahead." This volume is useful for a scholar searching for a printed copy of a given popular song.

105. Havlice, Patricia Pate. Popular Song Index. Metuchen, N.J.: Scarecrow Press, 1975. 933 pp. supplement. bibliography. index.

"The purpose of this volume is to provide a tool for finding words and music to folk songs, pop tunes, spirituals, hymns, children's songs, sea chanteys, and blues" (p. v). Among the 301 collections, indexed are Slave Songs of the United States, W. F. Allen et al., eds.; The Treasury of Negro Spirituals, H. A. Chambers, ed.; American Negro Songs and Spirituals, J. W. Work, ed.; Treasury of the Blues, W. C. Handy, ed. The black composers represented in the book include Fats Waller, Bob Cole, J. R. Johnson, James A. Bland, Eubie Blake, and Duke Ellington. The main body of the book consists of an alphabetical listing of the song title, the first line of the song, and first line of the song's chorus. Thus, each song indexed may have as many as three separate entries. The title entry itself contains the song title, as well as the first line of the song and of the chorus, and one or more numerals which refer to the anthologies in the bibliography. In addition, the two first-line entries are cross-referenced to the title entry, providing a point of access for the researcher who does not know the title of the desired song at hand. The index lists composers and lyricists.
Reviews: American Reference Books Annual 7:490 '76; Booklist 73:280 O 1 '76; Choice 13:44+ Mr '76; Library Journal 101:603 F 15 '76; Music Educators Journal 62:121 Mr '76; Notes 32:781 n4 '76; Reference Services Review 4:25 O '76; Reference Services Review 5:27 Ja '77; RQ 15:271-272 Spring '76; Wilson Library Bulletin 50:492 F '76

106. Library of Congress, Copyright Office. Catalog of Copyright Entries: Music. Washington, D.C.: Library of Congress Copyright Office, 1946-. each vol. approx. 800 pp.

This catalogue lists all the musical compositions registered with the United States Copyright Office from 1946 onward. It includes published and unpublished titles, as well as renewals entered during six-month periods. (Registrations were issued in monthly installments prior to 1946.) From 1946 through 1956, entries were listed by title. From 1957, entries come under main headings such as composer, editor, arranger, or (rarely) title. Information provided under each main heading includes: title; name(s) of author(s); name of publisher and place of publication; copyright data, including name and address of claimant, publication date, and copyright registration number. Through 1965, name indexes were included in each volume; from 1966 onward, name indexes are published as separate volumes. A perusal of the 1966 January-

106. Library (continued)

> June name index will reveal entries by a large number of black composers and arrangers, e.g., James Cleveland (7), Duke Ellington (39), Ulysses Kay (5), Hale Smith (2), Stevie Wonder (9), and Julian Work (33).

107. Library of Congress, Music Division. Negro Spiritual Card Index. n.d. 3 drawers.

> This card file is organized into two sections. The first is a short index of 119 collections of spirituals held by the Library of Congress at the time the index was compiled, probably in the 1930s. Organized by compiler's last names, the cards in this section contain complete bibliographical information and LC card catalogue numbers for each collection. The second section is the main file—a "Title and First Line" index—with each card bearing the title of a spiritual, the first line of that spiritual, and a letter symbol keyed to the anthologies in the index of collections.

108. Library of Congress, Music Division. Whittlesey File. n.d. fifteen drawers of catalogue cards.

> This research tool is divided into three main sections: Black Music Index (five drawers); Southern Instrumental Music (four drawers); and Southern Vocal Music (five drawers). The Black Music Index is organized by name of composer or performing group, and also by subject, i.e., publishers, bibliography, hymnbooks, violinists, etc. The Southern Instrumental Music section is organized by title of composition. The Southern Vocal Music section is organized by title and by subject, e.g., biography, broadsides, guitar music, theoretical works, and so on. This tool lacks documentation of the racial heritage of the individuals listed; therefore, it may, in some cases, be inaccurate in this respect. However, it remains an invaluable research tool because it contains much information which can not be found in other sources.

109. Shapiro, Nat, ed. Popular Music: An Annotated Index of American Popular Songs. 5 vols. New York: Adrian Press, 1964. each vol. approx. 300 pages.

> Shapiro presents "the significant songs of our time" (p. ix)—songs that "1) achieved a substantial degree of popular acceptance, 2) were exposed to the public in especially notable circumstances, or 3) were accepted and given important performances by influential musical and dramatic artists" (p. x). Indexed items are song titles; names of composers, publishers, and copyright holders; discographical information for the best-selling records, and the sources of the songs. Spanning the years 1920-1964, each volume covers a ten-year period (except for Volume 3, which covers the years 1960-1964). Each volume in the set includes a List of Titles and a List of Publishers.

109. Shapiro (continued)

> Reviews: Billboard 77:16 N 20 '65; Library Journal 89:4331 '64;
> Library Journal 92:3425 '67; New Yorker 40:230 O 17 '64;
> Recorded Sound 21:30-31 Ja '66

110. Voigt, John, and Randall Kane. Jazz Music in Print. Winthrop, Mass.:
Flat Nine Music, 1975. 66 pp.

> This compendium of published music by leading jazz musicians
> contains the titles of original compositions, arrangements, lead
> sheets, notated solos, methods books, and anthologies. It is
> organized alphabetically by composer/performer/arranger, and
> contains listings by such musicians as Count Basie, Ornette
> Coleman, Erroll Garner, Dizzy Gillespie, Billy Taylor, and many
> others. A valuable feature of the book is Andrew White III's long
> list of transcribed solos of John Coltrane. Although most of the
> music listed comes in the form of "piano arrangements" or lead
> sheets, listings of scores and charts, with and without parts, are
> also included. Among the latter listings are compositions by J. J.
> Johnson, Thad Jones, and John Lewis. This tool is a good source for
> the location of jazz works published prior to 1975.
> Reviews: Notes 33:84 n1 '76

# VIII

# Dictionaries
and Encyclopedias

## *GENERAL MUSIC*

111. Fink, Robert, and Robert Ricci. The Language of Twentieth Century Music: A Dictionary of Terms. New York: Schirmer Books; London: Collier Macmillan Publishers, 1975. viii, 125 pp. musical examples. bibliography.

Since much of the terminology of twentieth century music cannot be found in standard reference works, this book fills a great need. Its rather comprehensive contents cover much of the terminology of jazz, rock, electronic music, multimedia, twelve-tone music, chance music, and other genres, including that of the more traditional styles; new instruments and performance practices are also defined. Approximately seventy terms, including octad, dodecuple scale, blue note, antimusic, harmonic dualism, boogaloo, avant-garde, honky tonk, doink, fuzz bass, head riff, off-note, rip, quarternion, as well as some of the more traditional terms, grace its pages. This little book is an important contribution to contemporary music scholarship.

Reviews: American Music Teacher 27:38 n2 '77; American Reference Books Annual 7:477 '76; Choice 12:14-24 Ja '76; Choral Journal 16:32 n3 '75; Clavier 14:8 n8 '75; Diapason 66:12 N '75; Instrumentalist 30:18 Ja '76; Journal of Research in Music Education 24:90-91 n2 '76; Library Journal 100:1810 O 1 '75; Making Music 92:18 Fall '76; Musical Times 117:657-658 Au '76; Music Review 37:234-235 n3 '76; Music Teacher and Piano

111.  Fink (continued)

> Student 55:22-23 Jy '76; NATS Bulletin 32:33 n2 '75; Notes 32:555 n3 '76; Notes 32:774-775 n4 '76; Reference Services Review 5:23 Ja '77

112.  Jablonski, Edward.  The Encyclopedia of American Music.  Garden City, N.Y.:  Doubleday & Co., 1981.  xii, 629 pp.

> At this writing, this encyclopedia is the only such work devoted exclusively to American music.  Its 1,200 entries cover a wide range of pertinent topics, giving appropriate attention to black Americans.  The work is divided into seven major sections, each covering a major period in American music history.  Each section contains a brief introductory essay on appropriate historical and cultural influences and occurrences.  The entries within each section appear as composers' names, titles of compositions, names of musical genres, musical terminology, and other pertinent listings.  The work contains more than one hundred listings that pertain specifically to black music, including A. J. R. Connor, Blue Note, Pine Top Smith, William Grant Still, Funky, Motown, Hale Smith, Race Record, and Charlie Parker.
> Reviews:  Library Journal 106:2127 N 1 '82; Notes 38:607 Mr '82; Quill & Choir 48:39 Ja '82; Stereo Review 46:113 D '81

113.  Sadie, Stanley, ed.  The New Grove Dictionary of Music and Musicians. 20 vols.  London:  Macmillan Publishers; Washington D.C.:  Grove's Dictionaries of Music; Hong Kong: Peninsula Publishers, 1980.  each vol. approx. 900 pp.  musical examples, drawings, photographs.

> This comprehensive and monumental work contains 448 entries on black music, sixty-four pertaining to Africa alone.  The black music entries fall into such categories as blues, jazz, gospel, popular, South America, performance practice, biography, and several others, making this dictionary the most complete such reference work available for researchers new to the field.  The biographies carry "works" lists and bibliographical citations; the "genre" entries also carry citations, and are as thorough and as complete as space would allow.  The "Blues" entry, for example, has nine subsections: Definition; Origins; The 1920s; First Recordings; Piano Blues and the Northern Migration; 1930s Blues; Urban Blues; Postwar Blues; Blues and the White Audience; and Conclusion.
> Reviews:  Gramophone 58:1467 My '81; High Fidelity/Musical America 31:52-53 F '81; Musical Times 122:171-175 Mr '81; Musical Times 122:241-242 Ap '81; Musical Times 122:304-305+ My '81; Musical Times 122:375+ Ju '81; Music Educators Journal 67:85 F '81; Music Scene n318:16 Mr/Ap '81; Notes 38:45-59 n1 '81; Opera 32:338-339 Ap '81; Saturday Review 8:87-88 Ja '81; Soundboard 8:207-210 n3 '81; Strad 91:814-816 Mr '81; Strad 91:897-898 Ap '81

# JAZZ AND POPULAR

114. Feather, Leonard. The Encyclopedia of Jazz. Rev. ed. New York: Horizon Press, 1960. 527 pp. photographs, musical examples. bibliography.

   First published in 1955, this valuable reference work contains biographical sketches of more than three thousand jazz musicians. The work is divided into several sections of narrative text and lists, covering such topics as jazz history, chronology, "The Anatomy of Jazz," the role and place of jazz in American society, recommended "histories of jazz" on record, and the results of international jazz polls. Of significant value to researchers will be the section titled "Musicians' Birthdays" and "Musicians' Birthplaces." The biographical section is composed of entries giving the name of the performer; instrument(s) played; place and dates of birth and death; and the performer's career development, beginning with the subject's earliest musical experiences.
   Reviews: Billboard 72:45 O 17 '60; Downbeat 27:56 D 8 '60; Gramophone 39:137-138 Au '61; International Musician 59:35-36 F '61; Jazz Journal 14:36 Ju '61; Jazz Monthly 7:28 O '61; Library Journal 86:799 '61; Metronome 78:52 Ja '61; Neue Zeitschrift für Musik 123:245-246 My '62

115. Feather, Leonard. The Encyclopedia of Jazz in the Sixties. Foreword by John Lewis. New York: Horizon Press, 1966. 312 pp. photographs. bibliography.

   A compilation of a "representative cross-section" of jazz performers prominent in the 1960s, this is the second issue in the author's "Encyclopedia of Jazz" series. It is divided into several chapters that cover topics such as "The Blindfold Test," poll tabulations, "A Selected List of Recordings from the Sixties," and others. Accompanied by more than 250 photographs, the biographical sketches include the name of the performer; instrument(s) played; vital data; and a career trace.
   Reviews: American Literature 39:266 My '67; Antiquarian Bookman 39:391 Ja 30 '67; Billboard 79:58 Ja 28 '67; Choice 4:398 Ju '67; Downbeat 34:42 Mr 23 '67; International Musician 66:19 Jy '67; Jazz 6:53 Mr '67; Library Journal 92:763 F 15 '67; Orkester Journalen 35:5 S '67; Saturday Review 50:65 F 11 '67; Saturday Review 50:50 My 20 '67

116. Feather, Leonard, and Ira Gitler. The Encyclopedia of Jazz in the Seventies. Introduction by Quincy Jones. New York: Horizon Press, 1976. 393 pp. bibliography.

   This third volume in the "Encyclopedia of Jazz" series covers the ten years since the "Sixties" volume appeared. It includes sketches of prominent musicians who were active in the 1970s, regardless of how long they might have been active prior to that period; hence, this volume includes players ranging from Eubie Blake to Anthony Braxton. Aside from the biographies themselves, other sections of

116.  Feather (continued)

interest to researchers are the chapters on "Critics' and Readers'
Polls," "A Guide to Jazz Films," and "Recommended Recordings of
the Decade 1966-1975."
Reviews:     American Reference Books Annual 9:467 '78;
Billboard 89:88 Mr 12 '77; Booklist 74:948 F 1 '78; Cadence 2:20
Mr '77; Choice 14:830 S '77; Commonweal 104:510 Au 5 '77;
Contemporary Keyboard 3:6 Jy '77; Downbeat 44:52 D 15 '77;
Guitar Player 11:8 Ju '77; High Fidelity 27:148 Mr '77; Jazz
Forum 48:56 '77; Jazz Journal International 30:25 S '77; Jazz
Magazine (U.S.) 1:76 '77; Jazz Magazine 61:16 Ja '78; Jazz
Podium 26:39 My '77; Kirkus Reviews 44:504 Ap 15 '76; Library
Journal 101:1778 S 1 '76; Melody Maker 53:37 Jy 8 '78; Music
Journal 35:80 Jy '77; New Republic 175:35 S 25 '76; New York
Times Book Review p18 Jy 10 '77; New York Times Book
Review p37 O 24 '76; New York Times Book Review p27 Au 28
'77; Publishers Weekly 209:51 Ap 26 '76; Publishers Weekly
211:81 Ju 6 '77; Radio Free Jazz 18:13 '77; Variety 286:75 Mr
23 '77

117.  Gold, Robert S.  A Jazz Lexicon.  New York: Alfred A. Knopf, 1964.
xxvi, 363 pp. bibliography.

This study of the language of the jazz world contains definitions of
nearly seven hundred slang words that have evolved from a fusion of
aspects of the vocabulary of traditional black culture and that of
the urban jazz community.  The author defines and briefly explains
such diverse terms as "ax (axe)," "barrelhouse," "bebop," "chart,"
"jive," "mary jane," "pad," "pot," "running changes," "spasm band,"
"stretch out," "swing," "wail," and many others.  Each entry
contains notes on the origin and development of a particular term
and gives reference citations.  In preparing the dictionary, the
author combined personal interviews with a number of jazz
musicians and research in more than ninety periodicals and over 150
books and monographs.
Reviews:  Booklist 61:417 Ja 1 '65; Book Week p40 D 6 '64;
Choice 2:151 My '65; Downbeat 31:35 O 8 '64; Ethnomusicology
9:184 '65; International Musician 63:31 D '64; Jazz Monthly
10:30 F '65; Library Journal 89:3505 '64; Library Journal
89:3143 '64; Music Journal 22:70 S '64; New Republic 151:34 N
28 '64; New York Times Book Review p4 Au 16 '64; Orkester
Journalen 34:17 S '66; Saturday Review 48:31 Mr 20 '65

118.  Gold, Robert S.  Jazz Talk.  New York: Bobbs-Merrill Co., 1975. xii,
322 pp. bibliography.

Slang terms that originated in the jazz world from the turn of the
century to the early 1970s are defined in this volume.  The entry for
each expression includes information about the origin of the term; a
statement concerning the approximate dates during which the term
was in use; a concise definition; and a chronological list of
references to or quotations from periodical literature showing the

118. Gold (continued)

use of the expression in the context of daily conversation. Such terms as "axe," "woodshed," "ghost note," and "changes" are among the many jazz slang terms to be found in this useful book.
Reviews:   American Reference Books Annual 7:490 '76; Christian Science Monitor 67:22 O 8 '75; Journal of Popular Culture 10:475-476 n2 '76; Kirkus Reviews 43:559 My 1 '75; Library Journal 100:971 My 15 '75; Music Journal 33:26 N '75; Notes 32:302 n2 '75; Orkester Journalen 45:2 My '77; Publishers Weekly 207:44 Ap 28 '75; Wilson Library Bulletin 50:265 N '75

119. Hardy, Phil, and Dave Laing, eds. The Encyclopedia of Rock. 3 vols. St. Albans, [England]: Panther Books, 1976. each vol. approx. 330 pp. index.

The three volumes of this work provide information about a wide range of people who have contributed to the field of rock music— the artists, songwriters, record producers, record company owners, session musicians, and others. Inclusion is based on two criteria: commercial success in the United States or England, and the determination by the editors and contributors of the "historical influence and artistic significance" of the individual; the length of the entries is determined by the editors' opinion on the relative importance of the subject. Entries may also be found for influential record companies and cities that have served as centers of activity for rock music. The entries for individuals provide vital data, a brief overview of the person's career and association with various record companies, and the citation of some of his or her hit recordings. Entries for record companies and cities contain information about their important contributions to the field. Within each volume, the entries are arranged alphabetically; the three volumes treat the periods 1955-1959, 1960-1969, and 1970-1979, respectively.
Reviews:   Melody Maker 51:20 Jy 3 '76; Reference Services Review 5:28 Ja '77; Reference Services Review 6:15 Jy '78

120. Kinkle, Roger D. The Complete Encyclopedia of Popular Music and Jazz, 1900-1950. Introduction by George T. Simon. 4 vols. New Rochelle, N.Y.: Arlington House Publishers, 1974. each vol. approx. 650 pp.

This set provides information about popular music, jazz, and Broadway and movie musicals produced in the United States between 1900 and 1950, and includes biographical information on a large number of American popular and jazz musicians. Volume 1 lists the popular songs for each year; Volumes 2 and 3 carry biographical sketches of artists in the jazz and popular fields; and Volume 4 contains indexes and appendixes to the set. In Volume 1, the section on "Fifty Years of Popular Music and Jazz" lists the titles of the music, year by year, in three sections:   Broadway musicals, popular songs, and representative recordings. Among the popular tunes for 1917 can be found the following songs by black

120.  Kinkle (continued)

composers:  "Beale Street Blues" by W. C. Handy; "Every Body Gone Crazy 'Bout the Doggone Blues" and "Sweet Emalina, My Gal" by Turner Layton and Henry Creamer; "Little Mother of Mine" by Harry T. Burleigh; "Rockaway" by C. Luckeyeth Roberts, Alex Rogers, and Howard Johnson; and "You're Some Pretty Doll" by Clarence Williams.  One of the two "jazz" groups recorded in that year (1917) was the W. C. Handy Orchestra, with six sides—"That Jazz Dance"/"Livery Stable Blues"; "Old Miss Rag"/"The Hooking Corn Blues"; and "Fuzzy Wuzzy Rag"/"The Snakey Blues."  The biographies in Volumes 2 and 3 carry the following information: name of the artist/composer/lyricist; aka or nickname; vital data; brief career sketch; and recordings/shows/songs/arrangements. Volume 4 contains five appendixes and four indexes.  Among the former are included a list of jazz poll winners for the period 1937-1972 and a list of the principal record labels from the mid-1920s to the early 1940s.    The extensive indexes of personal names, Broadway musicals, musical movies, and popular songs with numerous cross-references, carry the names and the titles of products of a large number of black song writers and jazz musicians.

Reviews:   Audio 60:36 Ju '76; Best Sellers 34:443 Ja 1 '75; Billboard 87:6 Ja 4 '75; Booklist 71:1200 Jy 15 '75; Catholic Library World 47:128 O '75; Catholic Library World 48:221 D '76; Choice 12:198 Ap '75; Coda 12:27 '75; High Fidelity/ Musical America 25:MA37 Jy '75; Jazz Journal 28:17 Ma '75; Jazz Report 9:18 '76; Jazz Research 6/7:277 '74/'75; JEMF Quarterly 11:115 '75; Library Journal 100:467 Mr 1 '75; Matrix 107/108:24 D '75; Music Educators Journal 61:83 Mr '75; National Observer 14:23 N 8 '75; National Review 27:466 Ap 25 '75; Notes 32:44 S '75; Popular Music and Society 4:111 '75; Reference Services Review 3:127 Ja '75; Reference Services Review 3:20 Jy '75; Saturday Review 2:43 F 22 '75; Second Line 27:23 Spring '75; Variety 277:34 D 25 '74; Wilson Library Bulletin 49:532 Mr '75

121.  Nite, Norm N., and Ralph M. Newman.  Rock On:  The Illustrated Encyclopedia of Rock 'N Roll.  2 Vols. Introduction to Vol. 1, The Solid Gold Years, by Dick Clark.  New York:  Harper & Row Publishers, 1974.  Introduction to Vol. 2, The Modern Years:  1964-Present by Wolfman Jack.  New York: Thomas Y. Crowell Publishers, 1978.  722; xv, 590 pp. photographs. appendix. indexes.

These two volumes offer short biographical sketches and lists of hit songs of popular singers who had top one hundred singles during the 1950s, 1960s, and the early to middle 1970s.  Although the work is devoted primarily to rock artists, it also includes outstanding performers in country, popular, and novelty musics.  Among the black artists listed are Johnny Ace, Ray Charles, Bill Doggett, LaVerne Baker, Hank Ballard, Otis Redding, Dinah Washington, Johnny Mathis, Nat Cole, Cozy Cole, Earl Bostic, George Benson, The Commodores, Roberta Flack, Isaac Hayes, Lou Rawls, The

121. Nite (continued)

Emotions, and Earth, Wind and Fire.  Each entry carries the name
or names of the individual or group; vital data; a short biographical
sketch; and a list of the artist's national hit songs, giving the month
and year of their top one hundred successes and the labels on which
they were recorded.  Scattered throughout the set are classic
photographs of the artists in their peak years. Each volume carries
an index of song titles.  For researchers of Afro-American popular
music, this is an indispensable set.

Reviews:     American Reference Books Annual 7:491  76;
American Reference Books Annual 10:487 '79; Booklist 71:705
Mr 1 '75; Booklist 75:1650 Jy 15 '79; Choice 12:372 My '75;
Creem Magazine 6:55 Mr '75; Library Journal 103:2096 O 15
'78; Popular Music and Society 4:55 '75; Publishers Weekly
214:73 Au 7 '78; Society 17:80 My '80; Variety 277:34 D 25 '74;
Wilson Library Bulletin 49:458 F '75; Wilson Library Bulletin
53:469 F '79

122. Roxon, Lillian.  Lillian Roxon's Rock Encyclopedia.  The Universal
Library. New York: Gross & Dunlap, 1971. 611 pp. appendix.

This is a wide ranging encyclopedia of popular music that includes,
not only legitimate rock groups such as The Jimi Hendrix
Experience, but also performers such as Anthony and the Imperials,
the Albert Ayler Trio, King Curtis and the Kingpins, Willie Dixon,
Dionne Warwick, and Muddy Waters.  In addition, performance halls,
musical events, and musical styles related to black music and
popular music in general are also included—the Apollo Theater,
Discothetique, and acid rock, for example.  The entries provide a
description of the person, group, event, or location, and list the
record albums and singles of the performers, as well as other
records on which they appeared.  The appendix lists Cash Box Top
Albums (1960-1968), Cash Box Singles (1949-1968), and Billboard's
Number 1 Weekly Hits.

Reviews: AB Bookman's Weekly 44:2023 D 15 '69; American
Musical Digest 1:40 '70; Billboard 81:6 D 6 '69; High
Fidelity/Musical America 20:30 Mr '70; International Musician
69:16 Jy '70; Jazz and Pop 9:48 My '70; Library Journal 95:652
F 15 '70; Library Journal 95:1975 My 15 '70; Music Educators
Journal 56:113 Mr '70; New York Times Book Review, Part Two
p3 F 15 '70; Notes 28:694 Ju '72; Partisan Review 37:301 Spring
'70; Publishers Weekly 196:52 O 13 '69; Rolling Stone 51:34 F 7
'70; RQ 10:174 Winter '70; Saturday Night 85:34 Mr '70;
Saturday Review 52:50 D 6 '69; Saturday Review 54:43 Jy 24
'71; Saturday Review 54:47 Jy 31 '71; Variety 257:53 D 17 '69;
Wilson Library Bulletin 44:563 Ja '70

123. Stambler, Irwin.  Encyclopedia of Pop, Rock & Soul.  New York: St.
Martin's Press; London:  St. James Press, 1977.  [xxxiii], 609 pp.
photographs. bibliography.

123.  Stambler (continued)

> This work contains comparatively substantive articles on the major
> figures in traditional and contemporary American popular music.
> Among the black artists whose biographies and/or professional
> sketches appear are Bill Doggett, James Brown, Edwin Hawkins,
> John Lee Hooker, The Impressions, Quincy Jones, Gladys Knight and
> the Pips, Little Anthony and the Imperials, Otis Redding, Ruth
> Brown, Brook Benton, Ike and Tina Turner, and others.  Each entry
> contains the name of the individual or group; profession; places and
> dates of birth and death; discussion of the individual's or group's
> career.  The volume also contains a special article titled "R&B, Soul
> and the Roots of Rock."  The appendixes list Gold Record awards,
> Grammy winners, and nominees and winners of music category
> awards of the Academy of Motion Pictures Arts and Sciences.
>     Reviews:     American Reference Books Annual 7:492 '76;
> American Reference Books Annual 9:469 '78; Best Sellers
> 34:552 Mr 15 '75; Booklist 71:1204 Jy 15 '75; Catholic Library
> World 47:90 S '75; Choice 12:372 My '75; Guitar Player 9:71 O
> '75; Library Journal 99:3192 D 15 '74; Melos/Neue Zeitschrift
> für Musik 2:160 '76; Music Educators Journal 66:98 D '79; Music
> Journal 34:14 Ja '76; Reference Services Review 3:127 Ja '75;
> Reference Services Review 6:7 Jy '78; Wilson Library Bulletin
> 49:667 My '75; Wilson Library Bulletin 49:672 My '75; Wilson
> Library Bulletin 51:602 Mr '77

124.  Woll, Allen L.  Songs from Hollywood Musical Comedies, 1927 to the
      Present:  A Dictionary.  New York:  Garland Publishing, 1976.  128 pp.
      photographs.  appendix.

> This book is divided into four sections which, when used in
> combination, can provide the user with information about the
> musical comedies in which more than seven thousand songs
> appeared and the sound recordings upon which some of them may be
> found.  The first section is an alphabetical list of the song titles;
> each is followed by one or more numerals that refer the user to the
> second section.  Contained in the second section is an alphabetical
> listing of 1,186 musical comedies produced between 1927 and 1976;
> each show title is accompanied by the date the musical was
> produced, the name(s) of the star(s), and the name(s) of the
> director(s); many entries also carry listings of the songs that
> appeared in the show, together with the name(s) of composer and
> lyricist and the record label number of a recording of the sound
> track.    The third section is a "Chronology of the Hollywood
> Musical," and the final section is an index of composers and
> lyricists.    The book indexes songs by composers, including Fats
> Waller, Eubie Blake, Duke Ellington, Ford Dabney, W. C. Handy, and
> James P. Johnson.
>     Reviews:  American Reference Books Annual 8:472 '77; Fontes
> Artis Musicae 23:202 '76; Library Journal 101:1408 Ju 15 '76

125.  Wood, Graham.  An A-Z of Rock and Roll.  London:  Studio Vista, 1971.
      128 pp. photographs.

125.  Wood (continued)

This little volume contains short biographical sketches of individual and group stars of the 1950s and 1960s.  Each sketch carries, to some degree, vital data and information regarding the performer's early preparation, professional chronology, and important recorded titles.  Among the black individuals and groups included in the book are Chuck Berry, Bo Diddley, The Drifters, The Flamingoes, The Platters, and Jackie Wilson.  The appendixes have information on "Major US Films Featuring Rock Performers, 1955-61" and "A Listing of Million Sellers by Rock Artists, 1955-61."

Reviews:  Blues Unlimited 82:19 Ju '71; Jazz Journal 24:5 Ju '71

## *BIOGRAPHICAL*

126.  Anderson, Ruth E.  Contemporary American Composers: A Biographical Dictionary.  Boston:  G. K. Hall & Co., 1976.  vi, 513 pp.

This work contains approximately four thousand brief biographies of contemporary composers.  Each entry in the work fulfills the following criteria:  "birth date no earlier than 1870; American citizenship or extended residence in the United States; and at least one original composition published, commercially recorded, performed in an urban area, or selected for an award in composition" (p. iii).  Each entry contains the composer's date of birth and/or death; information about his or her education, awards received, and positions held; a list of important compositions; and the composer's address at the time of publication.  Much of the information contained herein was acquired directly from the composers themselves; those entries containing information from other sources are marked with an asterisk.  This is a useful source of biographical information about minor composers as well as major figures.  Among the black composers included are:  H. Leslie Adams, Margaret Bonds, William S. Fischer, Talib Rasul Hakim, Ulysses Kay, Carman Moore, Oliver Nelson, Howard Swanson, and George Walker.

Reviews:    American Reference Books Annual 8:466 '77; Bibliographical Society of America—Papers 71:404 Jy '77; Brio 13:52 '76; Choice 13:1267 D '76; Library Journal 101:1758 S 1 '76; Music 10:8 O '76; Musical Times 118:476 Ju '77; Music Educators Journal 63:129 S '76; Notes 33:603 Mr '77; Reference Services Review 5:22 Ja '77

127.  Chilton, John.  Who's Who of Jazz: Storyville to Swing Street.  Preface by Johnny Simmen.  Philadelphia:  Chilton Book Co., 1972.  x, 419 pp. photographs.

This biographical dictionary contains sketches of more than one thousand jazz musicians who were born in the United States before 1920.  The entries appear alphabetically by the musician's last name as it is generally known, and include other information such as the

127.  Chilton (continued)

"real name" in parentheses, instrument, vital data, and career
information which traces the musician's progress from earliest
known musical experiences.  Although the sketches are brief, the
work is nonetheless a valuable reference source since it includes
many names that do not appear elsewhere.
   Reviews:  AB Bookman's Weekly 49:1951 My 22 '72; Choice
9:953 O '72; Downbeat 39:30 F 17 '72; Hip 10:13 '71; Jazz
Digest 1:27 Ju '72; Jazz Report 8:13 '73; Music Journal 30:40 S
'72; National Observer 11:21 Ju 17 '72; Notes 29:719 Ju '73;
Point du Jazz 6:114 Mr '72; Reference Services Review 1:18 Jy
'73; Second Line 25:29 Winter '73; Times Literary Supplement
p287 Mr 12 '71

128.  Claghorn, Charles Eugene.   Biographical Dictionary of American
Music.  West Nyack, N.Y.:  Parker Publishing Co., 1973.  491 pp.

This is a handy source of the most essential information on more
than 5,200 American composers, performers, singers, hymnodists,
and lyricists.  It includes musicians and writers from all genres of
the art, from obscure sidemen of early jazz bands to librettists of
little-known operas.  Black musicians and writers are identified as
such, except in the many instances in which the information was
apparently not available to the author.  Among the wide variety of
black figures included are:  Henry Creamer, Tommy Ladnier, Paul
Freeman, Jay McShann, John Turner Layton, Harry Lawrence
Freeman, Noah Ryder, Julia Perry, Samuel Snaer, Lucien Lambert,
Curtis Fuller, Russell Procope, Langston Hughes, Andy Razaf,
Basile Bares, Arthur Prysock, and Will H. Tyers; even obscure
bands, such as the Southern Syncopated Orchestra, are included.
Each of the book's entries contains the following information:
name; vital data; professional activity; and a list of selected
compositions, special accomplishments, or tributes.  This is a good
source of quick-reference information.
   Reviews:  Booklist 71:580 F 1 '75; Hymn 25:62 '74; Music
Trades 122:28 Ja '74; Stereo Review 33:14 Jy '74

129.  Harris, Sheldon.   Blues Who's Who:  A Biographical Dictionary of Blues
Singers.  New Rochelle, N.Y.:  Arlington House Publishers, 1979.  775
pp.  photographs. bibliography. index.

This reference work, the most comprehensive biographical source
available on blues singers, carries 571 sketches that contain the
following  information:      the  performer's  name,  nickname,
pseudonymn, or title; dates of birth and death; biography, including
career  dates;   non-musical  activities;  personal  information;
professional billings; books about the singer; titles of songs written
by the singer; awards/honors/influences; photographs; and other
information.
   Reviews:  American Reference Books Annual 11:447 '80;
Billboard 91:78 O 13 '79; Cadence 5:23 O '79; Choice 17:518 Ju
'80; Coda 176:22 D 1 '80; Downbeat 47:72 Ap '80; Guitar Player

129. Harris (continued)

> 13:130 N '79; Jazz Journal International 32:10 D '79; Jazz
> Magazine 4:45 '80; JEMF Quarterly 15:237 '79; Library Journal
> 104:1441 Jy '79; Melody Maker 55:35 S 18 '80; Music Educators
> Journal 66:17 My '80; New York Times Book Review p13 N 11
> '79; Notes 37:327 D '80; Radio Free Jazz 20:16 D '79; Record
> Research 171:2 Mr '80; Reference Services Review 9:38 Ap '81;
> Sing Out 27:42 '79; Variety 296:141 O 10 '79; Western Folklore
> 39:338 '80; Wilson Library Bulletin 54:398 F '80

130. Rich, Maria. Who's Who in Opera. New York: Arno Press, 1976. xxi,
684 pp.

> Among the numerous biographical sketches in this work are those of
> Betty Allen, Martina Arroyo, Ester Hinds, Eugene Holmes, Jessye
> Norman, Leontyne Price, Faye Robinson, and twenty other black
> opera singers.    Appearing alphabetically, each entry carries the
> following information:    personal data; education; debut; previous
> occupations and positions; awards; related professional activities;
> opera companies with which the artist performed; repertoire;
> recordings, films, and television events in which the artist
> appeared; world premieres; and the artist's sponsoring agent or
> management. The book also contains a list of 140 opera companies
> in   thirty-three   countries;   a   dictionary   of   more   than   125
> international artists' agents; and profiles of domestic and foreign
> companies, including location, home theater, address, telephone
> number, founding date, information on the seasons between 1973
> and 1975, budget, ticket sales, and other information.
> Reviews:    American Music Teacher 27:35 '77; Central Opera
> Service Bulletin 19:19 '77; High Fidelity/Musical America
> 26:102 N '76; Music and Musicians 25:38 D '76; Music Journal
> 36:41 F '78; Musikrevy 31:237 '76; NATS Bulletin 33:41 '77;
> Notes 34:91 '77; Notes 34:340 '77; Opera Canada 18:52 '77;
> Opera Journal 10:38-39 '77; Opera News 41:12 N '76; Saturday
> Review 4:46 O 16 '76

131. Slonimsky, Nicholas, ed. Baker's Biographical Dictionary of Musicians.
6th ed., rev.  New York: Schirmer Books; London:  Collier Macmillan
Publishers, 1978. xxvi, 1955 pp.

> This work carries among its numerous entries brief biographical
> sketches of ninety-two black musicians.  Included are composers of
> concert and recital music, opera singers, recital instrumentalists,
> conductors, jazz and blues artists, and others representing the
> United States as well as other countries.   The diverse entries
> include sketches for Thomas Green Bethune, James Bland, Jules
> Bledsoe, Johnny Hodges, Frank Johnson, Quincy Jones, Ulysses Kay,
> Huddie Ledbetter, Dorothy Maynor, Julia Perry, and other famous
> and lesser known Afro-American musicians. The sketches contain
> important factual information, presumably based on the biblio-

131. Slonimsky (continued)

    graphic citations given at the end of each entry. When appropriate, lists of works are included.

    Reviews: American Music Teacher 29:34 S/O '79; American Record 42:55 S '79; American Reference Books Annual 11:447 '80; Booklist 77:274 O 1 '80; Choice 16:505 Ju '79; High Fidelity/Musical America 30:MA18 Ja '80; Library Journal 104:618 Mr 1 '79; Musical Times 120:825 O '79; Music 6:52 Au 4 '79; School Musician 50:28 D '78; Wilson Library Bulletin 54:130 O '79

132. Southern, Eileen. Biographical Dictionary of Afro-American and African Musicians. The Greenwood Encyclopedia of Black Music. Westport, Conn.: Greenwood Press, 1982. xviii, 478 pp. appendixes. bibliography. index.

    In presenting the biographical sketches of more than 1,500 black musicians, this new and important work documents the history of black music and "assesses its achievements and its impact upon world music of contemporary times" (p. ix). The work includes the sketches of instrumentalists, singers, composers, conductors, critics, concert promoters, patrons, educators, and others who have made important contributions to black music history. Containing information that, in many instances, has never before been published, the book lists "living persons as well as figures from the past" (p. ix), ranging from Sebastian Rodriguez (ca. 1642–ca. 1726) to individuals who were born in 1945. Although the book is a "pioneering venture" (p. x), it is a comprehensive and quite representative source of fresh and important information. Appendix 1 lists the biographies according to "Period of Birth," i.e., "The Colonial Era: 1640–1775," "The New Nation: 1776–1839," "The Antebellum Period: 1840–1862," etc. Appendix 2 lists the entrants by "Place of Birth"; Appendix 3 organizes the names by "Musical Occupations"—"Blues Musicians and Boogie Woogie Pianists," "Choral Conductors," "Composers," "Concert Artists and Groups," etc. These three appendixes and the book's index make this work eminently useful and its information highly accessible.

    Reviews: Library Journal 107:85 Ja 1 '82

## MISCELLANEOUS

133. Raffe, W. G. Dictionary of the Dance. New York: A. S. Barnes and Co.; London: Thomas Yoseloff, 1965. 583 pp. bibliography. indexes.

    Among its diverse entries, this comprehensive work includes descriptions of black American dances such as the buck-and-wing, cakewalk, Charleston, jitterbug, calinda, and others; and discusses "Negro Dancing" in general. In addition, more than fifty dances of eighteen African countries are listed. Latin America is also represented—among the black dances included from this part of the world are the Xango and fourteen others from Brazil, the merengue

133. Raffe (continued)

from the Dominican Republic, and the mambo and seven others from Haiti. Dances of European provenance pertinent to black music research are also described—round and square dances such as the cotillion, quadrille, lancers, and polka. The book's Geographical Index lists the countries of origin of the dances described; the Index of Subjects Relating to Dance lists the various kinds of dances, the related institutions, cults, methods, and other miscellaneous items—reincarnation, schools of dance, myth and dance, and so on.

Reviews: Booklist 62:169 O 15 '65; College and Research Libraries 26:330 Jy '65; Library Journal 90:3014 Jy '65; Saturday Review 48:31 Mr 20 '65

134. Spalding, Henry D., ed. and comp. Encyclopedia of Black Folklore and Humor. Introduction by J. Mason Brewer. Middle Village, N.Y.: Jonathan David Publishers, 1972. xiii, 589 pp. drawings, musical examples. addenda. bibliography. index.

A general reference work on black folklore, this encyclopedia contains and discusses 1,500 parables, songs, poems, proverbs, and other folk materials as they relate to the economics, politics, and social activities of black culture. Representing the "convictions, customs, and associations" (p. xii) of Afro-American culture, this tool will provide the researcher with much background information, as well as with a "feel" for black folk culture. The section on music discusses and treats "Epic Ballads and Other Traditional Folksongs," "Dance Songs or Reels," and "Songs About Animals" "from slave days to the advent of jazz"; the section also includes "spirituals, gospels, work and love songs, 'hollers'," the blues, and other song types (p. 232). The practical value of the book lies not only in its music section however. In the section on poetry, for example, the reader will readily recognize relationships between the poems and the texts of the published black popular songs of the 1870s, 1880s, and 1890s.

Reviews: Catholic Library World 44:311 D '72; Choice 10:66 Mr '73; Christian Century 89:466 Ap 19 '72; Kirkus Reviews 40:317 Mr 1 '72; Library Journal 97:2172 Ju 15 '72; Publishers Weekly 201:66 F 28 '72; Southwest Review 58:103 Winter '73

135. Wentworth, Harold, and Stuart Berg Flexner, eds. and comps. Dictionary of American Slang. 2nd supp. ed. New York: Thomas Y. Crowell Co., 1975. xviii, 776 pp. appendix. bibliographies. supplement. index.

Containing twenty-two thousand definitions of slang terms, this source book will be useful to researchers of jazz, black popular song, and Afro-American folk song. The work contains meanings for common musical slang terms such as "Ax/Axe," "gig," "jam," and "cut" as well as entries of rarer usages, such as "blackstick" for clarinet. Folk music researchers will find gullah–derived terms such as, for example, "gi gi," from gri gri, and others. Although the

135. Wentworth (continued)

accuracy of a few of the meanings and derivations might be
questioned, careful use in connection with entries number 117, 118
and 193 is recommended.  Organized alphabetically, each entry of
this encyclopedia includes the entry word; taboo and derogatory
designations; part of speech; definitions; some quotations and
citations in which the word has appeared; etymology and comments;
and cross references.  A valuable extra feature of the dictionary is
its Word Lists which contain black slang and pig Latin expressions,
onomatopoeia, "blend words," "Synthetic Slang Expressions," and
other categories.

Reviews:  American Reference Books Annual 7:545 '76; Best
Sellers 35:347-348 F '76; Booklist 72:484-485 Ju 15 '76; Choice
13:208 Ap '76; English Journal 65:91 My '76; Modern Age 20:451
Fall '76; Wilson Library Bulletin 50:408 Ja '76

# IX

# General Black Music Histories, Chronologies, and Cultural Studies

136. Baraka, Amiri. Blues People: Negro Music in White America. 1963. Reprint. Westport, Conn.: Greenwood Press, 1980. xii, 244 pp. index.

> Arranged in chronological order, this book examines the ways in which the changing sociological position of black Americans affected black American music ranging from the arrival of blacks in this country until the beginning of the 1960s. Jones regards the blues as the primary vitalizing force of black American music after the Civil War. He views the subsequent periodic dilution of black American music as a combination of white appropriation of the music and black assimilation into (rather than adaptation to) white culture of America. Each instance of popularization and denigration of the music was followed by a return to the blues for renewed vitality and validity as black music. Although Blues People presents a valuable perspective of black Americans and their music, the work is largely undocumented (it lacks a bibliography) and tends to present as fact some items that are necessarily speculative, such as the origins of the blues. The book is useful primarily as a view of historical events in the development of black American music rather than as an insight into the music itself. The book begins with a survey treatment of the African heritage, then progresses through the slave experience, the migration to the cities after emancipation, the growth of the black middle class in the first decades of the twentieth century, and moves on to "The Modern Scene," in which musical styles such as bebop, hard bop, funk, and free jazz are discussed. Throughout the book, the author treats blues and jazz styles, together with the social, cultural, and historical contexts in which the music developed.

137. Bardolph, Richard. <u>The Negro Vanguard</u>. New York:  Vintage Books, 1959. viii, 495, xvi pp. bibliography. index.

This volume consists of an overview of the contributions of black persons in all fields from 1770 to 1959.  Included among them are more than 150 persons who have been involved in musical entertainment—artists, composers, lyricists, publishers, arrangers, and the like.  The book covers the entire scope of black American music—spirituals, blues, jazz, gospel music, musical theater, concert and recital music, and so on.
Reviews:  American Historical Review 65:922 Ju '60; Booklist 56:233 D 15 '59; Chicago Sunday Tribune p4 D 13 '59; Christian Science Monitor p11 Ja 19 '60; Kirkus Reviews 27:714 S 15 '59; Library Journal 84:3577 N 15 '59; New York Herald Tribune Book Review p8 D 27 '59; Saturday Review of Literature p31 Mr 17 '62; School and Society 88:307 Summer '60; Springfield Republican p4D D 13 '59

138. De Lerma, Dominique-René, ed. <u>Reflections On Afro-American Music</u>. Kent, Ohio:  Kent State University Press, 1973.  271 pp.  appendixes. index.

This volume reflects the nature and the state of black musical thought as it existed at the beginning of the 1970s.  With contributions from over twenty-six musicians and scholars, the book is a collection of the thoughtful and thought-provoking comments that emerged from the second national black music seminar held at Indiana University in 1972.  Included are papers by musicologists, composers, anthropologists, and performers, as well as transcribed panel discussions of some of these and other professionals.  The book's seventeen chapters run the gamut from African music and spirituals to soul music, touching upon such topics as black music in education, the black composer's relationship to society, black music history, journalism, and others.  Individuals who made contributions to the book include Richard Abrams, Cannonball Adderly, Samuel Akpabot, T. J. Anderson, John R. Blacking, John Carter, Thomas A. Dorsey, Phyl Garland, Pearl Williams Jones, Portia K. Maultsby, Undine S. Moore, and Geneva Southall.  The book's four appendixes contain lists of:  1) European works that make use of Afro-American musical characteristics; 2) "Black Artists in Music and the Dance Available for Booking"; 3) college history texts that include information on black music; and 4) works of black music that had been performed publicly prior to 1972.  This book will be useful to researchers interested in black music philosophy, aesthetics, criticism, history, education, and sociology.
Reviews:  American Music Teacher 24:36-38 n1 '74; Choice 11:104 Mr '74; Coda 11:23 n8 '74; Jazz Forum n27:66 F '74; Jazz Journal 27:7 Mr '74; Jazz Research 5:166-167 '73; Library Journal 99:490 F 15 '74; Music 8:16 S '74; Music Educators Journal 61:123-124 S '74; Music Journal 32:32 F '74; New York Review of Books 21:14 O 17 '74; Notes 31:553+ n3 '75

139. Dixon, Robert M. W., and John Godrich. Recording the Blues. New
York: Stein and Day, 1970. 112 pp. photographs, drawings, charts,
graphs. index.

This book examines the general content of the various race record
series that were produced by record companies between 1920 and
1945; it represents a capsule history of the American race record
phenomenon. For background, the work begins with the "Birth of an
Industry" in Thomas A. Edison's first phonograph in 1877, then
discusses "The New Market" of black buyers which emerged
between 1920 and 1922 and "The Classic Blues" recordings of 1923-
1926, and progresses through other brief periods to discuss the "End
of an Era, 1941-1945" that was occasioned by the "Petrillo Ban" on
recordings that brought the commercial recording of music to a
temporary standstill.    The work discusses or mentions such
companies and labels as Black Swan, Black Patti, Columbia, Victor,
Paramount, Okeh, Gennett, and Aeolian-Vocalion; it treats blues
singers such as Bessie, Mamie, Clara, and Trixie Smith, Alberta
Hunter, Victoria Spivey, Ma Rainey, Ida Cox, Blind Lemon
Jefferson, Tampa Red, Georgia Tom (Thomas A. Dorsey), and
others; it also mentions the male quartets that performed spiritual
and novelty numbers during the period—The Norfolk Jubilee
Quartet, the Birmingham Jubilee Singers, and others.    Also
mentioned are "sermons-with-singing" such as Rev. J. M. Gate's
Death's Black Train Is Coming and those of Rev. A. W. Nix, Rev. E.
W. Clayborn, Joe Taggart, and others.    Also discussed are the
successes, struggles, and the failures of race labels as they
competed for success in the Afro-American market place.
Reviews: AB Bookman's Weekly 46:582 S 7 '70; Black World
20:90 Ja '71; Blues 76:21 O '70; Choice 8:399 My '71;
Ethnomusicology 16:134-135 n1 '72; Gramophone 48:677 O '70;
Jazz and Pop 10:40 Jy '71; Jazz Hot 264:35 S '70; Jazz Journal
23:8 S '70; Jazz Monthly 188:29 O '70; Journal of American
Folklore 86:79 Ja '73; Library Journal 96:292 Ja 15 '71; Library
Journal 96:481 F 1 '71; Matrix 89:16 S '70; Melody Maker 45:28
S '70; Musical Times 111:898 S '70; Storyville 30:236-237 Au/S
'70; Times Literary Supplement n20:1365 '70; Western Folklore
30:147-149 n2 '71

140. Gayle, Addison, Jr., ed.   The Black Aesthetic.   Garden City, N.Y.:
Doubleday & Co., 1971. xxiv, 432 pp. biographies. index.

This is a collection of thirty-two essays on "the black aesthetic,"
seven of which are devoted specifically to music.   Other essays
address the question as it relates to poetry, drama, fiction, and
general aesthetic theory. With each writer presenting his own view
of the subject, the work serves as an introduction to some of the
polemical and nontechnical thinking on the issue.    The music
category  includes,  among  others,  the  following  essays:
"Introduction to Black Aesthetics in Music" by Jimmy Stewart; "The
Black Aesthetic Imperative" by Ron Welburn; and "The Changing
Same (R&B and the New Black Music)" by LeRoi Jones.

140. Gayle (continued)

> Reviews: AB Bookman's Weekly 47:948 Mr 22 '71; Black World
> 20:51 O '71; Black World 21:51 Ju '72; Booklist 67:887 Jy 1 '71;
> Journal of Research in Music Education 20:195-197 n1 '72;
> Library Journal 96:79 Ja 1 '71; Music Clubs Magazine 51:30 n3
> '72; Music Educators Journal 58:96-98 N '71; Nation 214:533 Ap
> 24 '72; New York Times 120:27 Ja 23 '71; New York Times Book
> Review p5 F 28 '71; Notes 28:233 D '71; Publishers Weekly
> 198:53 N 9 '70

141. Hare, Maud Cuney. Negro Musicians and Their Music. 1936. Reprint.
Da Capo Press Music Reprint Series. New York: Da Capo Press, 1974.
xii, 439 pp. photographs, drawings, musical examples. appendix.
bibliography. index.

> A comprehensive history of black American music to 1936, this
> detailed work contains a wealth of information. Although it has
> been superseded by Eileen Southern's work (The Music of Black
> Americans: A History entry number 149), it remains a useful source
> of both details and contemporary perspective on the period from
> ca. 1900 to 1935. The work begins with the African heritage and
> proceeds by way of "African Influences in America," through
> discussions of black folk music, musical comedy, jazz, "Music in
> War Service," and concert/recital music.

142. LaBrew, Arthur. Black Musicians of the Colonial Period, 1700-1800.
Detroit: Arthur LaBrew, 1977. vii, 183 pp. appendix. index.

> Taken from seventy-four sources, more than six hundred names of
> eighteenth-century slave and black musicians are included in this
> "Bicentennial Report." The book is divided into two parts. The
> first part consists of historical commentary which reviews
> "structure in 18th century black America" (p. 3), musicians in
> civilian and military life and religion, and black musicians in other
> countries. The second part of the work lists black musicians who
> were active from 1695 through 1813. Each listing contains vital
> data; place and date of birth or dates of activity, if known;
> instrument; and descriptive information about the musician.

143. Locke, Alain. The Negro and His Music. 1936. Reprint. Kennikat Press
Series in Negro Culture and History. Port Washington, N.Y.: Kennikat
Press, 1968. 142 pp.

> Primarily, this book is a brief outline-history of black American
> music from the nineteenth century to ca. 1935. It begins with an
> overview discussion of black musical "types and periods," then
> proceeds to present information on the various black music genres—
> spirituals, work songs, minstrel music, jazz, ragtime, and musical
> comedy—and concludes with speculations about the future of
> "Negro music." Its primary value lies in the author's keen
> observations of contemporary popular and classical activities and
> trends of the period between ca. 1900 and 1935. In spite of its

143. Locke (continued)

brevity, it is a particularly valuable source of first-hand perceptions and generally reliable interpretations of the musical developments of the Harlem Renaissance. Any research on this renaissance period should begin with this work as a comprehensive secondary source.

144. Patterson, Lindsay, ed. and comp. The Afro-American in Music and Art. Preface by Charles H. Wesley. International Library of Afro-American Life and History. Crowell Heights, Penn.: Publishers Agency, 1976. xvi, 304 pp. photographs, drawings. bibliography. index.

This book consists of thirty-nine essays that outline the activity and artistic production of black persons in the fields of music and art. The essays are organized under sixteen topical headings, eleven of which deal with black American music from the folk music of seventeenth-century slaves to the musical activity of the present: "Spirituals," "Minstrel," "Post-Minstrel," "Ragtime," "Blues," "Gospel," "Jazz," "Rock and Roll," "Popular Composers," "Famous Singers," and "Classical Music." Among the authors whose essays are included in the book are Maud Cuney Hare, W. E. B. Du Bois, James Weldon Johnson, W. C. Handy, Arna Bontemps, Margaret Bonds, Alain Locke, Sterling A. Brown, David Ewen, and Raoul Abdul.

145. Ploski, Harry A., and Ernest Kaiser, eds. and comps. The Negro Almanac. 2nd ed. New York: Bellwether Co., 1971. 1110 pp. appendix. bibliography. index.

This book is useful as a quick-reference source for various kinds of information on the black experience in the United States. Included are biographical sketches on prominent Afro-American scholars, poets, authors, artists, and entertainers; listings of black newspapers and periodicals published in the United States, complete with addresses, circulation and frequency data; information on black American religious organizations and denominations, including historical sketches and directories; "significant documents" related to the black struggle for freedom, including the U.S. Constitution, the Compromise of 1850, the Emancipation Proclamation, Booker T. Washington's "Atlanta Compromise" speech of 1895, and the Civil Rights Acts of 1957 and 1960.

Reviews: American Libraries 8:77 F '77; American Reference Books Annual 8:223 '77; Booklist 68:569 Mr 15 '72; Booklist 73:501 N 15 '76; Choice 14:350 My '77; Journal of Negro Education 46:462 Fall '77; Library Journal 97:863 Mr 1 '72; Library Journal 102:594 Mr 1 '77; Negro Digest 18:73 F '69; Reference Services Review 6:39 Ja '78

146. Roach, Hildred. Black American Music: Past and Present. Boston: Crescendo Publishing Co., 1973. vii, 199 pp. maps, photographs, musical examples, drawings. bibliography and discography. appendix. index.

146. Roach (continued)

>This history treats black American music from the colonial era to
>the present, focusing largely on composers and composed music
>rather than performers and improvised music. The work is divided
>into three sections: I. The Beginning (1619-1870s), II. The
>Awakening (1870s-1950s), and III. Freedom Now (1950s-1970s).
>Part I treats African music as it relates to black American music,
>black folk music, and the spiritual. Part II deals with minstrelsy,
>jazz, and concert music in the first half of the present century.
>Part III treats contemporary African music as influenced by black
>American music, and the developments in jazz and concert music
>since the mid-twentieth century. In Parts I and II, the musical
>characteristics of the various genres of black American music are
>discussed. Parts II and III contain brief discussions of several black
>composers; each discussion contains a brief biography, a short
>explication of the composer's compositional style, and a list of some
>of the titles of works he/she has composed. Many of the discussions
>include a photograph of the composer.
>Reviews: Choice 11:105 '74; Ethnomusicology 19:490 n3 '75;
>Orkester Journalen 42:29 D '74; Publishers Weekly 204:63 O 15
>'73

147. Roberts, John Storm. Black Music of Two Worlds. New York: Praeger
Publishers, 1972. x, 286 pp. photographs. bibliography. discography.
index.

>Black Music of Two Worlds is an important source of information
>about the fusion processes between African and European musics of
>the Americas. The introduction sets the stage by discussing the
>basic elements of African music that are pertinent to the primary
>topic of the book, e.g., structure, instruments, rhythm, scale, and
>performance practices. Part I, entitled "Old Cultures in a New
>World," discusses the survival and adaptation of African
>characteristics in the music of the Americas; the African
>characteristics include instrumentation, religious and cult music,
>rhythm, structural format, and so on. More than one-half of the
>text is contained in Part II, "Black Music of the Americas," which
>treats the integration and syncretization of African and European
>music. Its five chapters treat black music in Central and South
>America and in the Caribbean; black folk music, spirituals, and
>blues in the United States; jazz, from its beginnings through be-bop;
>and jazz fusions with black Latin American and Caribbean music.
>Each chapter discusses the syncretic process in terms of musical
>elements such as rhythm, instrumentation, form, use of percussion,
>scale, melody, and so on. Part III treats the musics created by
>contact between European and African musics in twentieth-century
>Africa.
>Reviews: AB Bookman's Weekly 52:344 Jy 30 '73; Black
>Perspective in Music 1:183-184 n2 '73; Black World 23:95 N '73;
>Books and Bookmen 18:58 Au '73; Choice 10:110 Mr '73;
>Crawdaddy n22:92 Mr '73; Instrument 27:16-17 Ja '73; Jazz
>Journal 25:12-13 O '72; Kirkus Reviews 40:784 Jy 1 '72; Library

147. Roberts (continued)

> Journal 97:2844 S 15 '72; Music Educators Journal 59:88 Mr '73; Music Journal 31:4 Ja '73; New Statesman 86:707 N 9 '73; Notes 30: 62-64 S '73; Publishers Weekly 202:115 Jy 17 '72; Stereo Review 30:18 My '73; Times Literary Supplement p1323 O 26 '73; Triangle 67:28 n3 '73

148. Rublowsky, John. Black Music in America. New York: Basic Books, 1971. 150 pp. photographs. bibliography. index.

> Discussing black music in the context of an outline American history, this book is a short introduction and orientation to the African/Afro-American musical traditions. Through brief but comprehensive explications of African culture, African music, and the slave trade, the author follows African/Afro-American music from its beginnings to the evolution and development of ragtime, jazz, and rhythm & blues. In the process, he discusses the importance of music in West African life, the basic characteristics of African music, and African musical practices and procedures as these relate to Afro-American music. The latter is presented within the context of general American historical periods such as "The Colonial Period," "Independence," and "Emancipation." This book is a good encapsulated history of Afro-American music, and an effective, brief, preresearch introduction to the field.
>
> Reviews: AB Bookman's Weekly 49:264 Ja 24 '72; American Record Guide 37:655 My '71; Choice 8:1186 N '71; Journal of Library History, Philosophy and Comparative 199:58 My 17 '71; Kirkus Reviews 39:543 My 1 '71; Library Journal 96:3139 O 1 '71; Notes 29:454 n3 '73; Wilson Library Bulletin 46:189 O '71

149. Southern, Eileen. The Music of Black Americans: A History. New York: W. W. Norton & Co., 1971. xviii, 552 pp. plates, maps, drawings, photographs, playbills and programs. bibliography and discography. index.

> This book traces the participation of black Americans in the creation, performance, and evolution of music. The discussion begins with the West African roots of black music and progresses through events that took place in 1970. The book is organized into sections, each of which treats a different historical period. Each section is preceded by a chronology of important historical events, and begins with a discussion of the general state of the music of the period. The book also contains discussions of the sociological functions of music in the various historical periods, of African-derived instruments and performance practices, and of the manner in which the development of black music was influenced by societal institutions. An important feature of the book is the discussion of the structural elements in the music created and performed by black Americans—aspects of form, melody, rhythm, and texture. Also considered are minstrel songs, folk songs, spirituals, worksongs, ragtime, blues entertainment music, military songs, jazz, black gospel music, and concert music. Numerous primary

149. Southern (continued)

sources of information about black Americans in music are either
quoted or cited to portray and corroborate the author's accounts of
musical events.

Reviews: American Record Guide 37:654 My '71; Black World
21:97 D '71; Black World 21:84 Ja '72; Booklist 68:23 S 1 '71;
Choice 8:1186 N '71; High Fidelity/Musical America 21:MA29
30 Jy '71; Instrument 26:12 Au '71; Jazz Digest 1:40 S/O '72;
Jazz Journal 25:12-13 D '72; Journal of Negro History 57:306
Jy '72; Journal of Research in Music Education 20:410-411 n3
'72; Library Journal 96:837 Mr 1 '71; Music Clubs Magazine
51:30 n3 '72; Music Journal 29:12 S '71; Notes 28:43 S '71; Pan
Pipes 64:32 n2 '72; Western Folklore 32:60 n1 '73; Yearbook for
Inter-American Musical Research 7:175-177 '71; Yearbook of
the International Folk Music Council 4:17-16 '72

150. Southern, Eileen. Readings in Black American Music. New York: W. W.
Norton & Co., 1971. xvi, 302 pp. musical examples. index.

This anthology of writings by and about black American musicians
and their music is concerned with ideas and events, gathered from
eyewitness accounts (e.g., James Eight recounting the "Pinkster
Festivities in Albany"), the writings of important figures in black
history (e.g., W. E. B. Du Bois), and articles and publications by
black musicians and composers themselves (e.g., W. C. Handy).
Each excerpt is preceded by a brief biographical or explanatory
note that places the writing in its historical context. The readings
are arranged in chronological order and grouped under topical
headings, such as The African Heritage, Music on the Plantation,
and The Music of a Free People.

Reviews: AB Bookman's Weekly p25 Winter '72; Instrument
26:12 My '72; Library Journal 97:684 '72; Pan Pipes 65:33 n2
'73; Publishers Weekly 201:57 Ja 3 '72

151. Trotter, James M. Music and Some Highly Musical People, Containing
Brief Chapters on a Description of Music, the Music of Nature, a Glance
at the History of Music, Following Which Are Given Sketches of the
Lives of Remarkable Musicians of the Colored Race, with Portraits and
an Appendix Containing Copies of Music Composed by Colored Men.
1881. Reprint. New York: Johnson Reprint Corp, 1968. 352, 152 pp.
photographs. appendix.

This is the earliest published comprehensive treatment of cultivated
black musical activity in the United States. It begins with four
brief chapters devoted to general aesthetics and music history, then
proceeds to discuss the social and cultural contexts of over forty-
one black musical figures and groups who were active in the United
States prior to and during 1881. The careers of Elizabeth Taylor
Greenfield, Justin Holland, The Hyers Sisters, Joseph White, The
Colored American Opera Company, The Fisk Jubilee Singers, The
Georgia Minstrels, Frank Johnson, Joseph Anderson, Sam Lucas,

151.  Trotter (<u>continued</u>)

Samuel Snaer, and many other nineteenth-century black musicians in at least twenty American cities are discussed and described. The appendix contains the sheet music of compositions by thirteen composers.
Reviews: Negro Digest 18:49 S '69

# X

# Topical Studies

## FOLK MUSIC

152. Bodkin, B. A., ed. <u>Slave Narratives: A Folk History of Slavery in the United States From Interviews with Former Slaves.</u> 16 vols. Federal Writer's Project. Washington, D.C.: Library of Congress, 1941. pp. per vol. varies. photographs.

> These typewritten records of folk materials include interviews with former slaves; photographs of former slaves; transcripts of laws; advertisements; slave sale, transfer, and manumission records; and other documents. The following states are represented in the collection: Alabama, Arkansas, Florida, Georgia, Indiana, Kansas, Kentucky, Maryland, Mississippi, Missouri, North Carolina, Ohio, Oklahoma, South Carolina, Tennessee, Texas, and Virginia. Containing a wealth of folk songs and other folk literature, the collection constitutes valuable "indirect source material" for scholars working in the area of black American folk music.

153. Courlander, Harold. <u>Negro Folk Music, U.S.A.</u> New York: Columbia University Press, 1963. x, 324 pp. drawings, musical examples. bibliography. discography. sources of notated songs. index.

> Courlander discusses the anthems, spirituals, blues, and other songs in the folk tradition of black people in the United States, as well as cries, calls, whoops, and hollers. The book also covers the musical instruments of the black folk tradition, with brief histories, and approaches to playing them. An entire section of songs and lengthy song specimens is included. In the course of the discussions, the

153. Courlander (continued)

author questions some of the "conventional wisdom" pertaining to
the black folk music tradition and presents rational arguments,
based on solid facts, on behalf of more reasonable theories, beliefs,
and assumptions.   With this book, the beginning researcher is
provided with a sound general view of the research area, as well as
some of the best and most appropriate basic reading material in all
branches of black folk music.
        Reviews:   American Literature 36:125 Mr '63;  Christian
Science Monitor p10 O 1 '63; Downbeat 30:40 D 19 '63;
Ethnomusicology 8:187-190 n2 '64; Jazz 3:28 Mr/Ap '64; Journal
of the International Folk Music Council 17:26-27 '65; Library
Journal 88:4763 D 15 '63; Music Educators Journal 50:174-175
n4 '64; Music Journal 22:56 D '64; NATS Bulletin 20:33 n3 '64;
New York Times Book Review p22 N 17 '63; Notes 20:665 Fall
'63; Pan Pipes 57:35 n2 '65; Sing Out 13:59 n5 '63/'64; Times
Literary Supplement p524 Ju 18 '64; Western Folklore 24:59-60
n1 '65

154. Epstein, Dena J.  Sinful Tunes and Spirituals:  Black Folk Music to the
Civil War.  Music in American Life.  Urbana:  University of Illinois
Press, 1977.  xix, 433 pp. photographs, musical examples. appendixes.
bibliography. index.

This work traces the history of black folk music in the United
States from 1619 to 1867; it is a well-documented report on the
character and the state of this music as heard by contemporary
observers.   Based on "slave narratives, travel accounts, memoirs,
letters, novels, church histories, and polemics on slavery" (p. xiii), it
is the first systematic search of the historical record of slavery for
the purpose of documenting the origins, evolution, and status of
black folk music in the United States.   Part One of this
documentary survey reports on the "Development of Black Folk
Music to 1800"; Part Two chronicles "Secular and Sacred Black Folk
Music, 1800-1867"; and Part Three presents information on "The
Emergence of Black Folk Music During the Civil War."  The book's
seventeen chapters touch on such specifics as black folk
instruments, music and dancing, funerals and celebrations, African
survivals and acculturation in the United States, and all the Afro-
American folk song genres.   The lengthy and unusually specific
bibliography is tremendously valuable in itself—its specificity will
assist researchers who wish to retrace or replicate any aspect of
the study.
        Reviews: American Historical Review 84:557 Ap '79; Booklist
74:1239 Ap 1 '78; Choice 15:884 S '78; Fontes Artis Musicae
25:273-275 n3 '78; History 6:116-117 Ap '78; Hymn 30:140-141
n2 '79; JEMF Quarterly 14:219+ n52 '78; Journal of American
Folklore 65:446 S '78; Journal of American History 65:446-447
S '78; Journal of Southern History 45:147 F '79; Living Blues
42:30 Ja/F '79; Music Educators Journal 65:22 S '78; Notes
35:871-873 n4 '79; Tennessee Folklore Society Bulletin 44:148-

154. Epstein (continued)

    149 n3 '78; Times Literary Supplement 3983:882 Au 4 '78;
    Virginia Quarterly Review 54:109 Summer '78

155. Jackson, Bruce. The Negro and His Folklore in Nineteenth Century
    Periodicals. Austin: University of Texas Press, 1967. xxiii, 374 pp.
    musical examples. appendixes. bibliography. indexes.

    This collection of thirty-five articles, letters, and reviews is an
    attempt to present a wide range of writings on Afro-American
    culture and folklore as they appeared in nineteenth-century
    journals. It will serve as a good introduction to the study of the
    music of the period, especially since nearly one-half of the essays
    are devoted to black song. Appendix I is "A Slaveholder's Primer."
    Appendix II is a rather extensive guide to further reading in the
    area. The indexes are of authors, titles (of articles and periodicals),
    and songs and verses.
        Reviews: Antiquarian Bookman 41:2184 Ju 3 '68; Choice 5:834
    S '68; Journal of American Folklore 81:352-354 n322 '68;
    Journal of English and Germanic Philology 68:194 Ja '69;
    Library Journal 93:200 Ja 15 '68; Southern Folklore Quarterly
    33:54-55 n1 '69; Southwest Review 53:216 Spring '68

156. Katz, Bernard, ed. The Social Implications of Early Negro Music in the
    United States. The American Negro: His History and Literature. New
    York: Arno Press and The New York Times, 1969. xxx, 146 pp. musical
    examples, drawings. bibliography. index.

    This important volume presents complete or partial reproductions
    of eighteen writings by sixteen authors or collaborators writing
    between 1862 and 1939, with the majority before 1900. The authors
    are all pioneers in the documentation and collection of black
    American music and include such familiar and influential names as
    W. E. B. DuBois, Francis Allen, Lucy McKim Garrison, James
    Weldon Johnson, George Washington Cable, John Lovell, Jr., and
    J. Rosamond Johnson. The articles and excerpts are presented with
    their original examples of text and music resulting in a rich source
    of black folk music and spirituals; the index provides valuable
    access to the songs.
        Reviews: American Musical Digest 1:38-39 n5 '70; Yearbook
    for Inter-American Musical Research 6:127-130 '70

157. Krehbiel, Henry Edward. Afro-American Folksongs: A Study in Racial
    and National Music. 3rd ed. 1914. Reprint. New York: Frederick
    Unger Publishing Co., 1967. xii, 176 pp. musical examples. appendix.
    index.

    Despite a few interpretive and philosophical shortcomings due to its
    early date, and notwithstanding later writings on the subject, this
    book remains a significant and useful contribution to the field.
    First published in 1913, it stands as the first application of musical
    scholarship to the study of black folk songs; it also represents the

157. Krehbiel (continued)

first attempt, however superficial, to explain the music in terms of its African background. The author discusses "Folksongs in General," slave songs and their musical characteristics, poems, funeral music, Creole songs, and "Dances of the American Negroes." The appendix consists of "Ten Characteristic Songs."

158. Lawless, Ray M. Folksingers and Folksongs in America: A Handbook of Biography, Bibliography, and Discography. Rev. ed. New York: Duell, Sloan and Pearce, 1965. xviii, 750 pp. supplement. plates. indexes.

This volume contains a wide range of information for anyone interested in folk music; it is organized in three parts which treat biography of folk singers, bibliographies and folk song collections, and discography. In the first part, the brief biographies of folk singers include several of black musicians, although they are not so identified. The second part contains discussions of thirteen anthologies of black folk music including three by Alan Lomax; two bibliographies pertaining to black folk music are annotated. The final section of the book consists of 1) a list of more than eight hundred folk song titles; 2) a discography of works by individuals including Big Bill Broonzy, Harry Belafonte, Marian Anderson, Blind Lemon Jefferson, and Leadbelly; and 3) a discography of works by groups such as the Fisk Jubilee Singers, the Golden Gate Quartet, and by several performers recorded by the Library of Congress Music Division, Folkways Records, and others. The folk song titles are listed in alphabetical order and are accompanied by an indication of their location in one or more of thirty-eight anthologies. The individual discographies are arranged alphabetically by singer and include works recorded primarily between 1948 and 1958 on long-playing records. The group discographies are listed alphabetically by title of the recording. Information included in the discographical entries includes the name of the record company and label number, the size of the disc, and the titles of the songs performed. The three indexes list names and subjects, titles, and long-playing records. The supplement that concludes this revised edition has the same format as the main text and updates the book from 1960 to 1965.

Reviews: American Literature 37:527 Ja '66; Antiquarian Bookman 36:1222 O 4 '65; Catholic Library World 37:337 Ja '66; Catholic Library World 37:202 N '65; International Musician 64:18 Jy '66; Journal of Negro History 51:141 Ap '66; Library Journal 90:4641 '65; Music Educators Journal 52:107 n2 '65; Sing Out 15:84 n6 '66

159. Odum, Howard W., and Guy B. Johnson. The Negro and His Songs: A Study of Typical Negro Songs in the South. 1925. Reprint. Foreword by Roger D. Abrahams. Hatboro, Penn.: Folklore Associates, 1964. xix, 306 pp. bibliography. index.

This early sociological study of Afro-American song texts will be useful to researchers, despite over-generalizations, naiveté, and

159. Odum (continued)

errors. It is a study of the "full range of the song expressions" (p. vii) of the Southern rural Afro-American, an early attempt to "see far beyond the stereotypes," seeking to "reveal the character and quality of the Negro's way of thinking and self-expression" (p. viii). In attempting to "expose the 'inner life' of their informants" (p. vii), the authors discuss "The Singer and His Songs"; religious, social, and work songs; and "Imagery, Style, and Poetic Effort."
Reviews: Antiquarian Bookman 36:1424 O 18 '65; Journal of Negro History 50:137 Ap '65; Notes 23:60-61 nl '66

160. Odum, Howard W., and Guy B. Johnson. Negro Workaday Songs. Chapel Hill: University of North Carolina Press, 1926. xii, 278 pp. musical examples. bibliography. index.

This is a sociological study of the texts of more than two hundred Afro-American folk songs that "were taken directly from Negro singers" (p. x) in several Southern states during the years 1924-1925. In the first thirteen of the book's fifteen chapters, the author "presents a series of pictures of the Negro as portrayed through his workaday songs" (p. xi), both folk and semifolk—work songs, bad-man ballads and chain gang songs, songs of relationships between men and women, religious songs, and others. The final two chapters of the book discuss "Types of Negro Melodies" and "Types of Phono-photographic Records of Negro Singers." This is a good source for a wide variety of song texts and of discussions of the roles and interactions of these texts in Afro-American social contexts.
Reviews: AB Bookman's Weekly 64:367 N '26; Booklist 23:67 N '26; Boston Evening Transcript p3 Au 7 '26; Industrial and Engineering Chemistry 117:247 Au 28 '26; Nation 123:223 S 8 '26; New Republic 48:Supl62 S 29 '26; New York Herald Tribune Books p5 O 31 '26; New York Times Book Review p32 O 31 '26; Outlook 143:478 Au 4 '26; St. Louis 24:314 N '26; Saturday Review 3:52 '26; Survey 56:519 Au 1 '26; Wilson Library Bulletin 22:293 N '26

161. Sandberg, Larry, and Dick Weissman. The Folk Music Sourcebook. New York: Alfred A. Knopf, 1976. x, 260, xiv pp. photographs. glossary. index.

This excellent reference source on the "folk and folk-based music of North America in the English language" (p. ix) opens with a section on "Black American Music." Included are narratives on various genres and styles, biographical sketches on the principal performers, annotated record listings for each performer, and an annotated list of anthologies and collections. Treated are the blues in its various forms and manifestations, jug bands, string bands, ragtime, one-man bands, sacred blues, country spirituals, sanctified singing, gospel music, Creole blues, zydeco, and jazz.
Reviews: American Reference Books Annual 8:471 '77; Blue-grass Unlimited 11:32 D '76; Booklist 73:7 S 1 '76; Booklist

161. Sandberg (continued)

> 73:32 S 1 '76; Booklist 73:856-857 F 1 '77; Cadence 1:18 S '76;
> Choice 13:1307 D '76; Clavier 15:6 n8 '76; JEMF Quarterly
> 12:232 n44 '76; Library Journal 101:2559 D 15 '76; Music
> Educators Journal 63:83 N '76; Old Times Music 22:28-29 Fall
> '76; Reference Services Review 5:29 Ja '77; Rolling Stone p73
> Ju 17 '76; School Library Journal 23:149 S '76; Wilson Library
> Bulletin 51:681 Ap '77

162. Scarborough, Dorothy.  On the Trail of Negro Folk-Songs.  1925.
Reprint.  Foreword by Roger D. Abrahams.  Hatboro, Penn.:  Folklore
Associates, 1963.  ix, 295 pp.  musical examples.  index.

> This work discusses ballads, dance songs, lullabyes, animal songs,
> work songs, railroad songs, and blues, the latter in a separate
> section which is based on the author's revealing interview with
> W. C. Handy.  Also discussed are the author's search for these songs
> and "The Negro's Part in Transmitting The Traditional Songs and
> Ballads of whites ."  The index lists song titles and first lines.
> Written in the first person, the book is a unique and refreshing
> approach to folk song scholarship, despite its early date.
> Reviews:  Downbeat 30:40 D 19 '63; Ethnomusicology 8:313-314
> n3 '64; Journal of the International Folk Music Council 17:27
> '65; Journal of American Folklore 78:84-85 n307 '65; Notes
> 20:655-656 n4 '63; Sing Out 14:63+ n6 '64; Western Folklore
> 24:59+ n1 '65

163. White, Newman I.  American Negro Folk-Songs.  Cambridge:  Harvard
University Press, 1928.  501 pp.  bibliography.  musical examples.
appendixes.  indexes.

> Religious songs, animal songs, work songs, songs about women,
> "seamy" songs, blues songs, and other miscellaneous song texts are
> presented and discussed in this book.  Although based on the white
> origins theory, it is nevertheless a serious and scholarly study that
> recognizes the fact that "The songs . . . are beyond question the
> Negro's songs" (p. 25).     The book's fifteen chapters offer
> information about the character of Afro-American folk songs, their
> origins (according to the author), and the state of scholarship in the
> field.  The five appendixes contain song specimens of various kinds-
> tunes, "Negro Ballets and Related Songs," "Spiritual Songs and
> Camp-Meeting Songs of the White People," "Songs from the Old
> Minstrel Books," and "Songs from Antebellum Novels, Travel Books,
> Slave Autobiographies, etc."  The two indexes are for titles and for
> tunes.
> Reviews:     AB Bookman's Weekly 68:709 F '29; American
> Journal of Sociology 35:332 S '29; Nation 127:579 N 28 '28; New
> Republican 57:144 D 19 '28; New York Herald Tribune Books p4
> My 26 '29; St. Louis 26:384 D '28; Saturday Review of
> Literature 5:220 '28; Times Literary Supplement p797 N 1 '28;
> World Tomorrow 12:44 Ja '29

164. Work, John Wesley. Folk Song of the American Negro. 1915. Reprint. New York: Negro Universities Press, 1969. 131 pp. photographs, musical examples.

This book reflects the state of black musical thought at the turn of the century, presenting information and an important perspective on "African Song," "Transmigration and Transmission of Song," characteristics of Afro-American song, the origin and development of Afro-American song, the 1871-1878 tour of the Fisk Jubilee Singers, and other pertinent topics. The texts and the music of nine Afro-American spirituals are placed throughout the work.

## SPIRITUALS

165. Cone, James H. The Spirituals and the Blues: An Interpretation. New York: Seabury Press, 1972. viii, 152 pp.

This book offers a basic introduction to the spiritual and the blues. Although primarily about the spiritual, the work does present basic information about both genres and discusses relationships between them. The focus is on interpretation.
Reviews: AB Bookman's Weekly 2:304 Winter '72; America 127:128 S 2 '72; Black World 23:95 N '73; Black World 24:93 F '75; Booklist 69:19 S 1 '72; Choice 10:631 Ju '73; Christian Century 89:928 S 20 '72; Commonweal 97:481 F 23 '73; Ethnomusicology 17:132 n1 '73; Journal of American Folklore 87:105 Ja '74; Library Journal 97:1812 My 15 '72; Notes 30:62-64 n1 '73; Publishers Weekly 201:49 Mr 6 '72; Review for Religious 31:892 S '72; Theology Today 29:446 Ja '73

166. Fisher, Miles Mark. Negro Slave Songs in the United States. Foreword by Ray Allen Billington. 2nd ed. New York: Citadel Press, 1969. 223 pp. bibliography. index.

The primary importance of this book is that it presents views that differ from those of previous works on the Afro-American spiritual and, at the same time, debunks the "white-to-Negro" theory of the spiritual's origins. Treating the spirituals as "more than folk music"—a unique view at the time of the book's first edition (1953)—the author discusses the spirituals' origins and explores the variety of roles these songs played in slave life, treating their use of symbols, imagery, and concepts to foster various kinds of communication. The book's chapter on "Understanding Spirituals" is a good summary of the ideas presented in its preceding eight chapters, the first of which discusses "History in the Music of Negroes," the remainder being devoted to the major themes on which the spirituals were based, e.g., secret meetings ("Steal Away").
Reviews: Black World 24:93 F '75

167.  Jackson, George Pullen.  White and Negro Spirituals:  Their Span and
      Kinship.  1943.  Reprint.  New York:  Da Capo Press, 1975.  xiii, 349
      pp. photographs, tables, musical examples.  appendixes.

> This well-known book claims to provide the "true" story of the
> origins of the Afro-American spiritual.  The author discusses this in
> two parts:  "The whole story of American Religious Folk Song as the
> White People Sang It" and "The whole Story of American Religious
> Folk Song as the Negroes Sang It."  Jackson draws the conclusion
> that the slaves appropriated white folk songs and converted them
> into what came to be known as "Negro Spirituals."  This book is the
> most familiar and most complete manifestation of the "white
> origins" theory.   Although  its  claims  have  been  thoroughly
> disproved, black music scholars should be well familiar with its
> contents, its philosophy, and its methodology.
> Reviews:  Reprint Bulletin Book Review 20:33-34 Winter '75

168.  Lovell, John, Jr.  Black Song:  The Forge and the Flame.  New York:
      Macmillan Co., 1972.  xviii, 686 pp.  source notes.  index.

> A study of the social and literary development of "black song," this
> work is a thorough investigation of the creation and nature of the
> Afro-American spiritual, and the impact of that genre on aspects of
> American and world culture.  The book is divided into three main
> sections as follows.  Part I, "The Forge," is background information
> for the study of the spiritual; the author discusses the African
> musical experience and attacks the "white origins" theory of the
> rise of the Afro-American spiritual.  Part II, "The Slave Sings Free,"
> is a discussion of the role of the slave community in the
> development of black song; the African origins of the genre are
> linked to the Afro-American "poetic experience" in explaining
> literary meaning and transformation in black song.  Part III, "The
> Flame," presents information about the spread and the treatment of
> "The Spiritual as a World Phenomenon," from 1871, in performances
> and published collections; also presented is information on how the
> spiritual was used in and adapted to literary fiction, motion
> pictures, stage works, radio, and other communications media.  This
> work is one of several that should be read before launching a serious
> study of the Afro-American spiritual.
> Reviews:  Library Journal 97:2188 '72; Music 6:21+ N '72; Music
> Educators Journal 51:82-84+ My '73; Music Ministry 5:8-9 Ja '73

169.  Marsh, J. B. T.  The Story of the Jubilee Singers; With Their Songs.  Rev.
      ed. Boston:  Houghton Mifflin and Co., 1880. viii, 265 pp.  index.

> This volume contains the two earlier and separate accounts of the
> American and the European portions of the 1871-1874 tour of the
> Fisk Jubilee Singers, and bridges over the interval between the
> tours.  In addition, this volume adds more to the personal histories
> of the Singers and includes a large number of additional songs,
> bringing the total number of the latter to 128.   The anthology
> section of the work has its own preface and "Index to Music."

170. Pike, Gustavus D. The Jubilee Singers and Their Campaign for Twenty Thousand Dollars. Boston: Lee and Shepard Publishers; New York: Lee, Shepard and Dillingham, 1873. xiv, 272 pp. photographs. appendix. index.

This volume, the first of two books that discuss different portions of the 1871-74 tour of the Fisk Jubilee Singers, focuses on the United States portion of the two-continent sojourn. In addition, the work details information about the American Missionary Association, Fisk University, personal histories of the singers, and the group's journeys to and stops at Oberlin, New York, Hartford, and Boston, discussing the rigors of travel, the prejudice and discrimination they encountered, the rewards of performance, and the kindness of their supporters along the way. Sixty "Jubilee Songs," complete with preface and index, are appended.

171. Pike, Gustavus D. The Singing Campaign for Ten Thousand Pounds; Or The Jubilee Singers in Great Britain. 1875. Reprint. Introduction by E. M. Cravath. Freeport, N.Y.: Books for Libraries Press, 1971. 221 pp. plates. index.

This is an account of the Fisk Jubilee Singers' visit to Great Britain during the years 1871-1874. The book chronicles the group's preparation for the trip; preparatory performances in the United States; their arrival at Liverpool; their visits and performances at various locations in Great Britain; the closing of the campaign, during which they earned £10,000 to rescue their school from financial collapse; and their return to Nashville. Details of prejudice and discrimination, sickness, communications, command performances and invitations to perform, patronage, donations, concerts, and other trials and rewards are given. The appendix is a collection of jubilee songs complete with a preface and an index.

## MINSTRELSY

172. Haverly, Jack. Negro Minstrels: A Complete Guide. 1902. Reprint. Upper Saddle River, N.J.: Literature House/Gregg Press, 1969. 129 pp.

This guide to organizing and presenting "Negro minstrels" is a handy source for understanding how white men in blackface caricatured black life in America, creating, in the process, a stereotypical and negative image of the Afro-American. While the book is not about black music, it will be useful to students of black minstrelsy and of nineteenth-century black music, containing, as it does, "Recitations, Jokes, Cross-fires, Conundrums, Riddles, Stump Speeches, Ragtime and Sentimental Songs, etc." (title page).

173. Simond, Ike. Old Slack's Reminiscence and Pocket History of the Colored Profession from 1865 to 1891. [n.d.]. Reprint. Preface by Frances Lee Utley. Introduction by Robert C. Toll. Bowling Green, Ohio: Popular Press, 1974. xxxiv, 123 pp. appendix. index.

173. Simond (continued)

Simond's Reminiscence contains "a host of names of black artists, compiled by an eyewitness who was obviously a congenial man who knew 'everybody'. . . . The book, with all its errors, [is] a genuine primary document, recording history which [can] not be found in other sources, and providing a picture of artistic endeavor which long anticipated the successful arrival of Bert Williams and George Walker on the Broadway stage in 1900" (p. vii). The work is focused upon, but not limited to, the genre of black minstrelsy. Toll's introduction provides a brief overview of minstrelsy, a short bibliographical essay, and an introduction to Simond's work; the appendix consists of a bibliography of black minstrel songsters and a chronology of the "Major Dates in Black Minstrelsy." The lengthy index provided in the reprint gives invaluable access to Simond's document.

174. Toll, Robert C. Blacking Up: The Minstrel Show in Nineteenth-Century America. New York: Oxford University Press, 1974. x, 310 pp. appendixes. bibliography. index.

The author investigates and presents the cultural settings in which Negro (white) minstrelsy, as well as black minstrelsy, arose; he traces minstrelsy's development from its beginnings in the 1820s until the 1890s, citing the contemporary events and prevailing social and political attitudes that influenced its ever-changing character and evolution. Included in the discussions are the Georgia Minstrels, Callender's Minstrels, Haverly Colored Minstrels, Billy Kersands, Sam Lucas, W. C. Handy, and Tom Fletcher; Lew Johnson and Charles Hicks, black owners of minstrel troupes, also figure in the text. Further discussed is the impact that Negro minstrelsy had on black America, and how it shaped general American thought regarding black people during the mid-nineteenth-century controversy over slavery. This book, a sociopsychological study of a phenomenon which previously had not been adequately or properly investigated, is necessary reading for any scholar researching any aspect of show business history or late nineteenth-century popular music. The short appendix, "Note on Method," has potential implications for the researching of black popular culture.

Reviews: American Historical Review 82:452 Ap '77; American Literature 47:146 Mr '75; Booklist 71:664 Mr 1 '75; Books and Bookmen 20:58 My '75; Choice 14:1002 O '77; Educational Theater Journal 27:431-432 O '75; Journal of American History 62:678-679 D '75; Journal of American Studies 9:365-373 D '75; Kirkus Reviews 42:997 S 1 '74; Kliatt Paperback Book Guide 11:29 Spring '77; Listener 93:454 Ap 3 '75; Musical Opinion 99:69 N '75; New Statesman 90:63 Jy 11 '75; New York Times 124:27 Ja 18 '75; Publishers Weekly 206:58 O 7 '74; Sewanee Review 83:civ-cx Fall '75; Times Literary Supplement p218 F 28 '75; Virginia Quarterly Journal 51:R124 Summer '75

# RAGTIME

175. Berlin, Edward A.    Ragtime:    A Musical and Cultural History.
Berkeley:  University of California Press, 1980.  xix, 248 pp.  plates,
musical examples. appendix. bibliography. index.

The most complete available discussion of ragtime music, this work
treats the genre in its various manifestations—vocal ragtime, the
ragtime band, piano ragtime, and ragtime as it is performed by
various other instruments and instrumental combinations. It treats
some possible origins of the music and discusses various musical
sources for early ragtime—the march, the cakewalk, black
character pieces and patrols, coon songs, and Caribbean rhythms.
The author places ragtime in a historical perspective, discussing its
historiography and its "erosion as a distinctive style" (p. viii),
beginning in the 1920s.   The highlights of this work are its
treatment of the various ragtime styles as a single genre, its
presentation of a rather complete history of the genre, and its
identification of the music as representing "the first widespread
acceptance of a black cultural influence into the mainstream of
American life" (p. 196).  The book's "Location Index for Piano Rags"
in its Selected Anthologies is a valuable and useful feature.
   Reviews:  Choice 18:538 D '80; JEMF Quarterly 16:166-167 n49
'80; Journal of American History 68:157 Ju '81; Kirkus Reviews
48:170-171 F 1 '80; Library Journal 105:616 Mr 1 '80; New
Republic 184:25 Ja 24 '81; Notes 38:313 D '81; Ragtimer p17-19
N/D '80

176. Blesh, Rudi, and Harriet Janis. They All Played Ragtime. 3rd ed. New
York:  Oak Publications, 1966.  xxiv, 347, ix pp.  photographs, musical
compositions. music bibliography. rollography. discography. index.

This is both a history and a reference work, containing "The Story
of an American Music" as well as lists of ragtime and other sheet
music, player-piano rolls, and phonograph records.   After a brief
"prelude," the work begins with "The Sedalia Story," then traces the
development of ragtime from the first meeting of Scott Joplin and
John Stark to Joplin's experience with Treemonisha. Also discussed
are:  "Ragtime at the Rosebud," A Guest of Honor, "Ring-Shouts
and Rent-Shouts," and other topics.  This study of the personalities
and the various interrelationships of the ragtime era is loaded with
historical information; it is an impressive and influential work.  The
presence of copious and varied photographs of such personalities as
Joplin, Blind Tom, Blind Boone, Artie Matthews, Scott Hayden,
Arthur Marshall, Louis Chauvin, and Tom Turpin, and the complete
sheet music to sixteen piano rags, add to the book's interest and
value.
   Reviews:  Downbeat 33:42 N 17 '66; Jazz Report 5:4 n3 '66;
Second Line 17:160-161 N/D '66

177. Jasen, David A., and Trebor Jay Tichenor. Rags and Ragtime:  A
Musical History.  New York:  Seabury Press, 1978.  xii, 310 pp.
photographs, musical examples. appendix. index.

177. Jasen (continued)

The authors of this book define ragtime, and trace its development and modification through the folk, classic, popular, novelty, and stride styles. Finally, they discuss the ragtime revival of the period 1941-1978. The work discusses more than eight hundred important compositions and forty-eight major composers, the latter including Scott Joplin, Jelly Roll Morton, James P. Johnson, Willie "The Lion" Smith, Fats Waller, Euday Bowman, Scott Hayden, James Scott, Artie Matthews, Arthur Marshall, and Eubie Blake. More of a reference book than a narrative history, the work is a collection of separate "portraits" and biblio/discographies of the composers represented. For each individual, the authors have presented a biographical sketch and "have included for each rag the date of copyright, the name and location of the original sheet music publisher, a selected list of flat disc recordings and piano rolls and their subsequent reissue on LP records, a diagram of the musical structure and, finally, a commentary on the uniqueness of the rag" (dust cover). The book's 122 photographs of composers, sheet music, and other items complement both the text and the listings.
Reviews: Billboard 90:76 S 2 '78; Choice 15:1531 S 1 '78; Christian Science Monitor 70:23 N 24 '78; Kirkus Reviews 46:676 Ju 15 '78; Library Journal 103:1640 S 1 '78; Music Educators Journal 65:13-14 N '78; Notes 35:616-618 n3 '79; Ragtimer p15-16 S/O '78; Ragtimer p67 My/Ju '79; Record Research n161/162:6 F/Mr '79; Variety 293:84 Ja 17 '79

178. Schafer, William J., and Johannes Riedel. The Art of Ragtime: Form and Meaning of an Original Black American Art. Baton Rouge: Louisiana State University Press, 1973. xix, 249 pp. musical examples. bibliography. appendixes. index.

Basic information on ragtime and its composers is presented in this work which chronicles the genre's development from the 1890s to 1915. The work relates ragtime to other black music genres, discusses its impact on white culture, and examines ragtime style and performance. Classic ragtime, ragtime songs, and ragtime bands all receive attention. The book's four appendixes promise to be useful: "The Image on the Cover," "Ragtime versus Jazz Piano Styles," "Scott Joplin's Treemonisha," and "Bibliography of Ragtime."
Reviews: American Record Guide 40:61 N '76; Black Perspective in Music 3:105-107 n1 '75; Books and Bookmen 19:84 N '73; Choice 11:449 My '74; Coda 11:23 n7 '74; Jazz Digest 3:19 F '74; Jazz Forum n30:63 Au '74; Jazz Journal 27:6-7 Mr '74; Jazz Journal 27:3 My '74; JEMF Quarterly 10:38-39 '74; Journal of American Folklore 87:174-177 n344 '74; Library Journal 99:139 Ja 15 '74; Musical Times 116:45 Ja '75; Music Educators Journal 61:96-98 O '74; Music Journal 32:32-33 F '74 New York Times Book Review p4 F 3 '74; Publishers Weekly 203:49 Ap 30 '73; Ragtimer p8-9 S/O '73; Ragtimer p6-8 N/D '73; Ragtimer p14-15 My/Ju '74; Second Line 25:21-22 Fall '73; Stereo Review 33:54 S '74; Times Literary Supplement p1323 O

178. Schafer (continued)

> 26 '73; Yearbook for Inter-American Musical Research 9:192-193 '73

# BLUES

179. Garon, Paul. Blues and the Poetic Spirit. 1975. Reprint. Preface by Franklin Rosemont. New York: Da Capo Press, 1979. 178 pp. photographs. bibliography. index.

> Paul Garon's study of the blues represents a new and important approach to the analysis of the blues as a psychopoetic phenomenon. Garon treats the blues as it relates to aggression, eros, humor, work, crime, magic, and other matters, basing his exposition primarily on the theories and experimental findings of Karl Marx, Sigmund Freud and other psychologists, and on the surrealist poet-philosophers. Differing from all previous expositions on the blues, the book eschews the usual sociological-assimilative considerations and emphasizes the "psychological determinants of blues songs, and their poetic implications" (p. 18). This work is an important starting place for researchers who intend to investigate the essence of the blues.
> Reviews: Coda n169:16-17 O 1 '79; Radio Free Jazz 21:8-9 Mr '80; Reprint Bulletin—Book Reviews 25:12 n2 '80; Reprint Bulletin—Book Reviews 25:15 n4 '80

180. Guralnick, Peter. The Listener's Guide to the Blues. New York: Facts On File, 1982. 134 pp. index.

> This is a beginner's handbook to the study of the blues in its most basic manifestations—from its first commercial use in vaudeville to its present-day forms, from Ma Rainey and Bessie Smith to Professor Longhair, Bobby Blue Bland, and Jimmy Johnson. Each of the book's fifteen brief chapters is divided into two parts, the first being a narrative on a particular subject, the second consisting of a list of selected recordings that illustrate the subject. Throughout the Guide, the narrative sections discuss the lives, the influences, and the recordings of more than 150 important blues figures, guiding the novice listener from early blues songs and their African and New World antecedents, through city and country blues, Texas and Mississippi Delta blues, Chicago Jump, and other styles. Two of the book's chapters treat different pairs of blues artists—Chapter 9 is titled "Blues Stars: Lonnie Johnson and Leroy Carr," while Chapter 13 carries the title "B. B. King and T-Bone Walker." The Chicago "post-modern" school is also discussed, with emphasis on Otis Rush, Magic Sam, and Buddy Guy.

181. Keil, Charles. Urban Blues. Chicago: University of Chicago Press, 1966. ix, 231 pp. photographs. appendixes. index.

> "Primarily concerned with an expressive male role within urban

181.  Keil (continued)

lower-class Negro culture—that of the contemporary bluesman"
(p. 1), this sociological study of the blues discusses the character of
Afro-American music in general; blues styles, distinguishing among
country, city, and urban; the role of the blues singer and the
response of his audience; and "Soul and Solidarity." One of the
appendixes, "Blues Styles: An Annotated Outline," is a particularly
valuable feature of the book; it will serve as a good reference tool
and guide for researchers, teachers, and students.
    Reviews: American Anthropologist 69:786 D '67; Atlantic
Monthly 218:119 Au '66; Booklist 63:219 O 15 '66; Books Today
3:5 Au 7 '66; Book Week p2 Au 28 '66; Choice 3:1135 F '67;
Christian Century 83:964 Au 3 '66; Downbeat 34:40 My 18 '67;
Ethnomusicology 11:259 '67; Inter-American Institute for
Musical Research Yearbook 3:118 '67; Jazz Hot 224:9 O '66;
Jazz Journal 19:17 N '66; Jazz Magazine 138:18 Ja '67; Jazz
Monthly 13:27 Ju '67; Manchester Guardian Weekly 95:11 O 20
'66; Melody Maker 41:6 O 22 '66; Music Journal 24:105 S '66;
Negro Digest 15:51 Au '66; New York Times Book Review 71:22
Au 14 '66; Orkester Journalen 35:12 Jy/Au '67; Publishers
Weekly 189:120 Ap 25 '66; Publishers Weekly 193:103 F 19 '68;
Saturday Review of Literature p27 Jy 27 '68; Sing Out 17:37
'67; Times Literary Supplement p1005 N 3 '66

182.  Murray, Albert. Stomping the Blues. New York: McGraw-Hill Book
Co., 1976. 264 pp. photographs. index.

Essentially, this book is an exposition of some of the aesthetic
principles of blues music and the blues experience. It is a unique
approach in which the author, in criticizing prevailing dictionary
definitions of the blues, seeks to disprove the myths that have been
attached to the genre for decades. Making a distinction between
"the blues" proper and "blues music," the author presents the first
comprehensive consideration of the meanings of the term "blues."
Chapter titles such as "The Blues as Such," "Blues Music as Such,"
and "The Blues as Statement" reflect Murray's approach to the
subject. This is not a history, but a critical approach to a much
misunderstood subject. Using the term in its broadest sense, the
author mentions such diverse personalities as Muddy Waters, Bessie
Smith, W. C. Handy, Billie Holiday, Duke Ellington, Count Basie,
Louis Armstrong, Lester Young, Charlie Parker, Ornette Coleman,
John Coltrane, and many others. The inclusion of copious photographs of musicians is unusually effective. The captions are well-
done, and make the illustrations integral to the text. Although this
book contains no bibliography and no scholarly apparatus, it is indispensable reading for interpreters of the jazz and blues experiences.
    Reviews: Booklist 73:874 F 15 '77; Cadence 2:27 Jy '77;
Christian Science Monitor 69:23 Mr 17 '77; Coda n164:40 F 1
'79; Downbeat 44:51 O 20 '77; Jazz Journal International 31:25
S '78; Library Journal 102:388 F 1 '77; Living Blues n31:30
Mr/Ap '77; Music in Education 42:456 '78; Nation 224:55 Ja 15

182. Murray (continued)

'77; Newsweek 88:95 D 20 '76; New York Times 126:21 D 11'76; New York Times Book Review p6 D 26 '76; Rolling Stone p57 Ja 13 '77; Times Literary Supplement p840 Jy 28 '78

183. Oakley, Giles. The Devil's Music: A History of the Blues. New York: Harcourt, Brace, Jovanovich, 1976. 287 pp. photographs, map. bibliography. discography. indexes.

The author of this book purports to "trace the story of this music, and by it the history of Black Americans" (p. 1 ). He begins with Afro-American music in the slave experience and proceeds through country and city blues performers and styles, ending with post-war blues. Oakley presents the narrative in an effective, illuminating, and appropriate way, through numerous scattered quotations and photographs of luminaries such as Mamie Smith, Ma Rainey, Jimmy Yancey, Cripple Clarence Lofton, Gus Cannon, Memphis Minnie, Booker White, Little Walter, Eubie Blake, Jelly Roll Morton, and Muddy Waters; the interjection and spacing of blues lyrics throughout the book; and the layout of the pages.

Reviews: American Historical Review 83:815 Ju '78; Booklist 73:1395 My 15 '77; Books and Bookmen 22:51 My '77; Books West 1:28 O '77; Cadence 4:14 My '78; Choice 15:83 Mr '78; Downbeat 44:44 D 1 '77; Jazz Journal 30:41 Ja '77; Library Journal 102:1499 Jy '77; Melody Maker 51:19 D 18 '76; Music Journal 36:39 Ap '78; New York Times 127:C25 Mr 1 '78; Publishers Weekly 211:73 F 14 '77; School Librarian 25:191 Ju '77; School Library Journal 24:66 D '77; Stereo Review 40:15 Ja '78

184. Oliver, Paul. Aspects of the Blues Tradition. New York: Oak Publications, 1970. viii, 294 pp. musical examples. indexes.

Oliver's book deals with the origins and successive uses of several common subjects of blues lyrics. The first five chapters treat general subjects and their use by many artists in various blues lyrics. They are: "The Santy Claus Crave," Christmas themes; "Preaching the Blues," treatment of religious expressions in the blues; "The Forty-Fours," treatment of the interactions of blues by that title and blues titled Vicksburg Blues; "Policy Blues," treatment of the numbers as a theme; and "Joe Louis and John Henry," discussion of blues that treat those two hero figures. The final chapter consists of discussions of various aspects of sexual allusion and explicit treatment in the blues, including censorship by collectors and record companies, sexual imagery and symbolism, and the tracing of the changes in successive uses of four specific blues.

Reviews: AB Bookman's Weekly 46:582 S 7 '70; Booklist 67:211 N 1 '70; Choice 8:884 S '71; Hip 10:14 '71; Jazz and Pop 10:11 Jy '71; Jazz Report 7:14 '71; Library Journal 95:3474 O 15 '70; Notes 27:718 Ju '71

185.  Oliver, Paul.  <u>Savannah Syncopators:  African Retentions in the Blues</u>.
New  York:  Stein  and  Day,  1970.  112  pp.  photographs.  maps.
bibliography. discography. glossary. index.

This  book  discusses  the  connections  between  African  musical
characteristics--specifically  those  of  the  Savannah  regions--and
their  Afro-American  counterparts  in  United  States  blues  music.
After  describing  African  music  and  culture,  the  author  traces
musical survivals through "The Source of the Slaves," and goes on to
discuss  cross-cultural  similarities  in  a  chapter  on  "Africa  and  the
Blues."  The  Glossary  describes  more  than  eighty  African  musical
instruments.  The  index  is  an  "Index  of  Tribes  and  People"
mentioned in the text.

Reviews:  AB Bookman's Weekly 46:583 S 7 '70; Black World
20:90  Ja  '71;  Blues  Unlimited  75:29  S  '70;  Choice  8:76  Mr  '71;
Ethnomusicology  16:132  '72;  Gramophone  48:677  D  '70;  Jazz
and  Pop  10:41  Jy  '71;  Jazz  Hot  266:31  N  '70;  Jazz  Journal  23:8
S  '70;  Jazz  Monthly  188:29  O  '70;  Jazz  Research  2:164  '70;
Library  Journal  96:292  Ja  15  '71;  Library  Journal  96:481  F  1
'71;  Matrix  89:16  S  '70;  Melody  Maker  45:38  Au  15  '70;  Melody
Maker  45:28  S  12  '70;  Musical  Times  111:898  S  '70;  Negro
History  Bulletin  34:70  Mr  '71;  New  Statesman  81:23  Ja  1  '71;
Orkester  Journalen  39:26  F  '71;  Storyville  30:236  Au/S  '70;
Times  Literary  Supplement  p1365  N  20  '70;  Western  Folklore
30:150 '71

186.  Oliver, Paul.  <u>The Story of the Blues</u>.  London:  Barrie & Rockliff,
Cresset Press, 1969.  176 pp. photographs, musical examples, posters,
phonophotography graphs. discography and bibliography. index.

Through  its  many  photographs  and  their  accompanying  texts,  this
book  gives  an  overview  of  the  origins  and  development  of  the
blues.  Primarily  organized  on  a  chronological  basis,  the  book
discusses the development of the blues from its roots in the songs of
slavery,  work  songs  and  hollers;  to  the  delta  country  blues,  the
Memphis blues, minstrelsy, the classic blues, the blues in St. Louis
and Chicago, and the urban blues of the 1950s. Among the men and
women  included  in  the  discussion  are  Mississippi  John  Hurt,
Leadbelly, Blind Lemon Jefferson, Ma Rainey, Clara Smith, Jimmy
Rushing,  King  Oliver's  Creole  Jazz  Band,  Jimmy  Yancey,  Big  Bill
Broonzy,  Memphis  Minnie,  Blind  Boy  Fuller,  T-Bone  Walker,  Fats
Domino,  Bobbie  Blue  Bland,  and  B. B. King.  In  addition  to  the
treatment  of  the  blues  itself,  the  book  contains  a  valuable
introduction  to  phonophotography  as  a  method  of  collecting  and
precisely transcribing songs. The book is beautifully illustrated; its
photographs provide a view of the country and culture within which
the blues developed.

Reviews:  AB Bookman's Weekly 44:558 Au 25 '69; American
Musical  Digest  1:23  D  '69;  American  Record  Guide  36:912  Jy
'70;  Blues  Unlimited  65:20  S  '69;  Books  and  Bookmen  14:34  S
'69;  Choice  7:554  Ju  '70;  Economist  232:47  S  6  '69;  Guardian
Weekly 101:19 Au 7 '69; Guardian Weekly 101:19 D 20 '69; Jazz
Hot 259:15 Mr '70; Jazz Journal 22:11 S '69; Jazz Journal 22:40

186. Oliver (continued)

> O '69; Jazz Monthly 178:26 D '69; Jazz Research 3/4:256 '71/'72; JEMF Quarterly 6:184 '70; Library Journal 94:3847 O 15 '69; Library Journal 95:2482 Jy '70; Listener 82:419 S 25 '69; Melody Maker 44:12 Au 2 '69; Musical Times 111:48 Ja '70; Music Journal 27:18 D '69; Nation 209:673 D 15 '69; New York Times Book Review p18 O 19 '69; Orkester Journalen 38:2 Ja '70; Rolling Stone 58:48 My 14 '70; Saturday Review 52:53 D 13 '69; Second Line 25:26 Fall '71; Storyville 24:208 Au/S '69; Tempo 92:46 Spring '70; Times Literary Supplement p1092 S 25 '69

187. Sackheim, Eric, comp. The Blues Line: A Collection of Blues Lyrics. New York: Schirmer Books; London: Collier Macmillan Publishers, 1975. 499 pp. drawings.

> This is an anthology of 270 selected blues lyrics composed from the mid-1920s to the mid-1950s. Taken from the race records of the period, these faithful transcriptions of the lyrics of 125 major blues singers are treated as the great poetry that they are. Among the lyricists represented are Blind Blake, Lil Johnson, Bessie Smith, Victoria Spivey, Chippie Hill, Blind Lemon Jefferson, Leadbelly, King Solomon Hill, Robert Johnson, Sleepy John Estes, Blind Boy Fuller, Leroy Carr, Peetie Wheatstraw, Big Bill Broonzy, and Howlin' Wolf. Researchers will find this to be a handy work for poetic study and interpretation, and for historical and comparative study.
> Reviews: Jazz Journal International 30:32 Ju '77; Music Educators Journal 62:112 Mr '76; Music Journal 34:14 Ja '76; Stereo Review 37:13 D '76

188. Titon, Jeff Todd. Early Downhome Blues: A Musical and Cultural Analysis. Music in American Life. Urbana: University of Illinois Press, 1977. xvii, 296 pp. photographs, drawings, musical examples, plates. appendixes. bibliography. index. accompanying sound recording.

> Treating a music that writers have also called "country blues," this volume is divided into three sections: "The Music and the Culture," "The Songs," and "The Response." Part I provides background information about the culture that spawned the blues and about the singers and their creation of the blues. The three chapters of Part II present transcriptions and discussions of selected recorded blues songs, analytical discussions of the musical elements of "downhome" blues, and discussion of the structure and meaning of blues lyrics. Part III contains numerous reproductions of advertisements for blues recordings and discusses the history of the recording of the blues and of the advertising and marketing of those recordings. The book treats the music created by such men as Blind Lemon Jefferson, Son House, Charley Patton, Blind Willie McTell, Tommy Johnson, and Blind Blake.

188.  Titon (continued)

> Reviews: Booklist 74:790 Ja 15 '78; Bulgarska Muzika 29:67 Ap
> '78; Cadence 3:26 D '77; Choice 15:411 My '78; JEMF Quarterly
> 14:104 '78; Journalism Quarterly 54:838 Winter '77; Journal of
> American Folklore 93:81 Ja '80; Sing Out 27:36 '78

# JAZZ

189.  Berendt, Joachim E.  The Jazz Book:  From Ragtime to Fusion and
Beyond.  Translated by H. and B. Bredigkeit with Dan Morgenstern.  2nd
English ed.  Westport, Conn.:  Lawrence Hill & Co., 1982.  xi, 436 pp.
musical examples, table. discography. index.

> This book surveys the entire range of jazz, from ragtime (classic
> and New Orleans style) and Louis Armstrong to the AACM and
> electric jazz, jazz rock, and fusion.  In covering the whole scope of
> the genre, the book necessarily gives superficial and summary
> treatment to important musicians and significant events.  But it is a
> good introduction to the study of jazz, covering the various styles,
> the main figures, and the principal elements, instruments, vocalists,
> and ensembles of the genre.  The author's narrative on "A Definition
> of Jazz" is particularly informative and provocative.  The excellent
> and extensive discography is designed to be used in conjunction with
> the text.

190.  Blesh, Rudi.  Shining Trumpets:  A History of Jazz.  2nd ed., rev. and
enl.  New York:  Alfred A. Knopf, 1958.  xiv, 410, xviii pp.  chart,
photographs, musical examples. appendix. index.

> This work purports to "explore the beginnings and trace the progress
> of jazz , analyze and define its nature, evaluate and compare it
> with the kinds of music we know" (p. vii). Based on the assumption
> that "a thorough treatment of jazz as music not only deals with the
> American Negro but goes all the way back to Africa" (p. viii), the
> work is divided into two parts.  Book One treats "Black Music,"
> "Drums to Africa," folk songs, and the blues; Book Two treats the
> various jazz styles, starting with "New Orleans and the Beginnings
> of Jazz" and ending with the "Hot Piano."  The author's insights,
> perceptions and conclusions remain fresh today.  His treatment of
> jazz as black music is a relatively early recognition of the validity
> and propriety of that designation.  An interesting feature is the
> "Chart Showing  African  Survivals  in  Negro  Jazz  and  the
> Development of Negro Jazz."
>> Reviews: Jazz 3:239 Summer '59; Juilliard Review 6:25 Winter
>> '58/'59; Library Journal 83:3159 '58; Notes 16:254 Mr '59

191.  Brunn, H. O.  The Story of the Original Dixieland Jazz Band.  Baton
Rouge:  Louisiana  State  University  Press,  1960.  xx,  268  pp.
photographs, tables. appendix. index.

191. Brunn (continued)

The thesis of this book, that jazz was created by the ODJB, reveals it as part of the "white origins" literature. The book is a story of a white band in the jazz age; it traces the group's activities from the days before its recording of the first jazz record in 1917 until its final demise around 1940. Interesting, well-written, thorough, and authoritative in tone, it is nevertheless an example of the danger of relying on oral reports and conventional wisdom as evidence for conclusions. It is important that black music scholars be familiar with this version of the story and the methodology that produced it.

Reviews: Chicago Sunday Tribune p5 Jy 3 '60; Downbeat 27:40 My 26 '60; Gramophone 38:312 N '60; Library Journal 85:1914 '60; Melody Maker 35:8 My 8 '60; New York Times Book Review p7 My 22 '60; Notes 18:61 D '60; Saturday Review of Literature p84 My 21 '60; Second Line 11:15 '60; Variety 219:60 Ju 29 '60; Western Folklore 21:122 '62

192. Budds, Michael J.  Jazz in the Sixties:  The Expansion of Musical Resources and Techniques. Iowa City:  University of Iowa Press, 1978. xii, 119 pp.  musical examples.  appendix.  bibliography.  index.

The stylistic diversity, new resources, and advanced techniques that came to jazz in the 1960s are briefly discussed in this volume. The work treats the jazz of the 1960s as both a continuation of an evolutionary process that began with New Orleans jazz and as a process involving the disintegration of its structural foundations. After beginning with a "Survey of Jazz Styles Before 1960," the study treats 1960s jazz through its musical elements—"Color and Instrumentation," "Texture and Volume," "Melody and Harmony," "Meter and Rhythm," and "Structural Design."  The final two chapters treat "Other Influences" and the "Legacy of the Sixties to the Seventies." The "Jazz Styles Before 1960" section is valuable in itself; its brief but comprehensive treatment of the various pre-1960s jazz styles—"New Orleans Dixieland," "Chicago Dixieland," "Swing," "Bop," "Cool," and "Hard Bop"—is a convenient and concise review.  The chapter on "Color and Instrumentation" treats the employment of new sound sources and new timbres, including African and previously unused European acoustical instruments, electronic modification, synthesizers, and tape music.  The "Texture and Volume" chapter treats textural density; the "Melody and Harmony" chapter includes discussion of modal scales, quartal harmony, and atonal techniques.  Regular, irregular, and free rhythm are discussed in the chapter on "Meter and Rhythm," and the "Structural Design" chapter focuses on Third Stream structural concepts, "free form," and free group improvization. The appendix, which lists seventy-five recordings, is a valuable selection of important works of the period.

Reviews: Cadence 5:28 Au '79

193. Burley, Dan.  Dan Burley's Original Book of Harlem Jive. Foreword by Earl Conrad. New York: Dan Burley, 1944. 157 pp. drawings. index.

193. Burley (continued)

This book is a narrative presentation of black slang as it was manifest during the period of its crystallization; it is a key to understanding aspects of black urban culture, and, consequently, to understanding the jazz life. The first part of the book introduces the subject; the remainder of the work presents information on the etymology, syntax, and social background of the terminology. Chapter titles include "Jive for Jivers and Those Who Are Not," "Joe Q. Hipp," "The Book of Hypes," "Hit That Jive," and "Book of Jive Backcaps." Placed at the end of the work is "The Jiver's Bible," a dictionary of nearly four hundred slang words. The index is designed more as a table of contents.

194. Charters, Samuel and Leonard Kunstadt. Jazz: A History of the New York Scene. New York: Doubleday & Co., 1962. 383 pp. photographs. bibliography. appendix. index.

This book is the most complete existing account of black music in New York from the 1890s to around 1960, beginning with "Egbert Thompson, 'The Black Sousa'," and ending with "Dizzy" and speculations about the future of the genre. In between, the authors discuss James Reese Europe and his activities, the musical Shuffle Along, Florence Mills, Fletcher Henderson, music in the Harlem night clubs, the Ipana Troubadors, Willie "The Lion" Smith, Cab Calloway, Count Basie, and many other pertinent individuals, events, and movements.
      Reviews: Downbeat 29:36 Jy 5 '62; Instrumentalist 16:14 My '62; International Musician 61:27 Ja '63; Library Journal 87:1138 '62; Library Journal 87:2434 '62; Musical America 82:71 S '62; Music Educators Journal 48:82 '62; Music Magazine 164:47 Au '62; Orkester Journalen 30:13 N '62; Record Research 43:9 My '62

195. Collier, James Lincoln. The Making of Jazz: A Comprehensive History. New York: Dell Publishing Co., 1978. xi, 543 pp. photographs. bibliography. discography. index.

Unlike many books on the subject, this book is a history of the music itself, not of the performers or the recordings. The book's primary value lies in the author's approach to aural analysis and the way in which he communicates his musical perceptions and analyses to the reader. This aural/discussion approach to jazz analysis is more communicable than those which rely on musical notation, and it uses terminology that is acceptable and useful to both jazz musicians and jazz scholars. The discussions in the book range from "The African Roots" to "The Modern Age" and focus upon the musical styles and contributions of the musicians who most influenced the evolution and development of the genre. This book is recommended as an analytical model for inexperienced researchers in jazz music.

195. Collier (continued)

> Reviews: Booklist 74:1156 Mr 15 '78; Book World pE6 Au 20
> '78; Cadence 4:39 Au '78; Downbeat 45:59 '78; Jazz Journal
> International 32:16 Ap '79; Jazz Magazine 2:56 '78; Jazz
> Podium 27:38 Au '78; Kirkus Reviews 46:277 Mr 1 '78; Kirkus
> Reviews 46:315 Mr 15 '78; Kliatt Paperback Book Guide 14:63
> Winter '80; Melody Maker 54:55 Ap 7 '79; New Boston Review
> 5:9 S '79; New Statesman 97:123 Ja 26 '79; New Yorker 55:142
> O 29 '79; Notes 35:634 Mr '79; Observer (London) p33 D 17 '78;
> Orkester Journalen 47:16 Ap '79; Publishers Weekly 213:120 F
> 13 '78; Publishers Weekly 215:121 Ju 25 '79; Punch 275:774 N 1
> '78; Reference Services Review 6:14 Jy '78; School Library
> Journal 25:171 S '78; Second Line 32:41 Fall '80

196. Ellison, Jno. W., ed. Ellison's Clef Club Book for New York, Chicago and Boston Colored Musicians: A Standard Clef Club Diary and Daily Reminder for Members and Patrons. 1916 ed. New York: Jno. W. Ellison, 1916. 69 pp. photographs.

> This rare book contains advertisements for both individual
> musicians and firms (musical and nonmusical); a list of officers for
> 1916; a preface; a page for the owner's identification and important
> information such as telephone numbers and insurance company
> name; a brief explanation of the "History of Music" and "Rudiments
> of Music"; a page for cash account records; "A Brief History of the
> Mandolin, Guitar, Banjo, Etc."; a street directory; and a date
> record. The list of members is divided into sections by instrument,
> followed by an alphabetical list of names. Each entry contains the
> address and phone number of the musician along with a statement
> about the person's performing ability. A typical sample entry is:
> > JORDON, JOE.—Plays the Violin well, doubles on Bass and
> > Piano, also arranges and composes music. Address, CLEF
> > CLUB. 'Phone 1176 Circle.

197. Feather, Leonard. The Book of Jazz, From Then Til Now: A Guide to the Entire Field. Foreword by John "Dizzy" Gillespie. Rev. ed. New York: Bonanza Books, 1965. viii, 280 pp. musical examples. index.

> This is a somewhat unusual approach to the understanding of jazz,
> being organized into four main sections in an unusual grouping:
> Part I: The Sources (early history, with a chapter on "Jazz and
> Race"); Part II: Introduction to Instruments and Their Primary
> Performers; Part III: Discourse on the Nature of Jazz; and Part IV:
> The Future of Jazz. Part II contains a chapter on each of the
> principal instruments of jazz, each chapter discussing a particular
> instrument's role or roles in the history of the genre. The chapter
> titled "The Guitar," for example, treats the guitar and the banjo,
> tracing the musical development of these instruments from the
> American Revolution, through their roles in early jazz, to the status
> of the guitar in the early 1960s. It cites early jazz banjoists such as
> Charlie Dixon, Fred Guy, Johnny St. Cyr, and Lonnie Johnson;
> intermediate guitar greats Freddie Green and Charlie Christian; and

197. Feather (continued)

  guitarists from the 1950s and 1960s such as Bill Harris, Jim Hall,
Joe Pass, and Wes Montgomery. The focus is on the genres and the
people that influenced the development of jazz guitar, with
comments on the various roles played by the instrument(s), from
accompanist to a provider of "melodic continuity and depth." Part
II also treats "The Other Instruments," "The Blues and the Human
Voice," "Small Combos," "The Big Bands," and "Composers and
Arrangers." Parts III and IV discuss, among other things,
improvization and "Jazz in 1984."
  Reviews: Antiquarian Bookman 36:2281 D 13 '65; Booklist
62:806 Ap 15 '66; Christian Science Monitor 57:B2 D 2 '65;
Choice 3:891 D '66; Downbeat 33:49 Ap 21 '66; Wilson Library
Bulletin 40:644 Mr '66

198. Feather, Leonard. Inside Be-Bop. New York: J. J. Robbins & Sons,
1949. [vi], 103 pp. photographs, musical examples. discography.

  A discussion of the history and the music of be-bop, this book is
divided into three sections. Part I, "When," sketches the history of
the be-bop movement beginning with its immediate precursors in
the late 1930s and ending with the events of 1948; the discussion,
which is not documented, enumerates the important engagements,
recordings, and contributions of Charlie Parker and Dizzy Gillespie
as the movement's formative figures. Part II, "How," consists of an
analysis of the music; the topics chosen for discussion are blues
patterns and their expansions, melody, rhythm, melodic phrasing,
intervals, and passing tones. The musical examples that illustrate
the analyses are transcriptions of be-bop recordings, such as
"Anthropology" by Gillespie and Parker. Part III, "Who," contains
brief biographical sketches of ninety-two persons who have played
be-bop, including the greats (e.g., Kenny Clarke, Miles Davis, Oscar
Pettiford, and Max Roach), lesser known be-bop figures (e.g.,
Nelson Boyd, Wardell Gray, and George Wallington), and some
persons who are not considered be-boppers, but who have recorded
in that style (e.g., Mary Lou Williams and Nat Cole). The primary
value of the book lies in its analytical treatment of the music itself.
  Reviews: Billboard 61:20 Au 6 '49; Downbeat 16:8 Jy 15 '49;
Gramophone 27:33 Jy '49; International Musician 47:22 Ju '49;
Melody Maker 25:3 Jy 2 '49; Metronome 65:14 My '49; Notes
6:619 S '49; Variety 175:105 Jy 27 '49

199. Finkelstein, Sidney. Jazz: A People's Music. New York: Citadel Press,
1948. ix, 278 pp. drawings. discographies. index.

  While the author of this book considers jazz to be "the most
important single body of music yet produced in America," the work
is, ironically, "aimed at breaking down barriers," and seeks to "place
jazz as part of world music" (p. 2), eschewing the traditional
distinctions between " 'classical' and 'popular'," " 'highbrow' and
'lowbrow' " (p. 7). The book's unusual organization is revealed in its
seven chapter titles: "The Place of Jazz in Music History," "The

199. Finkelstein (continued)

Sound of Jazz," "The Blues and the Folk Song of Jazz,"
"Improvization and Jazz Form," "The Pop Tune, the Hot Solo & the
Large Band," "The Experimental Laboratory and the New Jazz," and
"The Future of Jazz."
Reviews: Booklist 45:189 F 1 '49; Downbeat 16:10 Ja 14 '49;
Horn Book 25:240 My '49; Library Journal 73:1666 '48; Listen
12:11 Ja '49; Metronome 65:21 F '49; Nation 167:584 N 20 '48;
New Yorker 24:114 D 18 '48; New York Herald Tribune Weekly
Book Review p29 N 28 '48; New York Times p30 O 31 '48; Notes
6:304 Mr '49; Record Changer 8:8 Ja '49; Saturday Review of
Literature p35 F 26 '49; Symphony 2:8 Ja '49; Wilson Library
Bulletin 45:64 Ap '49

200. Gitler, Ira. Jazz Masters of the Forties. The Macmillan Jazz Masters
Series, edited by Martin Williams. New York: Macmillan Co., 1966.
290 pp. bibliography. photographs. index.

This is one of a series of books that focus on the recorded music of
acknowledged master jazzmen. Spanning the entire history of jazz
(to 1969), the series covers numerous figures, from Buddy Bolden,
Bunk Johnson, and King Oliver through Cecil Taylor, John Coltrane,
and Ornette Coleman. (For titles of the other books in the series,
see entries number 201, 203, 218, 220, and 221.)
Reviews: American Record Guide 33:828+ My '67; Booklist
63:23 S '66; Book Week 7:11 Au '66; Choice 3:1022 '67;
Downbeat 33:41-42 N 17 '66; Jazz Journal 20:17 My '67; Kirkus
Service 34:569 Ju '66; Kirkus Service 34:583 Ju '66; Library
Journal 91:3954 S 1 '66; Library Journal 91:5264 O 15 '66; Music
Journal 24:105 S '66; Negro Digest 16:88 Mr '67; New York
Times 115:35m Au 4 '66; New York Times Book Review 71:10
Au 21 '66; Notes 23:746-747 n4 '67; Saturday Review 50:61 F
11'67

201. Goldberg, Joe. Jazz Masters of the Fifties. The Macmillan Jazz
Masters Series, edited by Martin Williams. New York: Macmillan Co.,
1965. 246 pp.

See entry number 200.
Reviews: American Record Guide 33:828 My '67; Antiquarian
Bookman 36:732 Au 30 '65; Booklist 62:39 S 1 '65; Choice 2:395
'65; Christian Science Monitor p13 N 23 '65; Downbeat 32:39 Jy
15 '65; Jazz Journal 20:17-18 My '67; Kirkus Service 33:424 Ap
1 '65; Library Journal 90:2557 Ju 1 '65; Library Journal 90:3139
Jy '65; New York Times Book Review 70:29 Jy 25 '65; Orkester
Journalen 35:13 Ap '67; Variety 239:59 Au 4 '65

202. Green, Benny. The Reluctant Art. New York: Horizon Press, 1963.
191 pp.

Three of the five musicians whose music is discussed in this book
are Afro-Americans—Lester Young, Billie Holiday, and Charlie

202. Green (continued)

Parker. The work is a series of first-person essays that discuss the individuals' significant output, their singularity, and their musical styles. The essays amount to exercises in jazz criticism which will be important contributions to the education of the inexperienced jazz researcher.
Reviews: Book Week p9 D 15 '63; Downbeat 30:35 Jy 4 '63; Jazz Hot 197:13 Ap '64; Jazz Journal 16:11 Ju '63; Jazz Magazine 9:13 Au '63; New Yorker 39:94 Au 7 '63; Reporter 28:56 Ap 25 '63; Times Literary Supplement p20 Ja 11 '63

203. Hadlock, Richard. Jazz Masters of the Twenties. The Macmillan Jazz Masters Series, edited by Martin Williams. New York: Macmillan Co., 1965. 255 pp. photographs.

See entry number 200.
Reviews: American Record Guide 33:828 My '67; Antiquarian Bookman 36:1098 S '65; Booklist 62:128 O '65; Downbeat 32:36 n4 '65; Education 86:447 Mr '66; Jazz Journal 18:24-25 O '65; Jazz Journal 20:17 My '67; Jazz Report 5:5 n6 ['66]; Kirkus Service 33:610 Ju '65; Kirkus Service 33:695 Jy '65; Melody Maker 42:15 My 20 '67

204. Hentoff, Nat. The Jazz Life. 1961. Reprint. New York: Da Capo Press, 1978. xiii, 255 pp.

This is a sociological study of the jazz musician and the jazz community. As such, it provides knowledge about and insight into the thought and behavior of those who participate in the jazz life, and details how jazz musicians relate to the people, the institutions, the events, and the ideas that affect their lives—club owners, agents, day people, recording sessions, the musician's union, law enforcement authorities, narcotics, racial discrimination, "paying dues," and so on. In discussing how successful jazzmen have functioned in and related to their world, the author has provided the examples of Count Basie, Charles Mingus, John Lewis, Miles Davis, Thelonius Monk, and Ornette Coleman, emphasizing the importance of the sociological and musical interactions on the development of contemporary jazzmen. Based on the author's first-hand observations and his readings of several decades, this book will complement and supplement studies that are historical, analytical, and biographical in nature.
Reviews: Kliatt Paperback Book Guide 13:56 Winter '79

205. James, Michael. Ten Modern Jazzmen: An Appraisal of the Recorded Work of Ten Modern Jazzmen. Foreword by Albert J. McCarthy. London: Cassell & Co., 1960. xix, 145 pp. photographs. index.

This is a collection of jazz criticism that can serve as a guide to pre-1960 recorded music of the figures discussed. Among the latter are seven black artists—Miles Davis, Dizzy Gillespie, Wardell Gray, John Lewis, Thelonius Monk, Charlie Parker, and Bud Powell—and

205. James (continued)

three whites—Stan Getz, Lee Konitz, and Gerry Mulligan.
Primarily, the work discusses the music of these jazzmen, but it
also includes comments on their influences, their musical growth
and development, and the social climates and conditions that
affected their work. As with any work of opinion, the content will
bring disagreements, but the book is honest and important, and the
appraisals that it contains can help listeners establish their own
criteria for listening, evaluation, and research.
Reviews: Jazz Hot 26:5+ O '60; Jazz Journal 13:16 Jy '60; Jazz
Monthly 6:24-25 Ju '60

206. Jost, Ekkehard. Free Jazz. Studies in Jazz Research, no. 4. Graz:
Institut für Jazzforschung, 1974.   214 pp.   musical examples.
discography. bibliography. index.

This work is a "critical exploration" of the "most essential musical
directions" (p. 7) of the new jazz of the 1960s, a study of the
divergent personal musical styles that developed in reaction against
traditional musical and sociological norms. The author discusses
the movement's renunciation of traditional harmonic concepts,
metrical patterns, and traditional structural concepts in its search
for new modes of musical expression. In presenting what he refers
to as "style portraits," the author examines the development of free
jazz in the United States and in Europe, focusing on the roles and
contributions of the main initiators of the movement:   John
Coltrane, Charles Mingus, Ornette Coleman, Cecil Taylor, Archie
Shepp, Albert Ayler, Don Cherry, the Art Ensemble of Chicago, and
Sun Ra.   Also mentioned are Pharoah Sanders, Marion Brown,
McCoy Tyner, Roswell Rudd, Roscoe Mitchell, Richard Abrams,
Anthony Braxton, and others.   Illustrated with copious music
examples, this is the definitive work on the "New Black Music," a
perceptive, penetrating, and scholarly resource.
Reviews: Hifi-Stereophonie 15:822 Au '76; Jazz Forum n38:63
'75; Jazz Journal 28:20 O '75; Jazz Podium 24:30 N '75; Musik
und Bildung 7:392-393 Jy/Au '75

207. Kofsky, Frank. Black Nationalism and the Revolution in Music. New
York: Pathfinder Press, 1970. 280 pp. appendix.

This is essentially a Marxist analysis of "the nature of the
connection between black nationalism and black music (jazz),"
based on what the author calls "a materialist understanding of the
political economy of jazz" (p. 5). Part I treats "The Society, The
Music, The Critic"; Part II discusses the origins and directions of
the revolution in black music following World War II, as well as
black radicalism, the jazz club, and John Coltrane/Albert Ayler;
Part III discusses "The Anatomy of the Coltrane Quartet," presenting Elvis Jones as a "polyrhythmic innovator," and ending with
interviews with McCoy Tyner and Coltrane; Part IV treats the
career of Malcolm X as it relates to black revolution and black
music.

207. Kofsky (continued)

Reviews: AB Bookman's Weekly 47:1047 Mr 29 '71; AB Bookman's Weekly 75:662 Au 27 '73; Black World 20:94 Au '71; Black World 20:83 O '71; Choice 8:76 '71; Jazz Journal 24:24 Ap '71; Jazz Magazine 191:7-8 Au '71; Jazz Research n3/4:284-288 '71/'72; Library Journal 96:1982 '71; Melody Maker 46:26 Ja 30 '71; Music Educators Journal 58:91-92 N '71; Negro History Bulletin 34:120 My '71; New York Review of Books 21:14 O 17 '74; Notes 29:236 D '72; Publishers Weekly 198:81 S 28 '70; Rolling Stone 82:52 My 13 '71

208. Leonard, Neil. Jazz and the White Americans: The Acceptance of a New Art Form. Chicago: University of Chicago Press, 1962. 215 pp. appendix. bibliography. index.

This work is a study of the extraordinary debate about jazz that began around 1917 and continued into the 1920s, ending with the general acceptance of the genre in the 1930s. It discusses the prevailing social, moral, and aesthetic values and concerns of white Americans—values and concerns that led to verbal and written assaults on jazz by its opponents. The author discusses the then-prevailing arguments, tactics, and campaigns of these critics and the counterattacks of jazz advocates. Also discussed are the use of jazz slang; the commercial and symphonic jazz of the 1920s and its role in making true jazz acceptable; censorship by government and public agencies; the centralization of the entertainment business in the 1930s and how it mitigated against the spread of hot jazz and blues; how the values of white America influenced the development of jazz; and the development of jazz criticism. This work is a valuable study of the social and cultural influences that affected the evolution of jazz.

Reviews: American Journal of Sociology 68:717 My '63; American Sociological Review 28:652 Au '63; Christian Science Monitor p11 My 23 '63; Downbeat 29:43 D 20 '62; Ethnomusicology 8:82-84 n1 '64; Jazz 2:12-13 F '63; Journal of American Folklore 76:356-357 n302 '63; Library Journal 87:3048 S 15 '62; Mississippi Valley Historical Review 49:727 Mr '63; Music Journal 21:110 Ja '63; Orkester Journalen 31:14 Ap '63; Tempo 64:37-38 Spring '63; Times Literary upplement p20 Ja 11 '63; Virginia Quarterly Review 39:xxxiv Winter '63; Western Folklore 23:67 n1 '64

209. McCarthy, Albert. Big Band Jazz. London: Barrie & Jenkins, 1974. 368 pp. photographs. index.

This book treats the history of the big band from early "syncopated" groups, such as the Clef Club Orchestras and the band led by James Reese Europe, to their demise following World War II. Richly illustrated, it is arranged in chronological order and covers bands that "concentrated primarily on jazz in the broad sense of the term" (p. 7). Not only are the big name bands treated here, but smaller

209. McCarthy (continued)

  regional groups are also included, with personnel lists appearing for
  many of them.
  Reviews: AB Bookman's Weekly 54:1936 n4 '74; Black World p4
  Au 4 '74; Black World p4 N 3 '74; Booklist 71:366 D 1 '74; Books
  West 1:27 O '77; Choice 11:1149 O '74; Guardian Weekly 111:21
  Au 3 '74; High Fidelity/Musical America 25:MA36-37 Ja '74;
  Jazz Forum n34:66 Ap '75; Kirkus Reviews 42:617 Ju 1 '74;
  Library Journal 99:1956 Au '74; Listener 92:252 Au 22 '74;
  Melody Maker 49:51 O 26 '74; Musical Times 116:45 Ja '75;
  Music Journal 32:24 '74; New York Times Book Review p33 Au
  21 '77; Times Literary Supplement p826 Au 2 '74

210. Meeker, David.  Jazz in the Movies: A Guide to Jazz Musicians, 1917-
  1977.  New Rochelle, N.Y.:  Arlington House Publishers, 1977.
  unpaged. photographs. index.

  Arranged alphabetically by film title, this book contains
  information about 2,239 films in which jazz musicians are featured
  either on or off the screen.  The films included are those that were
  and are available to theaters and/or individuals.  Each entry
  includes the title of the film, the alternate titles of any American
  or British reissues, the date the film was produced, the length of
  the film (in minutes), the name of the director or producer, and a
  brief annotation that includes the names of the featured
  performers.  Among the many performers chronicled here are The
  Count Basie Sextet, Clark Terry, Wardell Gray, Sarah Vaughn,
  Quincy Jones, Blind Lemon Jefferson, Amad Jamal, James P.
  Johnson, Mahalia Jackson, and Eubie Blake.
  Reviews:  American Reference Books Annual 9:469 '78;
  Billboard 90:113 Ja 28 '78; Booklist 74:1519-1520 My 15 '78;
  Books and Bookmen 23:64 Jy '78; Cadence 3:40 Ja '78; Coda
  n162:13-14 Au 1 '78; Jazz Forum n50:17 '77; Jazz Hot n347:30
  Mr '78; Jazz Journal International 30:25 S '77; Music Journal
  36:39 Ap '78; Notes 35:636 n3 '79; Orkester Journalen 46:30 My
  '78; Reference Services Review 6:11-12 Ju/S '78; Variety
  288:66 S 28 '77; Village Voice 22:53 O 31 '77; West Coast
  Review of Books 4:56 My '78

211. Ostransky, Leroy.  The Anatomy of Jazz.  Seattle:  University of
  Washington Press, 1960. xiii, 362 pp. musical examples. index.

  A somewhat scholarly approach to the analysis of jazz music, this is
  essentially a book on jazz styles.  Following an introductory chapter
  and chapters titled "Toward A Definition of Jazz," "The Musical
  Elements of Jazz," and "Understanding Style," the author discusses
  the styles of "New Orleans," "Preswing," "Swing," and "Modern,"
  then points "Toward the Future."  The work ends with a selected
  bibliography of appropriate books and articles.
  Reviews: Downbeat 27:51 S 29 '60; Ethnomusicology 6:132-134
  n2 '62; Jazz Journal 13:19 D '60; Library Journal 85:2794 '60;
  Melody Maker 35:13 Au 20 '60; Musica Jazz 16:24 O '60; Music

211. Ostransky (continued)

>and Letters 42:73-74 n1 '61; Notes 18:61-62 n1 '60; Second Line 11:24-25 n11/12 '60; Svensk Tidskrift für Musikforskning 44:97-98 '62; Western Folklore 21:142-143 n2 '62

212. Panassie, Hughes, and Madeline Gautier. Guide to Jazz. Introduction by Louis Armstrong. Translated by Desmond Flower. Boston: Houghton Mifflin Co.; Cambridge, Mass.: Riverside Press, 1956. vii, 312 pp. photographs. appendix.

>This encyclopedia treats jazz from 1900 to 1940, as viewed from the perspective of the French jazz critic Hughes Panassie. The entries include the names of jazz artists, subjects and terms, and tune titles of each period. The artists discussed encompass "true jazzmen . . . and in addition the most prominent among the 'fringe' musicians" (p. v), as determined by the author. The entries vary in length from a few lines (the entry for Sam Allen) to eleven columns (the treatment of Louis Armstrong). The discussion of an artist includes a synopsis of the biographical data, a brief discussion of his or her musical style, and a short discography; each term or subject is briefly defined. The entries concerned with a specific tune include the name(s) of the composer and lyricist, a brief description of the song, and a list of "Best recordings."
>Reviews: Booklist 53:220 Ja 1'57; Christian Science Monitor p7 Ja 3 '57; Downbeat 24:35-36 F 6 '57; High Fidelity 7:23 F '57; Jazz Journal 10:32 F '57; Jazz Today 2:49 Ja '57; Library Journal 82:86 Ja 1 '57; Manchester Guardian p4 N 20 '56; Nation 184:23 Ja 5 '57; New Statesman 53:22 Ja 5 '57; New Yorker 33:156 Ap 20 '57; Notes 14:362 Ju '57; San Francisco Chronicle p10 N 25 '56; Theatre Arts 41:63 Ap '57; Times Literary Supplement p713 N 29 '57; Variety 205:59 D 5 '56; Wilson Library Bulletin 53:283 Ja '57

213. Sargeant, Winthrop. Jazz: Hot & Hybrid. 1938. Reprint. New York: Da Capo Press, 1975. 302 pp. musical examples. bibliography. index.

>Despite shortcomings due in part to its early date, this book is a most important contribution to jazz scholarship. The earliest of the serious and scholarly approaches to the subject, the work represents an attempt to eliminate the confusion and end the speculation surrounding the jazz phenomenon at the time it was written; it is an attempt to view jazz as a part of Afro-American musical expression. Wideranging in its scope, the work discusses "Improvisation, Notation, and the Aesthetics of Folk Music"; "Jazz Origins and Influences"; jazz rhythm, scales, harmony, and form; "The Derivation of the Blues"; African influences; aesthetics; and "The Jazz Orchestra." The many music examples are effective in illustrating the author's points. This book is a basic source for jazz researchers.
>Reviews: American Music Teacher 27:41-42 S/O '77; Book

213. Sargeant (continued)

World p4 My 25 '74; Coda n148:6-7 Ju '76; Jazz Forum n37:24
'75; Musical Opinion 99:69 N '75; Musical Times 116:974-975 N
'75; Music Journal 33:30 My '75

214. Schuller, Gunther. Early Jazz: Its Roots and Musical Development.
The History of Jazz. New York: Oxford University Press, 1968. xii,
401 pp. musical examples, charts. appendix. glossary. discography.
index.

This is a scholarly work which treats the music itself, rather than
focusing on matters of social, historical, and stylistic interest. It is
a serious analytical approach to the understanding of jazz music.
The first of a proposed two-volume history of jazz, this book begins
with the prehistory of jazz and ends with events that occurred
around 1932. Its seven chapters discuss "The Origins," The
Beginnings," "The First Great Soloist," "The First Great Composer,"
"Virtuoso Performers of the Twenties," "The Big Bands," and "The
Ellington Style: Its Origins and Early Development," discussing
individual contributions of many significant jazzmen. The appendix
is an interview with violinist and band leader George Morrison. The
glossary defines a large number of terms used in jazz analysis. This
book is highly recommended.
Reviews:    America 119:84 Au 3 '68; American Literature
40:597 Ja '69; American Record Guide 35:881-883 My '69;
Antiquarian Bookman 41:1281 Ap 1 '68; Booklist 65:31 S 1 '68;
Choice 5:634 '68; Christian Century 85:489 Ap 17 '68;
Downbeat 35:26-27 My 30 '68; Ethnomusicology 13:562-565 n3
'69; High Fidelity/Musical America 18:MA30-31 Jy '68; Hudson
Review 22:540 Autumn '69; International Musician 167:18 N '68;
Jazz 6:31 n3 '67; Jazz Hot 247:5 F '69; Jazz Journal 21:15 D
'63; Jazz Monthly 176:25-31 O '69; Journal of the American
Musicological Society 22:135-138 n1 '69; Kirkus Service 36:172
F 1 '68; Library Journal 93:2660 Jy '68; Making Music 69:17
Spring '69; Melody Maker 43:13 D 7 '68; Musical Opinion 94:139
D '70; Musical Times 109:1120 D '68; Music Educators Journal
55:87-88 O '68; Music in Education 33:88 n336 '69; Music
Journal Annual p114 '68; New Statesman 76:328 S 13 '68; New
York Times Book Review 73:32 My 12 '68; Notes 25:227-229 D
'68; Orkester Journalen 37:2+ Ja '69; Performing Arts Review
1:191-193 n1 '69 Saturday Review 51:46 Jy 13 '68; Storyville
24:206-207 Au/S '69; Times Literary Supplement p1331 N 28
'68; Virginia Quarterly Review 45:R36 Winter '69; Yale Review
58:R27 Mr '69

215. Sidran, Ben. Black Talk. New York:    Holt, Rinehart and Winston,
1971. xvii, 201 pp. appendixes. index.

Unique among books on black music, this work discusses "the social
function of black music in America," taking the position that "black
music is not only conspicuous within, but crucial to, black culture"
(p. xiii). Stressing the oral bias of black life, the author dwells upon

215. Sidran (continued)

the importance of vocal expression and aural perception among black people, merging musical and social analysis in his exposition. The book's five chapters are: "Oral Culture and Musical Tradition: Prehistory and Early History"; "The Black Musician in Two Americas: Early History—1917"; "The Jazz Age: The 1920s"; "The Evolution of the Black Underground: 1930-1937"; and "Black Visibility: 1949-1969."

Reviews: American Music Teacher 21:32 n3 '72; Black World 23:95 N '73; Instrument 26:12 N '71; Jazz & Blues 3:17 Au '73; Jazz Digest 1:1+ Mr '72; Jazz Magazine n197:10 F '72; Journal of Aesthetics and Criticism 31:561-562 n4 '73; Kirkus Reviews 39:796 Jy 15 '71; Library Journal 96:3616 '71; Music Journal 30:82-83 Mr '72; New York Review of Books 21:14 O 17 '74; Notes 29:454-456 n3 '73; Publishers Weekly 200:48 Jy 26 '71; Saturday Review of Literature 54:86 O 30 '71

216. Simon, George T. The Big Bands. Foreword by Frank Sinatra. 4th ed. New York: Schirmer Books, 1981. xvii, 614 pp. photographs. index.

This book treats the swing bands that flourished in the United States between 1935 and 1946—the groups that played dance music in clubs and ballrooms across the country during that period. The work discusses more than seventy major big bands and at least mentions more than one hundred less-important groups. In discussing each band, the author superficially treats the many varieties of big band music—"hard-driving swing," "relaxed swing," "forceful Dixieland," "riff-filled swing," "commercial swing," "sweet," "intimate," and so on. Along with numerous white organizations, the author treats the major black bands of the period—bands led by Count Basie, Cab Calloway, Billy Eckstein, Duke Ellington, Lionel Hampton, Fletcher Henderson, Earl Hines, Andy Kirk, Jimmie Lunceford, and Chick Webb. Other black groups treated or mentioned include those of Louis Armstrong, Erskine Hawkins, Cootie Williams, Claude Hopkins, Teddy Hill, Jay McShann, Teddy Wilson, Bennie Moten, Noble Sissle, Lucky Millinder, and William McKinney. The information presented includes facts about, critiques on, and insights into the great swing ensembles—basic information from which to launch serious research.

Reviews: Human Events 41:11 S 26 '81

217. Stearns, Marshall, and Jean Stearns. Jazz Dance: The Story of American Vernacular Dance. New York: Macmillan Co.; London: Collier-Macmillan, [1968]. xvi, 464 pp. photographs. bibliography. appendixes. index.

This is a book about "American dancing that is performed to and with the rhythms of jazz" (p. xiv). Discussing dance forms ranging from minstrelsy to the jitterbug, it is an important source for the black music researcher. The work begins with a discussion of "Prehistory" in Africa and the West Indies, the American South, and

217. Stearns (<u>continued</u>)

the "Pattern of Diffusion" in the New World. It also discusses folkdancing and minstrel dances, dancing in road shows and carnivals, in ballrooms, in Broadway shows and revues. The book covers choreography, specialty dancing, acrobatics, and "class acts," and presents narrative portraits of Bill Robinson, John W. Bubbles, King Rastus Brown, and many others. The two appendixes are a selected list of films and kinescopes and analysis and notation of basic Afro-American movements. Copious and striking photographs and an extensive index complement the text.

Reviews: Arts and Society 7:237-239 n2 '71; Booklist 65:629 F 15 '69; Jazz and Pop 10:40 Jy '71; Journal of American Folklore; 82:275 Jy '69; Library Journal 94:565 '69; New Statesman 81:23 Ja 1 '71; Newsweek 73:120 Mr 17 '69; Notes 26:40 S '69; Orkester Journalen 37:20 D '69

218. Stewart, Rex. <u>Jazz Masters of the Thirties</u>. The Macmillan Jazz Masters Series, edited by Martin Williams. New York: Macmillan Co., 1972. 233 pp. photographs.

See entry number 200.

Reviews: Black World 23:96 N '73; Booklist 68:788 My 15 '72; Books and Bookmen 18:139 Ap '73; Coda 10:31-32 n9 '72; Downbeat 39:17+ O '72; Jazz and Blues 3:11-12 Ju '73; Jazz Digest 1:12-13 Jy '72; Jazz Journal 26:16 Ju '73; Kirkus Reviews 39:1305 D 1 '71; Music Journal 30:6 My '72; New York Review of Books 18:34 Mr 9 '72; Orkester Journalen 40:34-35 Ju '72; Point du Jazz 8:61-62 Ap '73; Publishers Weekly 201:56 Ja 3 '72; Second Line 25:23 Fall '73

219. Ulanov, Barry. <u>A History of Jazz in America</u>. New York: Viking Press, 1952. 382 pp.

This book discusses: 1) the nature and development of jazz in the United States, 2) primary jazz figures, 3) jazz music as it developed in the important cities in jazz history, and 4) the evaluation of jazz performance.

Reviews: Booklist 48:189 F 15 '52; Booklist 48:210 Mr 1 '52; Bookmark 11:157 Ap '52; Chicago Sunday Tribune p5 Mr 16 '52; Choice 9:825 '72; Christian Science Monitor p7 Ju 12 '52; Etude 71:6 Jy '53; Downbeat 19:5 Ap '52; International Musician 51:28 N '52; Kirkus Reviews 20:54 Ja 15 '52; Library Journal 77:532 Mr 15 '52; Melody Maker 28:9 Ap '52; Metronome 68:15 Ap '52; Musical America 72:31 D '52; New Leader 29:11 Mr '52; New York Herald Tribune Book Review p11 Jy 13 '52; New York Times Book Review p5 F 24 '52; New Yorker 28:32 Mr 29 '52; Notes 9:416 Ju '52; Record Changer 11:5-6+ Ap 7-8 N '52; San Francisco Chronicle p16 Mr 16 '52; Saturday Review of Literature 35:20 Mr 29 '52; United States Quarterly Book Review 8:130 Ju '52; Variety 185:61 F '52; Wilson Library Bulletin 48:89 Mr '52

220. Williams, Martin. <u>Jazz Masters in Transition, 1957-69</u>. The Macmillan
Jazz Masters Series, edited by Martin Williams. New York: Macmillan
Co., 1970. 288 pp. photographs.

    See entry number 200.
    Reviews: AB Bookman's Weekly 47:949 Mr 22 '71; Booklist
67:722 My 1 '71; Jazz Journal 24:25-26 O '71; Jazz Research
3/4:272 '71/'72; Library Journal 95:3474 '70; Musical Times
112:1075 N '75; Music Educators Journal 58:79 F '72; Music
Journal 29:60 Ja '71; Publishers Weekly 198:52 Au 10 '70

221. Williams, Martin. <u>Jazz Masters of New Orleans</u>. The Macmillan Jazz
Masters Series, edited by Martin Williams. New York: Macmillan Co.,
1967. xvii, 287 pp. photographs. index.

    See entry number 200.
    Reviews: American Record Guide 34:861 My '68; Antiquarian
Bookman 39: 1701 Ap 24 '67; Booklist 64:35 S '67; Downbeat
34:42 S 21 '67; International Musician 66:18 Ja '68; Jazz Journal
21:23 Mr '68; Jazz Monthly 167:30 Ja '69; Jazz Report 5:29 n6
'67; Kirkus Service 35:104 Ja 15 '67; Library Journal 92:2578
'67; Library Journal 92:2666 '67; Music Journal 25:60 My '67;
Negro History Bulletin 31:22 Ap '68; Orkester Journalen 35:24-
25 D '67; Publishers Weekly 190:92 D 26 '66

222. Williams, Martin. <u>The Jazz Tradition</u>. New York: Oxford University
Press, 1970. viii, 232 pp. discographical notes.

    This is an authoritative collection of sixteen essays by the author,
each devoted to a major figure or group in the history of jazz--Jelly
Roll Morton, Louis Armstrong, Bix Beiderbeck (not black), Coleman
Hawkins, Billie Holiday, Duke Ellington, Count Basie and Lester
Young, Charlie Parker, Thelonius Monk, John Lewis and The Modern
Jazz Quartet, Sonny Rollins, Horace Silver, Miles Davis, John
Coltrane, and Ornette Coleman. Taken together, the essays present
a comprehensive view of the first seventy years of the evolution of
jazz, focusing on the music by citing pertinent recordings, and
discussing the primary and unique contributions of each of the
artists. The introduction to the volume contains an excellent and
valuable commentary on the nature of jazz and jazz criticism. This
book serves as a good introduction to the music of the figures
discussed.
    Reviews: AB Bookman's Weekly 45:1882 Ju 1 '70; American
Music Teacher 20:38 n5 '71; American Record Guide 36:776-777
My '70; Booklist 67:26 S 1 '70; Booklist 67:54 S 1 '70; Choice
7:690 Jy '70; Christian Century 87:511 Ap 22 '70; Contemporary
Review 217:108 Au '70; Downbeat 37:30-31 O 15 '70;
Instrument 24:16 Ju '70; Jazz Journal 23:8-9 S '70; Jazz
Monthly n190:7 D '70; Jazz Reporter 7:3 n4 '70; Jazz Research
2:163-164 '70; Kirkus Reviews 38:312 Mr 1 '70; Library Journal
95:2482 Jy '70; New Statesman 81:23 Ja 1 '71; Notes 27:271-272

222. Williams (continued)

> D '70; Nuova Rivista Musicale Italiana 6:114-115 n1 '72; Orkester Journalen 38:24+ D '70; Publishers Weekly 197:86 F 2 '70; Times Literary Supplement p1004 S 11 '70

# BAND MUSIC

223. Jones, John Paul. The Black Man in Military Music of the United States Army. Jackson, Miss.: Westside Printers, 1978. 79 pp. photographs. appendix. bibliography.

> This book consists of a brief history of black bands in the U.S. Army, arranged chronologically by major wars as follows: the Revolutionary War, the War of 1812, the Civil War, the Indian Wars of 1866-1898, the Spanish-American War, World War I, World War II, and Korea and Vietnam. Each chapter gives a summary of the participation of black troops and black musicians during the period covered; some chapters also include information on the use or place of music in the army. The Appendix gives a list of black troops that participated in the Civil War and in World War I.

224. Schafer, William J. Brass Bands and New Orleans Jazz. Baton Rouge: Louisiana State University Press, 1977. ix, 134 pp. photographs, musical examples. appendixes. index.

> Based largely on oral history, this short work begins with a developmental history of brass instruments from the eighteenth century to the present. It then chronicles the development of the brass band and jazz movements in New Orleans, relating developments there to the general American brass band movement. Mentioned are groups such as the Eureka, Excelsior, Onward, Olympic, and Zenith bands that played for parades, circuses, political rallies, churches, funerals, and dances, playing both straight and improvised music—marches, popular songs, hymns, and dirges. The author discusses the roles played by such leaders as Barbarin, Cottrell, Tio, Dutrey, Baquet, and Humphreys in the evolution of the New Orleans brass/street band tradition. A vivid account of the New Orleans funeral tradition is given as the author discusses the function of the brass band in these burial rites. Naturally, the "second line" is given prominent discussion. Jazz is treated as a separate but contiguous movement, having influenced and having been influenced by the brass band movement. The appendixes carry a wealth of important information. Appendix I includes a Roster of Brass Bands, a Bibliography, and a Discography. The Roster lists the names of twenty-seven brass bands that were active in New Orleans at some period between 1880 and the present day. Each entry contains the name of the band, the dates during which the band was active, and the group's personnel. The Bibliography lists titles of books and articles that treat the band movement in America. The Discography is a listing of thirty

224. Schafer (continued)

recordings by nine New Orleans brass bands. Organized alphabetically by the names of the bands, each entry provides the name of the band, personnel, and record labels and numbers. Appendix II presents the complete score of a favorite funeral dirge of the New Orleans brass bands.

Reviews: Best Sellers 37:205 O '77; Choice 14:1374+ D '77; Coda 164/165:36-37 F 1 '79; Footnote 9:18 n2 '78; Jazz Journal International 31:36 Ja/F '78; Kliatt Paperback Book Guide 12:47 Winter '78; Library Journal 102:1022 My 1 '77; Music Journal 36:38 Mr '78; New York Times Book Review p26 Jy 24 '77; Orkester Journalen 46:5+ Jy/Au '78; Publishers Weekly 211:68 Ap 25 '77; Second Line 30:28 Spring '78; Swinging Newsletter 7:5 n34 '77

# GOSPEL

225. Heilbut, Tony. The Gospel Sound: Good News and Bad Times. Garden City, N.Y.: Anchor Books, Anchor Press/Doubleday, 1975. xxxv, 364 pp. photographs. discography. indexes.

This survey of gospel music and gospel singing is "must" reading for scholars researching black religious music in the United States. It is an important popular history of the most neglected area of research in black American music, discussing the unique contributions of various performing individuals, quartets, and groups, their singing techniques and performance characteristics, as well as the songs and their writers. The book covers gospel music from its beginnings with C. A. Tindley to James Cleveland and Andrae Crouch and the Disciples. A valuable bonus is the author's treatment of the interaction between gospel and rhythm & blues/soul music, and the movement of singers from one genre to the other. Although lacking scholarly apparatus, the real-life documentation—via interviews and personal observation—is, in this case, more than adequate. However, the lack of source data leaves the beginning researcher without much-needed information. The book communicates the essence of the gospel environment and the cultural behaviors and interactions of its participants.

Reviews: AB Bookman's Weekly 48:1904 D 13 '71; Booklist 68:546 Mr 1 '72; Booklist 68:612 Mr 15 '72; Kirkus Reviews 39:982 S 1 '71; Library Journal 96:2776 S 15 '71; Library Journal 97:1630 Ap 15 '72; Music Educators Journal 66:91 D '79; Music Journal 33:26 Mr '75; Nation 214:153 Ja 31 '72; New York Review of Books 17:45 N 18 '71; New York Times Book Review p18 D 19 '71; Publishers Weekly 200:48 S 20 '71

226. Ricks, George Robinson. Some Aspects of the Religious Music of the United States Negro: An Ethnomusicological Study with Special Emphasis on the Gospel Tradition. New York: Arno Press, 1977. [xvi], 419 pp. tables, musical examples, diagrams, charts, photograph. appendixes.

**226. Ricks** (continued)

This work is a socio-cultural, historical, and musicotheoretical study of the religious music tradition of black people on the North American continent. Spanning the period ca. 1750 to ca. 1959, the findings of the study are presented in two main parts. Part I is divided into three time-periods as follows: "The Early Period" (eighteenth century to the Civil War), "The Middle Period" (the end of the Civil War to the end of the nineteenth century), and "The Late Period" (early twentieth century to the 1950s). The author presents demographic and social data, as well as information about the religious, educational, and musical environments in which the music developed. Part II analyzes and compares the three primary black religious music genres—the spiritual, the jubilee, and the gospel song. Ricks' findings reveal information about the retention and reinterpretation of African cultural values in the United States, Afro-American religious practices, retention and utilization of African musical patterns, the influence of African music values on Euro-American music, and the origins and development of the three primary black religious musical genres and the relationships among them.

Reviews: Hymn 30:293-294 n4 '79

## *POPULAR*

**227. Burton, Jack.** Blue Book of Tin Pan Alley: A Human Interest Anthology of American Popular Music. Watkins Glen, N.Y.: Century House, 1951. 520 pp. photographs. indexes.

The Blue Book is a source of information about popular songs written between 1890 and 1950. The works of approximately one hundred composers are listed here. The first section of the book treats compositions and composers popular between 1776 and 1890; each succeeding chapter covers a single decade. Each chapter is organized alphabetically by the name of the composer. The entry for each composer or team of composers contains a brief biography, composition titles, and a brief list of record albums featuring works by the entry subject. The song titles are arranged in chronological order of copyright under the following rubrics: Popular Songs, Religious Songs, Stage Musicals, Instrumental Numbers, and Film Songs and Scores. Each song title may be followed by pertinent information such as the name of the lyricist, star(s) of the show/film, and a brief discography. The book is concluded by an index of composers and an index of lyricists. Among the black composers and lyricists treated are James A. Bland, Gussie Davis, Duke Ellington, W. C. Handy, J. Rosamond Johnson, Fats Waller, Bob Cole, Paul Lawrence Dunbar, Bob Miley, and Andy Razaf.

Reviews: International Musician 50:37 Ja '62; Notes 9:130-131 D '51

228. Coryell, Julie, and Laura Friedman. Jazz-Rock Fusion: The People, the
Music. Preface by Ramsey Lewis. New York: Delacorte Press, 1978.
xv, 297 pp. photographs. bibliography. discography.

This casual work is a collection of biographies and interviews in
which the authors/editors seek to present the narrative portraits of
"people in jazz who had a hand in shaping the course of the music
from the late sixties through the late seventies" (p. ix). Organized
by area of competency—i.e., bass, brass, drums, composers et al.—
the book discusses fifty-eight musicians who contributed to and
participated in the jazz-rock fusion movement. Ron Carter, John
Lee, Miles Davis, Freddie Hubbard, Gerry Brown, Billy Cobham,
Lenny White, Tony Williams, George Benson, Herbie Hancock, Keith
Jarrett, Patrice Rushen, Roy Ayers, Al Jarreau, Ronnie Laws,
Wayne Shorter, and Grover Washington, Jr. are among the black
musicians represented. Each entry includes a photograph of the
performer, a biographical sketch, and an interview with the
performer. The collective discography at the end of the work is
extensive. Arranged by performer alphabetically, the disco-
graphical citations list the albums on which each performer
appeared "as leader" and "as sidemen," and include titles and label
numbers.
Reviews: Booklist 75:590 D 1 '78; Book World pE9 D 3 '78;
Cadence 5:28+ F '79; Contemporary Keyboard 5:6 Ja '79; Guitar
Player 12:8 D '78; Jazz Journal International 32:27 Jy '79; Jazz
Magazine 3:54-55 n2 '79; Library Journal 103:2427 D 1 '78;
Publishers Weekly 214:166 Jy 17 '78; Punch 275:773-774 N 1
'78; School Library Journal 25:69 F '79

229. Craig, Warren. Sweet and Lowdown: America's Popular Song Writers.
Foreword by Milton Ager. Metuchen, N.J.: Scarecrow Press, 1978. xi,
645 pp. appendixes. indexes.

Short biographical sketches and catalogues of the songs of
American songwriters comprise the contents of this book. The
writer entries appear alphabetically by composers' last names. The
sketches are brief and give only bare essentials; the list of song
titles appears in chronological order by year of composition and,
where appropriate, includes the names of musical productions in
which specific songs were introduced or interpolated. The
appendixes carry information on comparative rankings of songwriters, sources for the data contained in the composer entries, and
a bibliography. The three indexes are: Index of Song Titles; Index
of Productions; and Index of Names. Among the black songwriters
whose sketches and lists appear in the book are James Bland, Bob
Cole, Cab Calloway, Duke Ellington, J. Rosamond Johnson, and Fats
Waller.

230. Dennison, Sam. Scandalize My Name. New York: Garland Publishing,
1982. xxiii, 594 pp. photographs, musical examples. appendixes.
bibliography. indexes.

230. Dennison (continued)

This is a revealing study of popular-song texts which treat Afro-Americans in the United States. Discussing the imagery of blacks in American popular music, the work reviews the role of song in creating, developing, modifying, and perpetuating the image of the Afro-American. Comic songs, songs of derision, sentimental songs and "carry me backs," coon songs, and others are all investigated for their role in portraying Afro-Americans as comic inferiors and as objects of ridicule or sympathy. Also discussed are the utilization, modification and transformation of black song, (e.g., pseudo-spirituals), both by its admirers and its detractors, in efforts to denigrate Afro-Americans on the one hand, and to elevate them on the other. The book's Index of Songs contains more than seven hundred titles, nearly all of which in some way malign black people. The Index of Names includes those of a number of black composers, some of whom participated, wittingly or unwittingly, in the image-making that is the subject of the book.

231. Ewen, David. <u>All the Years of American Popular Music</u>. Englewood Cliffs, N.J.: Prentice-Hall, 1977. xviii, 850 pp. index.

This work surveys the entire world of popular music, including songs of all kinds (standard, popular, blues, novelty, etc.); jazz; soul; country and western; hillbilly; musical theater; music in motion pictures, radio, and television; recordings; disco; and Muzak. The work discusses payola, licensing by ASCAP and BMI, and the places and locations from which important genres emanated—Storyville, Preservation Hall, Woodstock, Tin Pan Alley, 52nd Street, Roseland Ballroom, and others. The work also takes into account the social mores, customs, and political forces that have given meaning to our heritage of popular music. The index is valuable and impressive, containing approximately 13,420 entries. However, the absence of a bibliography is a handicap. Of the book's forty-two chapters, ten are particularly pertinent to black music research since they are devoted largely to black music genres. Generally, black music is discussed in the context of American popular music in general.
Reviews: Booklist 74:656 D 15 '77; Catholic Library Review 49:455 My '78; Choice 15:83 Mr '78; Journalism Quarterly 54:828 Winter '77; Kirkus Reviews 45:824 Au 1 '77; Musical Times 119:1049 D '78; Music in Education 42:335 n396 '78; New York Times Book Review p13 D 4 '77; Publishers Weekly 212:109 Au 1 '77; Reference Services Review 6:14 Jy '78; Wilson Library Bulletin 52:502 F '78

232. Ewen, David, ed. <u>American Popular Songs: From the Revolutionary War to the Present</u>. New York: Random House, 1966. xiii, 507 pp.

This is a comprehensive, alphabetical guide to songs that have been produced and sung by Americans since the eighteenth century—popular songs that span the years 1766 ("The Girl I Left Behind Me") to 1966 ("Ballad of the Green Berets"). The book also includes facts about the songs' composers and lyricists, performances, the con-

232. Ewen (continued)

texts in which the songs became popular, best-selling records,
and other pertinent information. The compiler has included
anecdotes and other comments that add interest and depth to
the entries. The work also lists more than 280 composers and
lyricists, more than six hundred musical comedies and motion
pictures, and a large number of American singers who have
performed the songs over the decades. Special features are the
book's chronological "All-Time Hit Parade" of more than 1,150
songs, its list of over 580 "All-Time Best-Selling Popular
Recordings" from the period 1919-1966, and its list of "Some
American Performers of the Past and Present (And Some of the
Songs with Which They Are Identified)." Throughout the book
there appear the names of black musicians such as James
Bland, Gussie Davis, Louis Armstrong, Fred Stone, Bert
Williams, Sheldon Brooks, and others. Listed songs by black
composers include "Canadian Sunset" (Eddie Heywood, 1956),
"Memories of You" (Eubie Blake, 1930), "St. Louis Blues" (W. C.
Handy, 1914), "I Ain't Got Nobody" (Spencer Williams, 1916),
"Honeysuckle Rose" (Fats Waller, 1929), "Charleston" (James P.
Johnson, 1923), "Carry Me Back to Old Virginny" (James Bland,
1878), and many others. Black music researchers will be
somewhat hampered by the absence of an index and because
the author did not identify the composers and lyricists by
race. Yet the book is still a valuable source for researchers
seeking limited information on specific song titles, lyricists,
and composers.
Reviews: American Literature 39:133 Mr '67; Booklist 63:428
D 15 '66; Books Today 3:18 O 23 '66; Choice 4:966 N '67; Kirkus
Service 34:805 Au 1 '66; Kirkus Service 34:919 S 1 '66; Library
Journal 91:3920 S 1 '66; Library Journal 91:6218 D 15 '66; Music
Journal 24:15 D '66; New York Times Book Review 71:40 O 23
'66; Notes 24:501-502 n3 '68; World Journal Tribune 1:40 O 5 '66

233. Garland, Phyl. The Sound of Soul. Chicago: Henry Regnery Co., 1969.
     iv, 246 pp. photographs. index.

This book is "an informal account" (p. [ix]) of "the total body of soul
music" (p. [viii]). The author defines and explains the idea of "soul"
as it applies to the varieties of Afro-American music, introducing
the reader to the public and the private worlds of soul. Organized
in three main parts, the work covers "The Roots of Soul," "The Soul
Scene," and "Soul in Jazz." Part I is devoted to discussions of the
functioning of the black musician both in the soul arena and in the
popular musical mainstream, and comments on the "cover" and
"crossover" phenomena of the 1950s and 1960s. Further, the
essence of Afro-American music is admirably summed-up; and the
origins, aesthetics, and sociology of black music are set forth in
discussions of the blues, cries and hollers, the ring shout, the
spiritual, and other Afro-American musical genres. The chapter
titled "A Concise Natural History of Soul" is an excellent synopsis
of the Afro-American musical tradition. Part II is devoted to the

233. Garland (continued)

careers and contributions of B. B. King, Nina Simone, and Aretha Franklin, with a discussion of "Recording in Memphis." Part III discusses soul as it relates to jazz; the section ends with a requiem for John Coltrane and with speculations on the future of the music.
Reviews: AB Bookman's Weekly 43:2023 D 15 '69; Best Sellers 29:332 N 15 '69; Booklist 66:947 Ap 1 '70; Christian Century 86:1522 N 26 '69; Jazz Hot 256:21 D '69; Jazz Hot 257:29 Ja '70; Jazz Magazine 176:16 Mr '70; Kirkus Reviews 37:901 Au 15 '69; Kirkus Reviews 37:948 S 1 '69; Library Journal 94:3649 O 15 '69; Library Journal 95:1214 Mr 15 '70; Music Educators Journal 57:70-71 O '70; Negro Digest 19:43 Ja '70; New York Times Book Review p18 Mr 8 '70; Pan Pipes 63:44-45 n2 '70; Review for Religious 29:467 My '70

234. Groia, Philip. They All Sang on the Corner: New York City's Rhythm and Blues Vocal Groups of the 1950s. New York: Edmundson Publishing Co., 1973. 147 pp. photographs. index.

Discussing the cultural and social "dynamics of the street corner," this book surveys and chronicles the activities and the contributions of the amateur black vocal quartets and quintets that engaged in a cappella street singing in New York City between 1947 and 1960. It opens with "How It All Began," discussing such early groups as The Ravens, The Orioles, The Five Keys, and the Moonglows, all of whom later emerged as nationally known groups. The discussion progresses through such groups as the Dominos, Checkers, Drifters, Vocaltones, Solitaires, Schoolboys, Pretenders, Chantells, Frankie Lymon and the Teenagers, and others. The book is an introduction to the "doo-wop" phenomenon that extended into other major cities during the golden years of rhythm & blues.

235. Haralambos, Michael. Right On: From Blues to Soul in Black America. 1974. Reprint. New York: Da Capo Press, 1979. 187 pp. photographs, charts, drawings. appendixes. bibliography. discography. index.

This book describes and defines both blues and soul music, comparing the one to the other. The book clarifies the differences between the two by concentrating on matters relating to musical style; text content; geographical, cultural, sociological, and demographic factors; radio communication; record sales; audience response; and artist/audience/public interaction. The author discusses the most important blues and soul singers, and their relationships with radio and with live audiences in Chicago, Detroit, New York, and Minneapolis. The study is fairly well documented with historical, sociological, and demographic data.
Reviews: Ethnomusicology 25:149-150 n1 '81; Journal of American Folklore 94:402 Jy '81; Reprint Bulletin—Book Reviews 26:9 n2 '81

236. Marsh, Dave, and Kevin Stein. The Book of Rock Lists. New York: Dell/Rolling Stone Press, 1981. xxviii, 643 pp. photographs. bibliography.

> Although this work is primarily a book of trivia, the dearth of substantive scholarly sources in this area of music makes this book useful to researchers. In addition, the book does give some insight into the culture about which it is written. There is a good amount of useful information among the thousands of items listed, although it should be checked for accuracy. Data contained in this volume includes items on the "great back-up bands," best harmonica players, band sidemen, rock opera, dance hits and steps, and protest songs. This information is not usually available in more conventional sources. Throughout the book's thirty-four chapters, there are scattered items that are pertinent to black music research, but of particular value are the items on black-owned and black-oriented record companies such as Motown, Stax, and Vee-Jay; and a chapter on rhythm & blues.
>
>     Reviews: Booklist 78:74 S 15 '81; Book World 11:12 O 18 '81; Library Journal 106:1915 O 1 '81; Observer p29 D 6 '81; Stereo Review 47:101 Ja '82; Wilson Library Bulletin 56:461 F '82

237. Nanry, Charles, ed. American Music: From Storyville to Woodstock. Foreword by Irving Louis Horowitz. New Brunswick, N.J.: Transaction Books, 1972. xiv, 290 pp.

> This collection of scholarly essays constitutes a sociological view of the development and the conditions of aspects of American music from the 1920s to the early 1970s. Providing both facts about and insights into the jazz life, the essays, although sometimes controversial, are thoughtful and valuable. The focus is on jazz and the rock revolution, with writings by sociologists, historians, and critics such as Morroe Berger, Neil Leonard, Nat Hentoff, Richard Peterson, Louis Horowitz, Howard Junker, and Jon Landau. Sample chapters: "The Culture and Career of the Dance Musician" by Howard S. Becker; "A Theory of the Jazz Community" by Richard A. Stebbins; "Ah, The Unsung Glories of Pre-Rock" by Robert R. Faulkner; and "Rock, Recording and Rebellion" by Horowitz.
>
>     Reviews: Booklist 68:964 Jy 15 '72; Choice 9:824 S '72; Library Journal 97:2176 Ju 15 '72; Library Journal 97:2495 Jy '72; Music Educators Journal 59:88 Mr '73; Popular Music and Society 1:245-246 n4 '72; Rolling Stone 110:68 Ju '72; Social Forces 52:141 S '73

238. Redd, Lawrence N. Rock Is Rhythm and Blues (The Impact of Mass Media). East Lansing: Michigan State University Press, 1974. xviii, 167 pp.

> This work discusses the relationship between rock music and rhythm & blues, treating the history of the two styles and the impact of the media on their popularity and acceptance. Focusing on how copyrights and music were stolen from black artists by whites, the work is a penetrating study of an aspect of the music world,

238. Redd (continued)

illuminated by interviews with B. B. King, Brownie McGhee, Dave
Clark, Arthur Crudup, Jerry Butler, and Jessie Whitaker.
Reviews:    Booklist 71:366  D  1  '74;  Choice 11:1150  O  '74;
Library Journal 99:2070 S 1 '74

239. Shaw, Arnold. Honkers and Shouters: The Golden Years of Rhythm and
Blues. New York:  Macmillan Publishing Co., 1978.  xxviii, 555 pp.
photographs. discography. bibliography. index.

This period study surveys the rhythm & blues scene from its
beginnings in the mid-1940s to the present day, focusing primarily
on the period between 1945 and 1960.  Emphasis is placed on the
singers, instrumentalists, composers, producers, and record
companies, while the genre itself is recognized and treated as "an
indigenous black art form and style" (p. xv).  As the author
elucidates the musical and social forces that combined to create
rhythm & blues, he also provides information on the business and
economic aspects of the phenomenon.  Also discussed are the
characteristics, peculiarities, developments, and contributions of
the blues genre in cities such as Philadelphia, Chicago, Newark, Los
Angeles, New York, and others.  The individual talents of such
musicians as Big Bill Broonzy, T-Bone Walker, Erskine Hawkins,
Louis Jordan, Lionel Hampton, Fats Domino, Jackie Wilson, and
many others are emphasized and showcased.  The blues are also
treated in their settings in the logging camps of the early twentieth
century.  Within its scope, the book is strikingly all-inclusive.  The
twenty-five interviews that are included are instructive and
valuable.   While the work does not carry the usual scholarly
apparatus, the first-hand experiences of the author authenticates,
tentatively at least, many of the statements for which the scholar
will need documentation.  This book is a good general reader for
beginning scholars in this branch of black music.
Reviews:    Audio 63:28-29 Ja '79; Billboard 90:87 Jy 22 '78;
Books of the Times 2:34 Ja 19 '79; Book World pF2 Jy 30 '78;
Book World pE2 Au 20 '78; Cadence 4:34 O '78; Choice 15:1383
D '78; High Fidelity/Musical America 28:168 N '78; Jazz
Journal International 31:19 N '78; JEMF Quarterly 15:240+ n56
'79; Kirkus Reviews 46:538 My 1 '78; Kliatt Paperback Book
Guide 12:54 Fall '78; Library Journal 103:874-875 Ap 15 '78;
Music Educators Journal 65:19 N '78; Music Educators Journal
66:91 D '78; Music Journal 36:50 D '78; New York Times pC21
Ja 19 '79; Notes 36:363/364 n2 '79; Publishers Weekly 213:69 Ap
17 '78; Rolling Stone 281/282:25 D 28/Ja 11 '79; Sing Out 27:36
n2 '78; Variety 291:83 Ju 28 '78; West Coast Review of Books
4:64 S '78

240. Shaw, Arnold. The World of Soul:  Black America's Contribution to the
Pop Music Scene. New York:  Cowles Book Co., 1970.  xiii, 306 pp.
photographs. discography. index.

240. Shaw (continued)

This is the story of the blues in several of its manifestations, beginning with "Country Blues and Bottleneck Bluesmen" and ending with the originators and the progeny of "Gospel Music and Soul"— James Brown, Ray Charles, Jimi Hendrix, and others. As he tells the story, the author discusses the classic blues singers; the jazz singers; black pop singers; rhythm & blues in various parts of the country; "The Big Three of R & B"—Motown, Stax, and Atlantic Records; and the modern bluesmen—Otis Spann, Ike Turner, Taj Mahal, and all the rest. The discography is a valuable addition to the text, which is a basic introduction to black popular music.

> Reviews: AB Bookman's Weekly 45:1882 Ju 1 '70; Booklist 66:1250 Ju 15 '70; Booklist 67:654 Ap 1 '71; Choice 8:1186 N '71; English Journal 62:303 F '73; Jazz and Pop 9:51 D '70; Jazz Research 3/4:280 '71/'72; Kirkus Reviews 37:1362 D 15 '69; Kirkus Reviews 38:190 F 15 '70; Library Journal 95:162 Ja 15 '70; Library Journal 95:1913 My 15 '70; Library Journal 95:1974 My 15 '70; Library Journal 95:4328 D 15 '70; Music Journal 28:63+ S '70; Notes 28:694-697 n4 '72; Pan Pipes 63:44-46 n2 '71; Publishers Weekly 196:46 D 8 '69; Publishers Weekly 199:72 Mr 8 '71; Top of the News 27:309 Ap '71; Variety 257:52 F 4 '70

# MUSICAL THEATER

241. Bordman, Gerald. American Musical Theatre: A Chronicle. New York: Oxford University Press, 1978. viii, 749 pp. appendix. indexes.

This is a broad historical survey which treats the subject of American musical theater, in discussions of short historical periods from its origins through the 1970s, e.g., "Origins to 1866," 1866-1878, 1878-1892, etc. The book presents discussions of opera buffa, operetta, the modern musical, Broadway and the swing era, new directions, and other areas of theatrical activity. The entries within the historical periods are arranged by show title; they include date of premieres, closing dates, names of composers and writers, story lines, principal actors, and other pertinent information. The book ends with three indexes: "Index to Shows and Songs," "Index: Songs," and "Index: People." Among the several all-black shows discussed in the work are Bandana Land, Blackbirds, Bubbling Brown Sugar and The Cannibal King; the index of names includes such personalities as Bert Williams, Eubie Blake, Arna Bontemps, Will Marion Cook, Cole and Johnson, James Reese Europe, and Fats Waller.

> Reviews: American Record 42:54 My '79; American Reference Books Annual 11:450 Ex '80; Booklist 76:785-786 F 1'80; Books of the Times 2:212 My '79; Central Opera Service Bulletin 21:28 n3 '79; Choice 16:86 Mr '79; Kirkus Reviews 46:911 Au 15 '78; Musical Opinion 103:2003 O 1 '78; Musical Opinion 102:396-397 Ju '79; New Boston Review 4:21 Ju '79; New Republic 179:42 N '78; Newsweek 92:120 N 20 '78; New York Times pC20 My 1 '79; Popular Music and Society 6:257-258 n3

241. Bordman (continued)

'79; Publishers Weekly 214:385 Au 28 '78; Stereo Review 43:13
D '79; Variety 293:107 N '78; West Coast Review of Books 5:46
Ja '79; Wilson Library Bulletin 53:405 Ja '79

242. Burton, Jack. The Blue Book of Hollywood Musicals: Songs from the
Sound Tracks and the Stars Who Sang Them Since the Birth of the
Talkies a Quarter-Century Ago. Watkins Glen, N.Y.: Century House,
1953. 296 pp. photographs, plates. discography. appendix. index.

Citations of musicals produced between October 6, 1927 and
October 31, 1952 comprise the contents of the book. Lists of
motion pictures made during each of these years are divided into
four categories: "Musicals," "Feature Films with Songs," "Western
Films with Songs," and "Full Length Cartoon Films with Songs."
Individual musicals are arranged alphabetically by title under each
category; the entries include a list of the cast, the name of the
director of the film, a list of the songs performed in the film, and
the names of their respective composers. Among the films treated
in the book are Cabin in the Sky and Stormy Weather. The index is
an alphabetical list of film titles; access to names of actors/
actresses or composers is not provided.
Reviews: Score 5:13 n2/3 '53

243. Fletcher, Tom. The Tom Fletcher Story: 100 Years of the Negro in
Show Business. New York: Burdge & Co., 1954. xx, 337 pp.
photographs.

More than an autobiography, Fletcher's book is a collection of
thirty-five vignettes on various aspects of the Afro-American
musical heritage, ranging from discussions of "The African
Company and Ira Aldridge" to comments on Fletcher's own life
"Until Now," touching on such subjects as black minstrelsy, Gussie
Davis, James Bland, the cakewalk, Abbie Mitchell, coon songs,
Shuffle Along, W. C. Handy, "James Reese Europe and the Clef
Club," and other topics of black music history. In a small way, the
book is a survey of the Afro-American secular music movement,
although the treatment is not complete. However, it is packed with
names and facts, and gives much "inside information," although it is
not a scholarly work. The absence of an index hampers its use.

244. Isaacs, Edith Rich. The Negro in the American Theatre. New York:
Theatre Arts, 1947. 143 pp. photographs.

This survey is a shallow but important presentation of information
about the participation of black performers and writers in the
theatrical world. It chronicles the accomplishments won and the
difficulties encountered by black show people in their quest to
achieve success in and contribute to the development of show
business in the United States. Heavily music-oriented, the book
provides career information on black musicians and composers and
possesses a scope which makes clearly evident the distance between

244. Isaacs (continued)

vaudeville and serious drama. Undocumented and without an index,
it is a brief historical sketch of black musical theater from ca.
1890-1946. The book is divided into three periods—Pre-1890
background, 1890-1917, and 1917-1946—and treats such figures as
James Hewlett, Ira Aldridge, James Bland, Ernest Hogan, Bert
Williams, Sissle and Blake, Josephine Baker, and others. It mentions
and discusses theatrical productions such as In Dahomey, Shuffle
Along, Blackbirds, Runnin' Wild, Porgy and Bess, The Green
Pastures, and many others. This survey is indispensable to novice
researchers of black musical theater or show business personalities.
Reviews: Library Journal 72:1472 '47; Saturday Review of
Literature p25 O 18 '47

245. Odell, George C. D. Annals of the New York Stage. 15 vols. New
York: Columbia University Press, 1927-1949. each vol. approx. 800
pp. photographs/plates. indexes.

A history of the New York stage from its beginnings to 1894, these
volumes contain accounts of performances presented at various
locations during most of the eighteenth and nineteenth centuries.
Each volume covers a particular time period (e.g., three years or
five years, etc.), and is organized by city or cities, and by
theater(s), and includes the names of actors and actresses, brief
biographies of important stage personalities, and reviews of the
various performances.      Information about concerts, opera
performances and entertainments presented by music societies is
also given. A search of the indexes will reveal the names of such
nineteenth-century musicians as Sisseretta Jones, Sam Lucas,
Horace Weston, A. A. Luca (of the Luca Family), Billy Kersands,
the National Sable Quintet, the Fisk University Jubilee Singers, and
others. The "Negroes" index entries will lead the researcher to
many unfamiliar names and facts, although most of the citations
are only brief mentions. An important feature of the book is the
presence of many photographs and drawings of individual
performers.
Reviews: Booklist 24:107 D '27; Books (New York Herald
Tribune) p5 Ju 5 '27; Nation 124:718 Ju 29 '27; New Republic
52:Sup182 D 5 '27; New York Times p8 N 6 '27; Outlook 146:224
Ju 15 '27; Saturday Review of Literature 4:451 '27; Saturday
Review of Literature 5:1188 '29; Yale Review 17:393 Ja '28

246. Sampson, Henry T. Blacks in Blackface: A Source Book on Early Black
Musical Shows. Metuchen, N.J.: Scarecrow Press, 1980. x, 552 pp.
photographs. appendixes. index.

Discussing such topics as "Black Power in the 1920s," "Pioneer
Black Show Producers," and "Black Musical Shows, 1900-1940," this
source book provides information on black musical shows that were
produced between 1865 and 1940. The work provides biographies on
important show people, a partial list of shows, and other pertinent
information. The entry for each show listed in the section on

246. Sampson (continued)

"Black Musical Shows, 1900-1940" contains data on the following items: date of first performance; acts and scenes; producer, author, lyricist, and composer; musical director; cast; story plot and scene synopses; and musical compositions used in the show. This is an important reference book.

Reviews: American Reference Books Annual 12:474 '81; Black Books Bulletin 7:52 n3 '81; Booklist 78:66 S 1 '81; Choice 18:805 F '81

## CONCERT AND RECITAL MUSIC

247. Abdul, Raoul. Blacks in Classical Music: A Personal History. New York: Dodd, Mead and Co., 1977. 253 pp. photographs. index. chronology of important music events.

A collection of vignettes, critiques, reviews, and interviews, the contents of this work aptly reflect its title. The work presents and describes events and individuals important to the history and development of black musicians in the concert and recital worlds. The composers treated range from Europe's Chevalier de St. George to America's Hale Smith; it is a survey of the concert world of Roland Hayes, Marian Anderson, Zelma Watson George, Andre Watts, Natalie Hinderas, Kermit Moore, Dean Dixon, Henry Lewis, and others. Opera companies, orchestras, and choruses that have been important to the development of black musicians in the concert world are also discussed.

Reviews: Book World pE3 Ap 2 '78; Booklist 74:723 Ja 1 '78; Kirkus Reviews 45:1295 D 1 '77; Library Journal 102:2434 D 1 '77; Publishers Weekly 212:60 N 14 '77

248. Baker, David N., Lida M. Belt, and Herman C. Hudson. The Black Composer Speaks. Metuchen, N.J.: Scarecrow Press, 1978. v, 506 pp. photographs. appendixes. index.

Fifteen contemporary black composers are discussed, through biographical sketches, interviews, and catalogues. T. J. Anderson, David N. Baker, Noel Da Costa, Talib Hakim, Herbie Hancock, Ulysses Kay, Undine Moore, Oliver Nelson, Coleridge-Taylor Perkinson, George Russell, Archie Shepp, Hale Smith, Howard Swanson, George Walker, and Olly Wilson are each represented by a chapter that contains a photograph of the composer, a list of the composer's achievements, the composer's thoughts on musical and aesthetic matters, and a complete list of his or her musical compositions. These are followed by a bibliography of writings by (where applicable) and about the composer. The entries in each composer's catalogue carry the title and date of composition; performing medium; author of the text (where applicable); dedication; performance time; first performance information; and other data. In addition, the appendixes list "Addresses of Publishers Appearing in the Text," "Addresses of Recording Companies Appearing in the Text," and "Compositions Classified by Medium"—

129

248. Baker (continued)

> all handy and valuable resource inventories. The index (of names and titles) effectively complements the body of the work. This is a good source with which to begin comprehensive research on black composers or research on any one or more of the composers included. This work can be supplemented by the volume entitled Fifteen Black Composers, edited by Alice Tischler (entry 249) which treats composers not included in the Baker volume.
>
> Reviews:   Cadence 4:14 My '78; Choice 15:1064 O '78; Library Journal 103:976 My 1 '78

249. Tischler, Alice. Fifteen Black American Composers: A Bibliography of Their Works. Detroit Studies in Music Bibliography, no. 45. Detroit: Information Coordinators, 1981. 328 pp. indexes. list of publishers.

> This reference source contains brief biographical sketches and bibliographical listings of the compositions of Edward Boatner, Margaret Bonds, Edgar Clark, Arthur Cunningham, William Dawson, Roger Dickerson, James Furman, Adolphus Hailstork, Robert Harris, Wendell Logan, Carman Moore, Dorothy Moore, John Price, Noah Ryder, and Frederick Tillis. Appearing in alphabetical order, each composer's section is organized as follows:   1) a short biographical sketch, followed by citations of the sources used in compiling the sketch; and 2) the composer's score bibliography, with the works listed in alphabetical order, giving, for each, complete available information on the year of publication, performance medium, commission, publisher, repositories at which the score is held, performance time, and other useful information.   We recommend this book as a companion to entry 248, The Black Composer Speaks.
>
> Reviews:   American Reference Books Annual 13:518 '82; Choice 19:492 D '81; Library Quarterly 52:168 Ap '82

# XI

# Collective Biographies

250. Handy, D. Antoinette. <u>Black Women in American Bands and Orchestras</u>. Foreword by Paul Freeman. Metuchen, N.J.: Scarecrow Press, 1981. xii, 319 pp. photographs, charts. appendix. bibliography. indexes.

This one-of-a-kind survey contains information that will not be found in any other secondary source, discussing black women musicians born between 1878 and 1953. Beginning with a historical overview of the American orchestra, it deals with black women as conductors and as performers in minstrel and dance bands, symphony and theater orchestras, jazz groups, "elite art" ensembles, and marching bands. The book's "Profiles" section features women who perform or performed on a number of instruments—violin, cello, string bass, guitar, sitar, ukulele, banjo, harp, and varieties of brass, woodwind, and percussion instruments. Significant emphasis is placed on the International Sweethearts of Rhythm, an all-girl band of the 1930s through the 1950s. Black women music administrators are also listed and discussed. Copious photographs illustrate the participation in American bands and orchestras.

Reviews: American Reference Books Annual 13:532 '82; Black Books Bulletin 7:52 n3 '81; Black Scholar 12:57 Jy/Au '81; Cadence 7:24 Mr '81; Choice 18:1275 My '81; Music Journal 39:48-49 My/Ju '81; RQ 20:306 Spring '81; Times Literary Supplement p750 Jy 3 '81; Wilson Library Bulletin 55:699 My '81

251. Handy, W. C. Negro Authors and Composers of the United States.
     1938. Reprint. New York: AMS Press, 1976. 24 pp. photograph.
     bibliography.

     Many composers and lyricists who made contributions to black
     American music in the opening decades of the century are included
     in this list. The composers named here are representative of the
     fields of opera, concert music, religious music, musical comedy,
     blues, motion picture music, popular music, and comic songs; also
     included is a category of women composers. This brief volume also
     contains a list of the winners of the first five Wanamaker contests.

252. Stewart, S. S. Sketches of Noted Banjo Players. Philadelphia: S. S.
     Stewart, 1881. 32 pp.

     Brief descriptions of the careers and abilities of sixteen banjoists
     who were prominent in 1881 constitute the first half of this
     pamphlet. The remainder of the work consists primarily of banjo
     anecdotes; a short explication of the "Theory of 'Fretting' or
     Dividing the String," "Stewart's Method of Putting on a Banjo
     Head," and a discussion of "Concert Pitch" are also included. A
     sample entry follows:
         Bohee, James, is a colored man, whose remarkable execution
         upon the instrument has won for him a great reputation. He
         has filled many engagements with various companies, and is, at
         the present time, with Haverly's Colored Minstrels.
     Among the musicians included in the book are Lewis Brimmer,
     James Bohee, Al Baur, Harry Budd, William Carter, William Carroll,
     Frank M. Cary, Andrew Collum, Chas. E. Dobson, Samuel Devere,
     Harry Stanwood, Charles Schofield, Harry Shirley, James Stanford,
     and Horace Weston.

## BLUES AND POPULAR

253. Bogle, Donald. Brown Sugar: Eighty Years of America's Black Female
     Superstars. New York: Harmony Books, 1980. 208 pp. photographs,
     drawings, posters. index.

     Treating black female performers in areas of entertainment ranging
     from music to dance to drama, this volume provides information
     about women who achieved "star" status from the beginning of the
     century to 1980, reaching from Ma Rainey to Donna Summer. The
     book is arranged in chronological order; its discussion of the
     contributions and interactions of female performers provides an
     overview of the changes that have taken place in the entertainment
     industry and the place of black women in that development. The
     value of the book is enhanced by the large number of photographs
     that illustrate the text.
         Reviews: Booklist 76:1479 Ju 15 '80; Library Journal 105:1405
         Ju 15 '80

254. Charters, Samuel. The Bluesmen: The Story and the Music of the Men Who Made the Blues. New York: Oak Publications; London: Music Sales, 1967. 233 pp. photographs, maps, musical examples. bibliography. index.

> This work begins with a section titled "The African Background," then presents large sections on the blues products of three states— Mississippi, Alabama, and Texas, giving information on the blues cultures of those states and on the primary bluesmen whom they produced. Biographies occupy the major portion of the book; these include extensive quotes from the singers themselves and transcriptions of their featured songs. Charley Patton, Son House, Skip James, Robert Johnson, Booker T. Washington, Bukka White, Blind Lemon Jefferson, Henry Thomas, Texas Alexander, and other singers from the three states covered are included.
>
> Reviews: Booklist 64:98 S 15 '67; Ethnomusicology 12:454 '68; Jazz Journal 21:23 Mr '68; Library Journal 92:2780 Au '67; Notes 24:719 Ju '68; Orkester Journalen 36:11 Jy/Au '68; Western Folklore 28:68 '69

255. Stewart-Baxter, Derrick. Ma Rainey and the Classic Blues Singers. New York: Stein and Day, 1970. 112 pp. posters, advertisements, photographs. bibliography. discography. index.

> This book is devoted entirely to the biographies of those women who sang in the classic blues style during the 1920s, 1930s, and 1940s (e.g., Bessie Smith, Sippie Wallace, Ida Cox, Rosa Henderson, Lucille Hegamin, and Victoria Spivey). After beginning with a chapter that seeks to define the term "Classic blues," the author presents the biographies, grouping them according to similarities in the styles of the singers and, to a lesser extent, chronologically. The book also contains information about the professional relationships between these women and such artists as Louis Armstrong, Perry Bradford, Willie "The Lion" Smith, Jimmy Dunn, Don Redman, Jimmie Lunceford, Duke Ellington, Fletcher Henderson, James P. Johnson, Tommy Ladnier, Charlie Green, Freddie Keppard, Little Brother Montgomery, and King Oliver.
>
> Reviews: AB Bookman's Weekly 46:1188 O 26 '70; Black World 20:90 Ja '71; Blues Unlimited n76:21 O '72; Choice 8:77 Mr '71; Ethnomusicology 16:136 n1 '72; Gramophone 48:677 O '72; Jazz and Pop 9:50 D '70; Jazz Journal 23:8 S '70; Jazz Monthly n188:29 O '70; Library Journal 96:292 Ja 15 '71; Library Journal 96:481 F 1 '71; Matrix n90:10 D '70; Music Teacher 111:898 S '70; Storyville n30:236-237 Au/S '70; Times Literary Supplement p1365 N 20 '70

# JAZZ

256. Borenstein, Larry, and Bill Russell. Preservation Hall Portraits. Baton Rouge: Louisiana State University Press, 1968. unpaged.

256.  Borenstein (continued)

> For scholars researching New Orleans jazz, this book of collective
> biographies can serve as one means of introduction to the
> musicians.  Each biographical sketch is accompanied by a
> photograph of the subject's Preservation Hall portrait, and provides
> the musician's name/nickname; instrument; vital data; and the
> musician's professional development, relations, and
> accomplishments.  Among those included in the work are Danny
> Barker, Emma Barrett, Alex Bigard, George Lewis, Kid Punch
> Miller, Emmanuel Paul, Joe Robichaux, and the members of the
> Eureka Brass Band.
>> Reviews:  International Musician 67:32 F '69; Jazz Monthly
>> 169:27 Mr '69; Matrix 81:14 F '69; Melody Maker 44:10 Ja 18
>> '69; Music Journal 27:76 Mr '69; Publishers Weekly 194:93 S 23
>> '68; Orkester Journalen 37:2 S '69

257.  Charters, Samuel B., IV.  Jazz, New Orleans, 1885-1963: An Index to
Negro Musicians of New Orleans.  Rev. ed.  New York:  Oak
Publications, 1963.  173 pp.  photographs, drawings, musical examples.
appendixes. indexes.

> All the great names are included here—Celestin, Piron, Bigard,
> Olympia Orchestra, Excelsior Brass Band, and all the other New
> Orleans jazzmen and ensembles.  More than eight hundred musicians
> and over 120 bands and orchestras are listed in four sections as
> follows:  1885-1899, 1899-1919, 1919-1931, 1931-1963.  Each
> section includes a valuable historical and explanatory narrative,
> followed by the main entries—biographical vignettes—each of which
> contains the name of the individual or group; the individual's
> instrument, or the number of pieces in the group; vital data, or the
> dates of the group's active period; and a biographical sketch.  The
> book has a "Discographical Appendix," and also an appendix
> containing "Some New Source Material On the Beginnings of Jazz in
> New Orleans."  There are included indexes to names, bands, "halls,
> cabarets, theatres, etc.," tune titles, and addenda.  This work is an
> excellent source book for research on New Orleans jazz.
>> Reviews:  Journal of American Folklore 77:364 '64

258.  Knauss, Zane.  Conversations with Jazz Musicians: Louis Bellson, Leon
Breeder, Dizzy Gillespie, Eric Kloss, Jimmy McPartland, Barry Miles,
Sy Oliver, Charlie Spivak, Billy Taylor, Phil Woods, Sol Yaged.
Conversations, vol. 2.  Detroit:  Gale Research Co., 1977.  [vii], 281 pp.
photographs.

> In compiling this book, the author had "three chief goals in mind:
> first, to provide a forum for the leading jazz men by preserving
> their comments on their work and careers; second, to provide
> readers with insights into the profession of musicianship in our
> time; third, to present an accurate image of the musicians as
> individuals—to reveal their aspirations, their feelings about music,

258. Knauss (continued)

and their responses to the world they live in" (Introduction,
unpaged).  Each interview is prefaced by a brief biography and
information concerning the interview, i.e., the relationship between
Knauss and the person being interviewed, and a description of the
setting of the interview itself.
Reviews:  Billboard 90:59 Mr 18 '78; Cadence 4:23 Ap '78;
Choice 15:700 Jy/Au '78; Jazz Journal International 31:31 Jy
'78; Music Educators Journal 65:23 S '78; Music Journal 36:35
My '78; Wilson Library Bulletin 52:645 Ap '78

259. Spellman, A. B.  Black Music/Four Lives:  Cecil Taylor, Ornette
Coleman, Herbie Nichols, Jackie McLean. New York: Schocken Books,
1970. xiv, 241 pp. index.

Originally published as Four Lives in the Bebop Business. n.p.: Pantheon
Books, 1966.

Four jazz musicians—Cecil Taylor (piano), Ornette Coleman (tenor
saxophone), Herbie Nichols (piano), and Jackie McLean (alto
saxophone)—were chosen as the subjects of this collective
biography.  In selecting individuals whose background and musical
contributions differ, the author seeks to demonstrate the common
problems faced by black American jazz musicians as they encounter
exploitation by record company and cabaret owners.  Much of the
book is composed of quoted material gleaned from personal
interviews with each of the four men.  In the process of relating the
biographies of these four jazzmen, the author includes information
about such artists as John Coltrane, Miles Davis, Duke Ellington,
Dizzy Gillespie, Milt Jackson, John Lewis, Charley Mingus,
Thelonius Monk, Charlie Parker, Bud Powell, Max Roach, Sonny
Rollins, Archie Shepp, and Lester Young.
Reviews:  American Anthropologist 73:1372 D '71; American
Journal of Sociologists 77:390 S '71; Antiquarian Bookman
39:2376 Ju 5 '67; Best Sellers 30:331 N 1 '70; Booklist 63:611 F
15 '67; Books Today 3:22 N 27 '66; Book Week p20 N 13 '66;
Choice 4:539 Jy '67; Christian Science Monitor p9 D 19 '66;
Commonweal 85:490 F 3 '67; Downbeat 33:40 D 15 '66;
International Musician 66:14 Ju '68; Jazz Monthly 13:30-31 O
'67; Journal of Popular Culture 4:807-808 n3 '71; Kirkus Service
34:1026 S 15 '66; Library Journal 91:5621 N 15 '66; Library
Journal 92:359 Ja 15 '67; Music Educators Journal 54:11 O '67;
Music Journal 25:88 Ja '67; Music Journal 28:82 D '70; Nation
204:378 Mr 20 '67; Negro Digest 16:53 Mr '67; New Statesman
74:261 S 1 '67; New York Times Book Review 71:32 N 20 '66;
Orkester Journalen 35:16 O '67; Publishers Weekly 198:61 S 21
'70; Rolling Stone n82:52 My 13 '71; Saturday Review 50:61 F
11 '67; Saturday Review 50:120 Mr 11 '67; Spectator 219:163 Au
11 '67; Times Literary Supplement p993 O 19 '67

260. Wilmer, Valerie. Jazz People. 3rd ed. London: Allison & Busby, 1977.
167 pp. index.

260. Wilmer (continued)

Interviews of the following fourteen musicians form the basis for this collective biography:  Art Farmer, Cecil Taylor, Lockjaw Davis, Thelonius Monk, Billy Higgins, Jimmy Heath, Randy Weston, Babs Gonzales, Clark Terry, Jackie McLean, Buck Clayton, Howard McGhee, Joe Turner, and Archie Shepp.  The subjects of the book were born within a twenty-five-year period from 1911 to 1936; they represent a cross-section of first-rate musicians who have contributed to the development of jazz.  The interviews demonstrate the diversity of interests and personalities that marks these jazz players and the similarities of problems that they encounter in the process of their careers.  Each discussion is accompanied by a photograph of the subject.

Reviews: Times Educational Supplement p35 Jy 7 '78; Times Literary Supplement p1031 S 15 '78

# CONCERT MUSIC

261. Layne, Maude Wanzer. The Negro's Contribution to Music. n.p., 1942. 88 pp. photographs. index.

This is a collection of short biographical sketches of eighty-five black musicians who were more or less contemporary with the author.  Among those included are Amanda Aldridge, Louis Armstrong, Melville Charlton, William Levi Dawson, Walter Dyett, Eva Jessie, J. Rosamund Johnson, Camille Nickerson, Florence Price, and other well-known as well as lesser known black musicians.  Although the work is undocumented, it is useful as a springboard for research on any of the figures included.  Many of the sketches are accompanied by photographs.

262. Lovinggood, Penman. Famous Modern Negro Musicians. Introduction by Eileen Southern. 2nd ed. New York: Da Capo Press, 1978. viii, 68 pp.

This is a collection of biographical vignettes that briefly survey the accomplishments of nineteen black musicians who were active in the second decade of the twentieth century.  Written by a contemporary of these musicians, the book is a "modest report" on the state of black concert music during the period.  All of the musicians covered here have made lasting contributions to American society:  Marian Anderson, Harry T. Burleigh, Melville Charleton, Samuel Coleridge-Taylor, Cleota Collins, Will Marion Cook, Robert Nathaniel Dett, Carl R. Diton, Joseph Douglass, E. Azalia Hackley, Helen E. Hagan, Roland Hayes, Kemper Harreld, J. Rosamund Johnson, R. Augustus Lawson, Eugene Mars Martin, William H. Richardson, Florence Cole Talbot, and Clarence Cameron White.

Reviews: Reprint Bulletin—Book Reviews 24:16 '79

# XII

# Iconographies

263. Berendt, Joachim-Ernst. Jazz: A Photo History. Translated by William Odom. New York: Schirmer Books, 1978. 355 pp. photographs. discography. index.

   This collection of 370 photographs of great jazz artists is presented in seventeen categories, ranging from "New Orleans" to "Free" to "Miles Davis and After." It includes photographs of instrumentalists, singers, and bandleaders from the United States, Europe, and Japan. A large-format "photographic history of jazz" (dust cover), this book contains striking photographs—mostly candid—by sixty-five different photographers. The pictures are accompanied by extended captions and excellent commentary on the "people, places, styles, and the social, political, and cultural background from which jazz arose" (dust cover). Also included are significant statements from the musicians themselves, from critics and jazz historians such as Martin Williams and Leonard Feather, and from black leaders and literary figures such as Martin Luther King, Langston Hughes, and Leroi Jones.
   Reviews: Booklist 76:747 F 1 '80; Coda 176:23 D 1 '80; Jazz Podium 27:50 N '78; Jazz Times p14 Au '80; Library Journal 104:2650 D 15 '79

264. Fernett, Gene. Swing Out: Great Negro Dance Bands. Midland, Mich.: Pendell Co., 1970. 175 pp. photographs. index.

   Essentially, this is an album of more than one hundred photographs, posed and candid, of groups and individuals who were active in the

137

264. Fernett (continued)

big band movement in the United States. More than seventy-five
big bands are featured, with the focus on the twenty-five most
important ones, ranging from the earliest (Fate Marable's) to that
of Dizzy Gillespie (1950s). Among others highlighted are the bands
of McKinney (Cotton Pickers), Alphonso Trent, Noble Sissle, Chick
Webb, Erskine Hawkins, Don Redman, Claude Hopkins, Cab
Calloway, Jimmie Lunceford, Harlan Leonard, Duke Ellington, and
Count Basie. Included also are: 1) brief discussions which serve as
introductions to the featured groups, 2) a list of dates and places of
birth for major figures, 3) a list of theme songs for the major bands,
and 4) an index of pictures.
Reviews: AB Bookman's Weekly 45:1880 Ju 1 '70; Billboard
82:8 My 16 '70; Black World 23:95 N '73; Booklist 67:24 S 1 '70;
Music Journal 28:91 D '70

265. Gottlieb, William P. The Golden Age of Jazz. Introduction by John W.
Wilson. New York: Simon and Schuster, 1979. 158 pp. photographs.
index.

The photographs in this book capture the essence of jazz musicians
both on and off the stage; all those here represented were
prominent performers during the late 1930s and the 1940s. The
wide diversity of persons included reaches from James P. Johnson,
Leadbelly, and Sidney Bechet to Miles Davis, Billy Eckstein, and
Oscar Pettiford. The accompanying text and the captions to the
photographs consist of the compiler's reflections on the various
musicians and serve to illustrate further this view of the jazz world.
Reviews: Best Sellers 39:245 O '79; Business Week p11 Au 20
'79; Christian Science Monitor 71:B10 N 13 '79; Coda 169:15 O
1 '79; Jazz Echo 9:13 '79; Jazz Journal International 33:36 F
'80; New Republic 181:39 O 29 '79; New Statesman 100:29 O 24
'80; New Yorker 55:144 O 29 '79; Notes 37:63 S '80; Orkester
Journalen 47:2 D '79; Punch 278:70 Ja 9 '80; Radio Free Jazz
20:15 D '79; West Coast Review of Books 5:82 S '79

266. Hughes, Langston and Milton Meltzer. Black Magic: A Pictorial History
of the Negro in American Entertainment. Englewood Cliffs, N.J.:
Prentice-Hall, 1967. 375 pp. photographs. index.

Numerous reproductions of posters, broadsides, programs, sheet
music covers, and photographs comprise the contents of this
volume. The book is a history of black entertainment, featuring
black performers from the slavery period to American television
entertainment. Photographs of actors, dancers, writers, television
personalities, and musicians are presented in sixty sections that
carry titles such as: "Early Musicals," "T.O.B.A.," " 'Shuffle
Along'," "The Federal Theater," "Dancers and Dancing," "The Negro
in Films," and "Television Opens Doors." Howard Swanson, Esther
Sutherland, Sidney Bechet, Miles Davis, Gussie L. Davis, The Fisk
Jubilee Singers, Roland Hayes, Ulysses Kay, Nathaniel Dett,
Martina Arroyo, Grace Bumbry, Robert McFerrin, The Clara Ward

266. Hughes (continued)

> Singers, Alex Bradford, Fats Domino, Billy Eckstein, Bessie Smith, Hazel Scott, and The Charioteers are among the many and diverse musicians pictured in the book.
>
> Reviews: Best Sellers 27:321 N 15 '67; Booklist 64:964 Ap 15 '68; Catholic Library World 39:602 Ap '68; Kirkus Reviews 35:1098 S 1 '67; Library Journal 93:315 Ja 15 '68; Library Journal 93:770 F 15 '68; Negro Digest 17:96 F '68; New York Times 117:25 Ju 1 '68; Publishers Weekly 192:274 Au 28 '67; Variety 248:66 N 15 '67; Wilson Library Bulletin 43:789 Ap '69

267. Jones, Max, comp. Jazz Photo Album. London: British Yearbooks, [1947]. unpaged. photographs.

> Photographs of more than sixty individuals or groups are featured in this book, arranged approximately in chronological order. Each photo is accompanied by a short biography of the subject(s). Among those included in the book are Sidney Bechet, Louis Armstrong, James P. Johnson, Duke Ellington, Chick Webb, Fats Waller, Lionel Hampton, the Jimmie Lunceford band, Count Basie and his band, Bessie Smith, and Leadbelly.

268. Keepnews, Orin, and Bill Grauer. A Pictorial History of Jazz: People and Places from New Orleans to Modern Jazz. Rev. ed. New York: Crown Publishers, 1966. 282 pp. photographs. index.

> Organized into twenty-one sections, each preceded by appropriate narrative, this book contains hundreds of photographs of numerous jazz musicians who contributed to the development and making of jazz music from its beginnings to the middle 1960s. The contents range from the early bands and individuals of New Orleans—The Original Creole Orchestra (1912), The Onward Brass Band (1913), Manual Perez's Band of 1915, Joe Oliver, Freddie Keppard and others—to 1960s artists such as Albert Ayler, Eric Dolphy, Roland Kirk, Charles Lloyd, John Coltrane, and Ornette Coleman. The photographs are graced with informative captions.
>
> Reviews: Choice 4:1390 F '68; Orkester Journalen 37:15 Jy/Au '69

269. Rose, Al, and Edmund Souchon. New Orleans Jazz: Family Album. Baton Rouge: Louisiana State University Press, 1967. viii, [338] pp. photographs. index.

> In this volume, approximately six hundred candid and posed photographs of individual New Orleans jazz musicians and groups are presented, and are accompanied by brief and appropriate biographical data. Dating from the turn of the century, the photographs are organized in six sections, each section preceded by an introductory narrative. The index is both extensive and valuable.
>
> Reviews: Antiquarian Bookman 40:2264 D 18 '67; Booklist 64:670 F 15 '68; Choice 5:495 Ju '68; Downbeat 35:39 F 8 '68; Ethnomusicology 12:295 '68; International Musician 66:18 Ja

269. Rose (continued)

'68; Jazz Journal 21:9 Ja '68; Jazz Journal 21:23 Mr '68; Jazz Monthly 14:30 Ap '68; Jazz Report 6:8 '68; Jazz Report 6:26 '68; Library Journal 93:755 F 15 '68; Melody Maker 43:8 Mr 30 '68; Musical Times 109:544 Ju '68; Music Journal 26:78 '68; Notes 25:33 S '68; Orkester Journalen 37:2 Ja '69; Publishers Weekly 192:52 O 2 '67; Second Line 19:15 Ja/F '68

270. Spitzer, David D. Jazzshots: A Photographic Essay. Miami: Zerkim Press, 1978. unpaged. photographs.

This is a well laid-out collection of 193 striking and exemplary candid photographs of mostly modern jazz greats and near-greats, among them Reggie Workman, Archie Shepp, Sam Rivers, Joe Henderson, Anthony Braxton, Jackie McLean, Leroy Jenkins, Count Basie, Betty Carter, Cecil Taylor, Sun Ra, Horace Silver, Herbie Hancock, and Billy Taylor.
Reviews: Jazz Journal International 33:17 Ap '80; Radio Free Jazz 21:8 Mr '80

271. Stock, Dennis. Jazz Street. Introduction and commentary by Nat Hentoff. Garden City, N.Y.: Doubleday & Co., 1960. 63 pp. photographs.

Contained in this book are 130 photographs divided into three groups titled "First Bar," "The Itinerant," and "Faces." The first group includes photographs of some of the artists who contributed to the beginnings of jazz (e.g., the Silver Leaf Brass Band) or whose artistry in another genre influenced its development (e.g., Mahalia Jackson). The second group of photographs all feature Louis Armstrong. The third and largest group includes photographs of such jazz greats as Roy Eldridge, Earl Hines, Sidney Bechet, Billie Holiday, Oscar Pettiford, Mary Lou Williams, and others. The book is concluded by a brief commentary that identifies the subjects of the photographs and presents other pertinent information.
Reviews: Book Review Digest N '61; Guardian p10 N 25 '60; Library Journal 85:3447 '60; New Yorker 36:208 O 15 '60; New York Times Book Review p7 S 11 '60; Notes 18:61 D '60; Times Literary Supplement p840 D 20 '60

272. Wilmer, Valerie. The Face of Black Music. Introduction by Archie Shepp. New York: Da Capo Press, 1976. unpaged. photographs.

This work is a photographic documentary of moments in jazz history that range, as the introduction points out, from backwoods "sukey joints" to avant-garde performances. The photographer's skill has not only captured "the essence of the music" called jazz, but also reveals the truth of her contention that, "For me, Ornette Coleman has only to play a handful of notes on the saxophone, Aretha Franklin to stand up and do it, and an entire Beethoven symphony is wiped away" (p. [xi]). Keith Jarrett, Coleman Hawkins, Wilbur Ware, Cecil Taylor, Harry Carney, Tadd Dameron, Sonny Payne,

272. Wilmer (continued)

B. B. King, Gus Cannon, and others are caught in candid shots. New Orleans "second line" participants, street singers in song, country guitar players pickin', musicians shaving, talking, at rest, are all parts of this photographer's larger picture of the jazz world.

Reviews: Cadence 2:15 D '76; Coda 152:28 D '76; Jazz Journal International 30:14 F '77; Jazz Journal International 30:37 Jy '77; Jazz Magazine 250:6 D '76; Jazz Report 9:20 '77; Kliatt Paperback Book Guide 11:34 Winter '77; Library Journal 102:204 Ja 15 '77; Musical Times 118:1013 D '77; Music Journal 35:18 Ja '77; Punch 272:556 Mr 30 '77; Reprint Bulletin—Book Reviews 22:28 '77; Sing Out 25:49 '77

# XIII

# Pedagogy

273. Coker, Jerry. Improvising Jazz. Forewords by Stan Kenton and Gunther Schuller. Englewood Cliffs, N.J.: Prentice-Hall, 1964. xii, 115 pp. illustrations, musical examples. appendixes.

> The chapter headings in this book indicate the scope of the material covered: 1) Basic Tools, 2) An Introduction to Melody, 3) The Rhythm Section, 4) The First Playing Session, 5) Development of the Ear, 6) Further Study of Chord Types, 7) Swing, 8) Diminished Scales, 9) Analysis and Development of Melody, 10) Chord Superimposition, and 11) Functional Harmony. Each chapter includes a cohesive presentation of concepts together with several specific exercises or projects dealing with the subject of that chapter. The appendixes also contain useful information concerning aesthetic criteria for the evaluation of a jazz artist, possible chord voicings, alternate chord progressions for the blues, common chord progressions, and a list of often-used tunes.
> Reviews: Downbeat 31:40 O 8 '64; Ethnomusicology 9:201 '65; International Musician 63:22 Mr '65; Jazz 4:16 '65; Saturday Review of Literature p40 D 26 '64; Second Line 15:24 '64

274. Coker, Jerry. Listening to Jazz. Forewords by Jamey Aebersol and David Baker. Englewood Cliffs, N.J.: Prentice-Hall, 1978. xii, 148 pp. glossary.

> For researchers new to jazz, this book is basic to the understanding of the genre from its beginnings to its "free form" manifestations.

274. Coker (continued)

An elementary approach to the perception of jazz structure and improvization, its explanations of various jazz concepts—i.e., "chorus," "fill," "playing outside," "side slipping,"—are clear, precise, informative, and useful. The author discusses such topics as the nature of the jazz tune and the nature of improvization, making distinctions that are important to the scholar and the researcher; distinctions such as between improvization and "change running," and between improvization on "contemporary tunes" and during "free form" performances provide definitions that" can make jazz research less cumbersome and more precise. For researchers, the author's "Criteria for Appreciation" section can serve as research criteria; the entire book can serve as a basis for an organized approach to investigation in this area of study. In focusing on the most important and the indispensable concerns of jazz study, the author has presented a brief and rather definitive list of the greatest jazz improvizers. To guide and to facilitate listening, short discographies are scattered appropriately throughout the book, and a list of "Dealers in Discontinued Records and Tapes" is provided at the end. The absence of an index should not hamper users.
Reviews: Choice 15:1064 O '78; High Fidelity 28:168 N '78; Jazz Journal International 31:20 O '78; Kliatt Paperback Book Guide 12:54 Fall '78; Musical Times 120:223 Mr '79; Music Journal 36:40 S '78; Orkester Journalen 47:2 Mr '79

275. Dankworth, Avril. Jazz: An Introduction to Its Musical Basis. London: Oxford University Press, 1968. xi, 89 pp. musical examples. appendixes. index.

Identifying jazz as being of a "minority interest—just like classical music," Dankworth has outlined what he refers to as the rules and the "musical basis" of jazz music. He treats, in turn, chords, forms, scales, rhythm, "tonal effects," and styles, giving concrete written musical examples as he proceeds, and explaining such concepts as blue notes, syncopation, muting, and other effects, techniques, and procedures of jazz. The "Index of Technical Terms, Styles, Etc.," brief though it is, will be found to be a useful aid, containing such terms as "comp," "flutter," "skiffle," and "vamp." This is a good and basic, albeit brief, introduction to jazz music, designed for the ordinary musical reader, music students, and teachers of music.
Reviews: Antiquarian Bookman 42:1074 S 30 '68; Choice 5:1315 '68; Jazz Report 7:30 '70; Making Music 69:17 Spring '69; Music in Education 32:258 '68; Musical Opinion 94:139 D '70; Music Teacher 47:19 N '68; Notes 25:743 Ju '69

276. Gridley, Mark C. Jazz Styles. Englewood Cliffs, N.J.: Prentice-Hall, 1978. x, 421 pp. photographs, drawings, musical examples. appendixes. glossary. discography. supplementary readings. index.

This text is a comprehensive introduction to the significant styles of jazz that emerged between 1917 and the 1970s. It is the first

276.  Gridley (continued)

detailed and systematic approach to the understanding, appreciation
and perception of jazz music.  In five parts, the work covers "Basics
of Jazz," "Premodern Jazz," "Modern Jazz, the Early 1940s to the
Early 1960s," "The Early 1960s to the Late 1970s," and presents a
four-part appendix which discusses the "Elements of Music,"
technical matters, the author's personal feelings about describing
jazz, and a "Guide to Record Buying."  While the book is designed as
a text, and while its emphasis is on the roles, contributions, and
innovations of jazz musicians, the book stands as a valuable review
of significant jazz literature.   While the text is didactic, it is
equally valuable for novice jazz researchers as for teachers of
undergraduate jazz classes.  Its definitions and its analyses and
delineations of the roles of musicians, groups, and procedures have
significant implications for future directions in jazz research.
Reviews:  Billboard 90:34 Au 26 '78; Cadence 4:14 My '78;
Choice 15:1065 O '78; Coda 176:24 D 1 '80; High Fidelity 28:168 N
'78; Jazz Journal International 32:36 Ja '79; Jazz Magazine 3:57
'78; Musical Times 119:1049 D '78; Reference Services Review
6:14 Jy '78; Village Voice 23:66 Jy 3 '78

277.  Nanry, Charles.  The Jazz Text.  Foreword by Dan Morgenstern.  New
York:  Van Nostrand Reinhold Co., 1979.  x, 276 pp.  photographs.
bibliography.  index.

This general introduction to jazz for the beginning student is an
ideal text for a course that is based largely on listening, and will
serve as a guide for the beginning jazz researcher.   It is an
instructive work that presents a minimum of historical and
biographical information while emphasizing the forces that shaped
the music.  The work's eight chapters are presented in three larger
sections:   An Introduction to Jazz; The Emergence and
Development of Jazz; and Jazz Research.  The third part contains
two chapters—"A Student's Guide to Research" and "Jazz and All
That Sociology," the two together serving as a general introduction
for the scholar new to jazz research.
Reviews:  Jazz Forum 71:57 '81; Library Journal 104:1061 My 1
'79; Music Educators Journal 66:82 Ap '80; Orkester Journalen
48:2 F '80; Reference Services Review 9:43 Ap '81

278.  Ricigliano, Daniel A.  Popular and Jazz Harmony.  New York:  Donato
Publishing, Co., 1967.  ix, 194 pp.  appendixes.  indexes.

This text is designed to "illustrate and explain the principles of
harmonic movement in the popular and jazz idiom" (p. vii).  It is
divided into three main sections, which cover "Fundamentals,"
"Harmonic Patterns and Progressions," and "Advanced, Creative and
Other Material."  These sections are broken into forty-two chapters
that treat such topics as circle sequential patterns, moving line
patterns, substitute alternate chords, modulation, blues,
embellishing and extension patterns, popular and jazz harmonic
movement, voice leading, revising lead sheet chord symbols, and

278. Ricigliano (continued)

harmonizing an original melody. The general index makes the book useful as a reference work.
Reviews: International Musician 66:19 Jy '67

279. Terry, Clark, and Phil Rizzo. The Interpretation of the Jazz Language. Cleveland: M. A. S. Publishing Co., 1977. 209 pp. musical examples.

The primary purpose of this book is to train novice jazz musicians in the rhythmic interpretation of notation in the jazz idiom. The underlying triple division of the beat is notated, and comparisons are made between classical and jazz interpretations of basic rhythmic patterns. In addition, jazz articulation of various note symbols is explained with the goal of teaching jazz phrasing. The majority of the book consists of two- to four-measure patterns, intended to be sung, in which rhythms are combined with pitches. Each pattern is provided with scat syllables and is notated both as it would be seen and as it should be interpreted. In the last half of the book, patterns commonly used by the various instrumental sections are presented; included are patterns for saxophone, trombone, trumpet, and the rhythm section.
Reviews: Instrumentalist 33:105 My '79; Music Journal 36:40 S '78

280. Tirro, Frank. Jazz: A History. New York: W. W. Norton & Co., 1977. xix, 457 pp. photographs, charts, musical examples. bibliography. discography. glossary. index.

This text treats the history of jazz from its beginnings to the free jazz of Ornette Coleman. It includes chapters on African music, black American music, ragtime, and the various manifestations of jazz during its approximately seventy years of existence—the period 1900-1917, the 1920s, "The Big Band Concept" and the Swing Era, bebop, cool jazz and hard bop, and free jazz.
Reviews: American Musicological Society Journal 31:535 Fall '78; American Music Teacher 29:36 '79; Best Sellers 37:346 F '78; Booklist 74:518 N 15 '77; Cadence 4:23 Ap '78; Choice 15:411 My '78; Instrumentalist 23:20 Ap '78; Jazz Magazine 2:56 '78; Jazz Studies 5:98 '78; Kirkus Reviews 45:1085 O 1 '77; Library Journal 103:567 Mr 1 '78; Musical Quarterly 64:407 Jy '78; Music Educators Journal 65:67 Ap '79; New Boston Review 5:9 S '79; Notes 35:885 Ju '79; Pan Pipes 70:26 '78; Publishers Weekly 212:129 S 12 '77; Radio Free Jazz 20:14 Ja '79; Reference Services Review 6:14 Jy '78; Village Voice 23:66 Jy 3 '78

281. Wiskerchen, George. Developmental Techniques for the School Dance Band Musician. Foreword by Stan Kenton. Preface by Charles Suber. Boston: Berkelee Press Publications, 1961. 212 pp. musical examples. appendixes.

This is a well-conceived and carefully prepared manual for musicians and teachers of high school dance bands. College level

281. Wiskerchen (continued)

> students and teachers might also find it useful. The author's systematic approach can be seen in the sequence of the book's chapter titles: I. "Problem and Its Approach," II. "Techniques for Developing the Entire Band," III. "Technical Problems of the Saxophone Section," IV. "Technical Problems of the Brass Section," V. "Technical Problems of the Rhythm Section," VI. "Improvisation," and VII. "Random Afterthoughts and Hints." Each chapter contains a narrative discussion of its subject, including comments on function, technique, common problems, and other pertinent matters; suggested exercises, explanations, and instructions for special effects are included where appropriate. Also included are a selected bibliography and discography, a "Glossary of Dance Band Terminology," and a "Glossary of Dance Band Symbols."
> Reviews: Downbeat 28:49 S 28 '61; Music Educators Journal 48:109 n2 '61

## OTHER

282. De Lerma, Dominique-René, ed. Black Music in Our Culture: Curricula Ideas on the Subjects, Materials and Problems. Kent, Ohio: Kent University Press, 1970. 263 pp. appendixes. index.

> This publication summarizes the presentations and the ideas that emerged from the first black music seminar held at Indiana University in 1969. It contains writings and discussions relating to curriculum, concert music, jazz, dance, teaching materials, administration, funding, and staffing as they relate to the broad field of black music. The question of defining black music is touched upon throughout the work, and is central to the section entitled "Black Composers and the Avant Garde." Among the book's twenty contributors are Lena McLin, Hale Smith, Verna Arvey, Nicholas V. D'Angelo, Eileen Southern, Richard Turner, and O. Anderson Fuller. The book's seven appendixes, taken as a unit, themselves constitute a sourcebook, containing as they do selective lists of scores, recordings, films, books, and articles, along with "Sample Curricular Syllabi" and a list of the individuals who attended the conference.
> Reviews: American Anthropologist 73:902 Au '71; American Music Teacher 20:38 n5 '71; Choice 8:74 Mr '71; Jazz Journal 24:30 Mr '71; Journal of American Folklore 84:357-358 n333 '71; Matrix 92:11 Ap '71; Music Educators Journal 58:91-92+ N '71; Music Journal 29:66-67 N ' 71

283. Standifer, James A., and Barbara Reeder. Source Book of African and Afro-American Materials for Music Educators. Contemporary Music Project. Washington, D.C.: Music Educators National Conference, 1972. xvii, 147 pp. musical examples. appendix. bibliography.

> This resource book for teachers is designed to strengthen the study of African and Afro-American musics through the "common ele-

283. Standifer (continued)

ments" approach advocated by the Contemporary Music Project. It is useful as an introductory research tool, and is also suitable as an introductory study to African and Afro-American musics as areas of specialization. The bibliography lists books on African music, Afro-American music, poetry, biography, research materials, collections, tapes, films, and publishers of reprints. The work also includes a list of black musicians and a discography. The list is divided into such categories as "Concert Music," "Performing Organizations," "Vaudeville and Musicals," and "Motion Picture and Television Composers."

Reviews: American Music Teacher 22:41:42 n6 '73; Australian Journal of Music Education n11:64 O '72; Ethnomusicology 18:321-322 n2 '74; Jazz and Blues 2:27-28 F '73; Journal of Research in Music Education 21:283-284 n3 '73; Music Teacher 52:25 Jy '73; Nutida Music 17:36-39 n4 '73/'74; School Media Quarterly 2:159 Winter '74

# XIV

# Periodicals

284. <u>Annual Review of Jazz Studies</u>. Dan Morgenstern, Charles Nanry, and David A. Cayer, eds. Newark, N.J.: Institute of Jazz Studies, 1982+. annual. each vol. approx. 160 pp. musical examples, charts.

This journal succeeds the <u>Journal of Jazz Studies,</u> and is the only jazz journal published in the United States that is devoted to serious jazz scholarship. Its wide variety of articles includes technical writings, essays on jazz history and analysis, interviews with jazz musicians, bio-discographical and sociological studies, book reviews, and indexes and registers of various kinds.

285. <u>Black Music Research Journal</u>. Samuel A. Floyd, Jr., ed. Nashville, Tenn.: Fisk University Institute for Research in Black American Music, 1980+. annual. each vol. approx. 110 pp. musical examples, charts.

This journal favors articles that attempt to break new ground in black music philosophy, aesthetics, analysis, and research. It is the "yearbook" of the Fisk Institute, and carries only articles generated or solicited by the Institute. Lengthy reviews of important books in the field are regular features.

286. <u>Black Music Research Newsletter</u>. Samuel A. Floyd, Jr., Orin Moe et al., eds. Nashville, Tenn.: Fisk University Institute for Research in Black American Music, 1976+. semi-annual.

286. BMR Newsletter (continued)

> Brief articles of one thousand to 2,500 words are carried in this
> four- to twelve-page bulletin. The articles address current and
> historical events and questions, and report on activities and
> institutions related to black music. Contributions are wideranging,
> treating Latin-American connections and black European
> composers, concert music by black composers, as well as blues,
> jazz, ragtime, and other Afro-American musical genres. Provision
> is made for readers to publish and receive answers to research
> questions.

287. The Black Perspective in Music. Eileen Southern, ed. Cambria Heights,
N.Y.:   The Foundation for Research in the Afro-American Creative
Arts, Inc., 1973+.   published semi-annually.   photographs, musical
examples. annual index.

> Regularly published in this journal are research articles, essays,
> interviews, and other features on black music and musicians, as well
> as items relating to the social and cultural aspects of the black
> musical experience in America and abroad.   Regular features
> include reviews of books, dissertations, periodicals, musical
> compositions, and recordings, as well as commentary on
> contemporary events.

# XV

# Anthologies and Collections of Printed Music

## FOLK

288. Carawan, Guy, and Candie Carawan. We Shall Overcome. New York: Oak Publications, 1963. 112 pp.

Compiled for the Student Non-violent Coordinating Committee, this collection contains the words, the notated melodies, and the chord symbols of Southern freedom songs from the early 1960s. It is a "kind of short history of many of the major developments and events of the non-violent movement in the South" (p. 7). The songs are those of mass meetings, prayer vigils, freedom rides, sit-ins, marches, and other activities and events of the movement. "We Shall Overcome," "We Shall Not Be Moved," "You'd Better Leave Segregation Alone," "Dog, Dog," "Get Your Rights, Jack," "If You Miss Me from the Back of the Bus," and "Woke Up This Morning with My Mind on Freedom" are among the forty-six songs included.

289. Gellert, Lawrence, comp. Negro Songs of Protest. Foreword by Wallingford Riegger. Arrangements by Elie Siegmeister. New York: American Music League, 1936. 47 pp.

These twenty-four songs, "reflecting as they do the contemporary environment . . . are human documents," embodying "the living voice of the otherwise inarticulate resentment against injustice. . . . They speak now mildly, now sarcastically, now angrily— but always in a firm and earnest manner" (p. 6). Included are "Scottsboro," "Lice in Jail," "Ah's de Man," "Wake Up Boys," and "Cause I'm a Nigger."

290. Hallowell, Emily, ed.   Calhoun Plantation Songs.   2nd ed. 1907.
Reprint. New York: AMS Press, 1976. 75 pp. index.

This is a compilation of songs that were collected at the Calhoun
Colored School in Calhoun, Alabama.   The editor states in the
preface that she has tried to keep the written version of the songs
as close as possible to the way they were actually sung by the
original performers.   The songs appear in a variety of textures and
arrangement  styles,  the  most  prevalent  of  which  are  1)  a
predominantly four-part setting, some with brief solos in the verses,
and 2) a four-part setting of the chorus with either a solo verse or a
call-and-response type of verse setting.   Several songs consist of an
unaccompanied melody with text.   The majority of the songs
included here do not appear in other such collections of the period.

291. Jackson, Bruce, ed. and comp.   Wake Up Dead Man:   Afro-American
Worksongs from Texas Prisons.   Cambridge:  Harvard University Press,
1972. xxii, 326 pp. photographs. glossary. appendixes. index.

Song texts and music specimens from at least three Texas prisons
are presented and discussed in this book.   The collector and editor
points out that they are "the property of black inmates exclusively,
and  they  are  clearly  in  a  tradition  going  back  beyond  the
importation of the first Negro slaves to the Virginia colony in 1631"
(p. xv).   The book's introductory material includes the comments of
"The Singers on Their Songs" and an explanation of "The Texas
Convict Worksong Tradition."   The body of the work contains sixty-
five solo and group song texts and music specimens on "Cotton and
Cane," axe songs (crosscutting and logging), and flatweeding songs,
all interspersed with the author's comments and explanations.   The
appendixes include "A Note on Nicknames" and an explanation of
the responsorial patterns found in the songs.   The index is an "Index
of Names" of Texas prison inmates, other performers mentioned in
the text, and authors of works discussed or cited in the text.
    Reviews:   AB Bookman's Weekly 75:661 Au 27 '73; Booklist
    69:224 N 1 '72; Books and Bookmen 18:134 Ju '73; Choice 9:160 F
    '73; Ethnomusicology 17:548-549 n3 '73; Jazz & Blues 3:11 S '73;
    Journal of American Folklore 86:305-307 n341 '73; Journal of
    American Folklore 87:182 Ap '74; Journal of Negro History
    58:212 Ap '73; Library Journal 97:3593 N 1 '72; Musical Times
    114:604 Ju '73; New Yorker 48:74 Jy 8 '72; Publishers Weekly
    204:83 O 1 '73; Times Literary Supplement p852 Jy 27 '73

292. Johnson, J. Rosamund, ed. and arr.   Rolling Along in Song:   A
Chronological Survey of American Negro Music, With Eighty-Seven
Arrangements of Negro Songs, Including Ring Shouts, Spirituals, Work
Songs, Plantation Ballads, Chain-Gang, Jail-House, and Minstrel Songs,
Street Cries, and Blues. New York: Viking Press, 1937. 224 pp.

This anthology of eighty-seven arrangements of both authentic and
not-so-authentic  Afro-American  folksongs  includes  seven  ring
shouts, thirteen spirituals, twelve jubilees, eight "Plantation Ballads
and Love Pastimes," six minstrel songs," six "jail-house songs," five

152

292. Johnson (continued)

street cries, five "blues fragments," one blues, eight chain-gang songs, one "Negro Love Song," and one excerpt from George Gershwin's Porgy and Bess. Among the titles in this comprehensive collection are "Many Thousand Gone," "Hush, Somebody Callin' My Name," "Now, Let Me Fly," "Listen to the Mockin' Bird," "In the Evenin' By the Moonlight," "Shoo Fly, Don't Bother Me," "Shortnin' Bread," "John Henry," "Watermelon," "Stagolee," "Them Lonesome Moanin' Blues," "Lit'l Gal," and others. The twenty-seven page Introduction contains notes on the song categories, on some of the songs themselves, and on the characteristics of Afro-American music. This is a ready-made source for genre comparisons, notwithstanding questions about the reliability and validity of some of its entries.

293. Kennedy, R. Emmett. Mellows: A Chronicle of Unknown Singers. New York: Albert and Charles Boni, Publishers, 1925. 185 pp. drawings.

This collection of "himes," "ballets," "mellows," and "make-up" songs includes street cries (six), work songs (five), folk songs, and spirituals totaling forty-eight, several of which cannot be found elsewhere. Narrative accompanies the songs throughout.
Reviews: Bookman 62:490 D '25; Boston Evening Transcript p2 D 26 '25; Literary Review p3 D 5 '25; New Republic 45:169 D 30 '25; New York Times p19 D 20 '25; New York Tribune p7 D 20 '25; New York World p6m Ja 10 '26; Saturday Review of Literature 2:54 O '26

294. Landeck, Beatrice. Echoes of Africa in Folk Songs of the Americas. Instrumental arrangements by Milton Kaye. Translation of lyrics by Margaret Marks. New York: David McKay Co., 1961. 184 pp. drawings. discography. bibliography. index.

This collection contains the words and the music of ninety-two folk songs from Africa, Haiti, Trinidad, Cuba, Puerto Rico, Mexico, Brazil, Venezuela, Panama, and the United States. All of the songs are purported to contain African musical survivals. Those of the United States include Creole songs, street cries, spirituals, shouts, work songs, blues songs, and minstrel songs. The book is divided into four parts, with fifteen subsections, each introduced by narrative comments on its subject. Pertinent and useful comments on the music and the text precede each song.
Reviews: Booklist 57:601 Ju 1 '61; Library Journal 86:2108 Ju 1 '61; New York Times Book Review p21 Ju 25 '61; Notes 18:584 S '61; Western Folklore 22:281-282 n4 '63

295. Niles, John J. Singing Soldiers. New York: Charles Scribner's Sons, 1927. x, 171 pp.

This book contains running commentary on the words and the music of songs sung by black American soldiers during World War I.

295. Niles (continued)

Perceived by the author/editor as "a kind of folk music, brought up to date and adapted to the war situation," the songs were recorded by this white pilot whose duty carried him to "practically every area occupied by American troups" (p. ix).
    Reviews: Booklist 24:15 O '27; Boston Evening Transcript p4 Ap 23 '27; Cleveland Open Shelf p65 My '27; Independent 118:400 Ap 9 '27; Library Journal 52:423 '27; Literary Review p2 Ap 9 '27; New Republic 51:76 Ju 8 '27; New York Herald Tribune Books p15 My 22 '27; New York Times Book Review p7 Ju 12 '27; Pittsburgh Monthly Bulletin 32:511 O '27; Saturday Review of Literature 143:640 Ap 23 '27; Spectator 138:765 Ap 30 '27; Springfield Republican p7F Jy 3 '27; Times Literary Supplement p358 My 19 '27

296. Work, Frederick J., ed. Folk Songs of the American Negro. Introduction and preface by John W. Work, Jr. 1st ed., rev. Nashville, Tenn.: Work Bros. & Hart Co., 1907. 63 pp. index.

This is a collection of sixty-two "plantation songs," of which many, at the time of their publication, were the rarest of Afro-American spirituals. Collected by the editor in his search for authentic songs of syncopated, religious songs, they have numbered among them: "A Little Talk with Jesus," "By and By," "Going to Shout All Over God's Heaven," "I'm So Glad," "Listen to the Lambs," "Live A-Humble," "No Hiding Place," "O Mary Don't You Weep, Don't You Mourn," "Plenty Good Room," "Steal Away," "Swing Low," and "Were You There."

297. Work, John W., ed. American Negro Songs and Spirituals: A Comprehensive Collection of 230 Folk Songs, Religious and Secular. New York: Crown Publishers, Bonanza Books, 1940. 259 pp. bibliography. index.

This collection of 230 Afro-American folk songs is preceded by forty-six pages of valuable commentary on their origins and on the various folk music genres—the spiritual, the blues, work songs, and social and miscellaneous songs. The commentary and the songs reflect the best of the Afro-American folksong scholarship of the period.
    Reviews: Booklist 37:289 Mr 1 '41; New Republic 105:164 Au 4 '41; New York Herald Tribune Books p4 F 9 '41; Saturday Review of Literature 23:16 Ja 11 '41

## RELIGIOUS

298. Allen, William Francis, Charles Pickard Ware, and Lucy McKim Garrison, eds. Slave Songs of the United States. 1867. Reprint. The Black Heritage Collection. Freeport, N.Y.: Books for Libraries Press, 1971. xxxviii, 115 pp.

298.  Allen (continued)

>   This collection consists of 136 songs that were collected, during the
>   Civil War, from black folk in the southern United States.
>   Containing mostly religious music, with some secular songs
>   interspersed, it is a result of the first known efforts to collect and
>   preserve the folk music of black Americans. The book is divided
>   into five parts, corresponding to the five sections of the slave-
>   holding territory: Southeastern slave states, Northern seaboard
>   slave states, inland slave states, Gulf states, and the Mississippi
>   valley area. In his lengthy preface, the principal editor discusses
>   performance practices, the slave method of originating the songs,
>   and considerations relating to dialect; an early description of the
>   Shout is also included. The songs are presented without
>   accompaniment of any kind—only the melodies and the words are
>   included. Commentary occasionally appears with individual
>   examples.

299.  Ballanta–(Taylor), Nicholas George Julius. Saint Helena Island
      Spirituals: Recorded and Transcribed at Penn Normal, Industrial and
      Agricultural School. Introduction by George Foster Peabody. New
      York: G. Schirmer, 1925. xx, 93 pp.

>   This anthology contains 114 spirituals, 103 of whose melodies were
>   transcribed by Ballanta-Taylor on Saint Helena Island in South
>   Carolina; the remaining songs are also contained in other
>   contemporary anthologies. The spirituals appear in one of three
>   types of settings: unaccompanied, single-line melody; call-and-
>   response format with the responses in four-part harmony; and four-
>   part chorale style throughout. Of equal importance to the spirituals
>   themselves is the foreword by Ballanta-Taylor, who was a native of
>   Sierra Leone, Africa. It consists of an explication of the rhythmic,
>   melodic, cadential, scalar and harmonic characteristics of African
>   music.

300.  Brown, William W., comp. The Anti-Slavery Harp: A Collection of
      Songs for Anti-Slavery Meetings. Boston: Bela Marsh, 1848. 48 pp.
      index.

>   This small book contains the texts of forty-eight emancipation
>   hymns; many include the title of the tune to which they were sung.
>   A few of the texts are also accompanied by such information as the
>   name of the person to whom they are dedicated or a brief
>   description of the circumstances in which they were composed.

301.  Cleveland, J. Jefferson and Verolga Nix, eds. Songs of Zion.
      Supplemental Resources 12. Nashville, Tenn.: Abingdon, 1981. xvii, 252
      pp. index.

>   Consisting primarily of songs from the black religious tradition, this
>   collection contains 250 pieces, ranging from traditional spirituals to
>   contemporary gospel songs. This important work, nondenomi-
>   national both in character and in content, includes the music and

301.  Cleveland (continued)

> words to songs by Charles Albert Tindley, Thomas A. Dorsey, Lucie
> Campbell, Mahalia Jackson, Lena McLin, Walter Hawkins, and a
> variety of other black writers of religious song.  Hymns by white
> writers such as Lowell Mason are also included; they are sometimes
> arranged to conform to black musical style.  Unlike many hymnals,
> this one carries considerable narrative on interpretation and
> performance, black religious history, and the history of black
> religious song.  Each of the book's four sections of song—i.e., of
> hymns, spirituals, gospel song, and service music—is, in fact,
> preceded by appropriate explanatory narrative.  The songs are
> indexed by classification and by first lines and common titles.
> Unfortunately for scholars, the book lacks a composer index.  This
> work, the only one of its kind, is a valuable sourcebook for scholars
> studying the general field of black religious music.

302.  Dett, R. Nathaniel, ed.  Religious Folk-Songs of the Negro, As Sung at
Hampton Institute.  6th ed.  Hampton, Va.:  Hampton Institute Press,
1927. xxvii, 236 pp. indexes.

> Contained here are more than 150 Afro-American spirituals,
> arranged as they were sung at Hampton Institute between 1868 and
> 1926 and, perhaps, beyond.  The songs are grouped in categories such
> as "Hymns of Admonition," "Hymns of Aspiration," "Hymns of
> Penitence," "Hymns of Praise," and "Hymns of the Second
> Coming."  The three indexes, which appear immediately following
> the foreword, are:  "Index of Subjects," "Index of Titles," and "Index
> of First Lines."

303.  Fischer, William Arms, ed.  Seventy Negro Spirituals.  Boston:  Oliver
Ditson Co.; New York:  Charles H. Ditson & Co.; Chicago:  Lyon and
Healy, 1926. xix, 212 pp. bibliography.

> This collection of selected Afro-American sacred songs represents
> an early effort to treat the spirituals in a scholarly manner.  The
> editor's opening comments are at once a review of the literature on
> the spiritual from 1856; a survey account of the gradual public
> recognition of the spiritual as authentic and aesthetically valid
> Negro folk song and the transformation of the purely folk spiritual
> into arranged solo song and choral composition by such musicians as
> Harry T. Burleigh, Robert Nathaniel Dett, Carl Diton, J. Rosamund
> Johnson, Roland Hayes, and Paul Robeson; and an analysis of the
> musical content of the songs.  The work also carries very brief
> biographical sketches of Johnson, Burleigh, and Edward Boatner,
> notes on the songs themselves, and a bibliography containing titles
> of forty-seven books and articles on the Afro-American spiritual,
> spanning the years 1856-1925.

304.  Hayes, Roland.  My Songs:  Aframerican Religious Folk Songs Arranged
and Interpreted by Roland Hayes.  Boston:  Little, Brown, and Co.,
1948. x, 128 pp.

304. Hayes (<u>continued</u>)

> This is a selective anthology of thirty tastefully arranged Afro-American spirituals organized into three "panels"—1) Events in the Old Testament, 2) Abstractions from the Teaching of Both Old and New Testaments, and 3) The Life of Christ. The songs are introduced and accompanied by valuable and informative narratives on performance practice, cultural considerations, and interpretation.
>
> Reviews:     Library Journal 73:1666 '48;  New York Herald Tribune Weekly Book Review p3 N 21 '48; New York Times Book Review p13 D 19 '48; Wilson Library Bulletin 4:212 D '48

305. Jackson, Judge. <u>The Colored Sacred Harp</u>. Rev. ed. 1934. Reprint. Montgomery, Ala.: Paragon Press, 1973. 96 pp. photographs. index.

> This is a collection of the music and the words to seventy-seven religious songs, the compiler having "composed some of the songs, added parts to others" (front matter, unpaged). Shape notes are used in the notation.

306. Johnson, James Weldon, and J. Rosamund Johnson.  <u>The Book of American Negro Spirituals, Including The Book of American Negro Spirituals and The Second Book of Negro Spirituals</u>. New York: Da Capo Press, 1942. 376 pp.

> This edition of the Johnsons' collected spirituals is a combination of the original editions that were first published separately in 1925 and 1926, and reissued in one volume by Da Capo Press in 1942. This edition of 120 Afro-American spirituals, presented in a performing edition for solo voice with piano accompaniment, is basic to the understanding of these songs. The editing is both scholarly and sensitive, and the lengthy prefaces discuss the origins, development, quality, and historical significance of the songs. The text also refers to related genres such as the work song and the shout, and explains black dialect and its use in the spirituals. Included are songs such as "Didn't My Lord Deliver Daniel," "Ev'ry Time I Feel the Spirit," "I Couldn't Hear Nobody Pray," "Steal Away to Jesus," and "Zekiel Saw the Wheel."

307. McIlhenny, E. A., comp.  <u>Befo' de War Spirituals: Words and Melodies</u>. Boston:   Christopher Publishing House, 1933.   255 pp.   photographs. index.

> This anthology contains more than one hundred spirituals, presented in dialect and four-part harmony. The twenty-two-page introduction contains notes on the white editor's view of black life in the United States during and after Reconstruction, and relates the traditional Southern white mythology that all slaves on the large plantations were "cared for in the most careful and considerate manner" (p. 12). Also presented are details of what the editor believes constituted slave life on the plantations. While admitting that "to correctly transcribe the tones of the old Negro

157

307. McIlhenny (continued)

music to written notes is quite impossible" (p. 24), the collector, with the aid of a transcriber, attempted to present the songs "exactly as they were sung or as near as the harmonies and rhythmic tones of the Negro voice can be represented by written notes" (p. 33).
Reviews: Journal of Religion 14:246 Ap '34; New York Times Book Review p5 F 11 '34

## RAGTIME

308. Blesh, Rudi, comp. Classic Piano Rags. New York: Dover Publications, 1973. xi, 364 pp. index.

This diverse and valuable collection contains "81 of the best" (cover) classic ragtime compositions of fourteen composers—Scott Joplin, Joe Jordan, Arthur Marshall, Artie Matthews, James Scott, and Tom Turpin among them. The works are reproduced with their sheet music covers. The author's introduction provides background information.
Reviews: AB Bookman's Weekly 53:1085 Mr 18 '74; Choice 11:769 '74

309. Lawrence, Vera Brodsky, ed. The Collected Works of Scott Joplin. Introduction to vol. 1 by Rudi Blesh; to vol. 2 by Carman Moore. New York: New York Public Library, 1971. each vol. approx. 315 pp. appendixes. index.

This set contains the published works of Joplin—forty-four original piano pieces, seven collaborative works, one arrangement of a rag by another composer, the School of Ragtime—6 Exercises for Piano, nine songs, and the opera Treemonisha, each complete with sheet music covers. The appendixes include a rollography and two discographies.

310. Morath, Max, comp. Giants of Ragtime. New York: Edward B. Marks Music Corp., 1971. 64 pp. photographs.

Included in this anthology are thirteen rags by Scott Joplin, Eubie Blake, Luckey Roberts, James Reese Europe, and Tom Turpin. Most of the pieces were copyrighted between 1907 and 1914.
Reviews: Coda 10:35 n9 '72

311. Morath, Max. Max Morath's Guide to Ragtime: A Collection of Ragtime Songs and Piano Solos. New York: Hollis Music, 1964. 128 pp. index.

Forty-five ragtime songs and piano solos make up this collection. Cakewalks, rag songs, and classic ragtime pieces are all included. This is a source for studying all of ragtime's varieties, with pieces by black composers Scott Joplin and Arthur Marshall, Scott Joplin

311.  Morath (continued)

   and Louis Chauvin, Tom Turpin, James T. Brymn, and—a surprise—
   Gussie Davis. This collection is useful as a broad introduction to
   the study of ragtime. Researchers will need to search out
   additional individual copies of rag songs and popular ragtime pieces
   by black composers.
   Reviews: Jazz 5:19 n4 '66

312.  Morath, Max, comp. 100 Ragtime Classics. Denver: Donn Printing Co.,
   1963. vii, 366 pp.

   More than one half of the rags in this collection were composed by
   Scott Joplin, James Scott, and Joseph Lamb; others represented
   include Tom Turpin, James Reese Europe, Eubie Blake, Arthur
   Marshall, Luckey Roberts, Artie Matthews, and Charles H. Hunter.
   The works date from 1896 to 1922. The introduction contains
   performance suggestions; no covers are included in the musical
   reproductions.

313.  Tichenor, Trebor Jay, comp. Ragtime Rarities: Complete Original
   Music for Sixty-three Piano Rags. New York: Dover Publications,
   1975. x, 305 pp. index.

   Included in this anthology are ragtime pieces written by fifty-two
   composers between 1897 and 1916. Each rag is reproduced with its
   cover. The composers represented include many who are not
   included in other similar collections, e.g., Blind Boone, Harry P.
   Guy, Charles Hunter, and Fred S. Stone; two ragtime greats, Scott
   Joplin and Tom Turpin, are omitted here. The introduction contains
   a brief history of ragtime, discussion of ragtime publishers, and an
   introduction to the various pieces in the collection.
   Reviews: Choice 13:234 Ap '76; Coda n146:29 Ap '76; Jazz
   Journal 30:40-41 Mr '77; Ragtimer p12 Ja/F '76; Reprint Bulletin
   Book Reviews 21:29 Spring '76

## BLUES

314.  Glover, Tony. Blues Harp Songbook. New York: Oak Publications,
   1975. 79 pp. photographs. phonorecord. bibliography.

   This book will serve as an introduction to blues "harp" playing,
   although it is "semi-advanced" in difficulty. It contains very brief
   biographical sketches of blues harp artists; transcriptions, in cryptic
   notation, of one recorded composition by each artist; and comments
   on the compositions. The book's front matter contains an
   introduction, a foreword, a section titled "Blues Harp Mouth Data,"
   and an explanation of the book's, and the genre's, esoteric
   notation. Will Shade's "Harmonica Blues," Sonny Terry's "Beautiful
   City" and "Harmonica Stomp," Little Walter's "Juke," and Howlin'
   Wolf's "Sitting on Top of the World" are among the twenty-one

314. Glover (continued)

   compositions included.
   Reviews: Living Blues n24:48 N/D '75

315. Handy, W. C., ed.  A Treasury of the Blues: Complete Words and Music
   of Sixty-Seven Great Songs from "Memphis Blues" to the Present Day.
   Introduction by Abbe Niles.  New York:  Charles Boni, 1949.  258 pp.
   drawings. notes.

   Originally published as Blues/An Anthology: Complete Words and Music
   of Fifty-Three Great Songs. 1926. Reprint. New York: Macmillan Co.,
   1972.

   This anthology contains sixty-four blues and "Blues Songs" plus
   three excerpts from extended compositions.  Included are
   representative pieces from the period 1912 through 1926, most of
   them having been written or arranged by Handy himself.  Among
   the other composers represented are Spencer Williams ("Basin
   Street Blues"), Clarence Williams ("Gulf Coast Blues"), and Earl
   Hines ("Boogie Woogie on St. Louis Blues").  The main body of this
   anthology is preceded by a narrative section which includes a short
   history of the blues, an explication of blues form and harmony, and
   a concise biography of W. C. Handy.  Musical examples by Handy
   are included to illustrate the text.  A Treasury of the Blues was
   published as an expanded version of Blues/An Anthology and
   contains twenty-five pieces not included in the earlier work; Blues,
   however, contains twelve blues songs which were omitted from
   A Treasury.
      Reviews:  Chicago Sunday Tribune p4 D 11 '49; New York Herald
   Tribune Book Review p4 D 11 '49; Record Changer 8:22 N '49

316. Shirley, Kay, ed.  The Book of the Blues.  Introduction by Orin
   Keepnews.  Annotations by Frank Driggs.  New York: Crown Publishers
   and Leeds Music Corp., 1963.  301 pp.  diagrams.

   From this compilation of ninety blues lead sheets, the researcher
   will be able to get started on an understanding of all aspects of the
   blues.    Containing  tunes  and  lyrics  of  blues  compositions
   copyrighted between ca. 1927 and the 1960s, the book is a good study
   source  that  can  be  used  alone  or  in  conjunction  with  recorded
   versions of the compositions. Each entry includes notes on the song
   under consideration, a discography on the song, guitar diagrams of
   chords used in the song, and the melody and lyrics of the song itself.
      Reviews:   Ethnomusicology 8:317-319 n3 '64; Jazz 3:28-29
   Mr/Ap '64; Library Journal 88:3625 O 1 '63; Saturday Review
   47:65 Ju 13 '64

## CONCERT MUSIC

317. Patterson, Willis, comp.  Anthology of Art Songs by Black American
   Composers.  Preface by George Shirley.  Introduction by Wendell P.

317. Patterson (continued)

Whalum. New York:  Edward B. Marks Corp., 1977.  xi, 148 pp.

This collection of forty-two art songs by twenty-four black
American composers is one of only two such collections that have
been published.  The composers whose works are included range
from those who were active in the 1920s and 1930s, such as Florence
Price (1888-1953) and Cecil Cohen (1894-1967), to younger
composers, such as Maurice McCall (b. 1943) and Charles Lloyd, Jr.
(b. 1948).  Among the most prominent composers included are Hale
Smith, Undine Moore, George Walker, and Olly Wilson.  The songs,
which are settings of poems by such writers as Claude McKay,
Langston Hughes, Paul Lawrence Dunbar, Alexander Pushkin,
Robert Browning, and others, are of varying degrees of difficulty,
some being "difficult and challenging."  Accompanying parts are
scored for the piano, although other instruments—the cello (Dorothy
Moore) and percussion (Wilson)—are used in a few isolated cases.
Together, these pieces make up a high-quality collection of songs
that represent several of the idioms in which black American
composers have worked over the past forty-odd years.  The front
matter includes brief but informative biographical sketches of the
composers whose works comprise the anthology.

# XVI

# Records and
# Record Collections

318. <u>Recorded Anthology of American Music</u>. New York: New World Records, 1975+.

> This collection consists of more than one hundred discs containing all forms of music produced in America from the 1770s to the present decade. Comprising concert and recital music, marches, folk music, jazz, and all varieties of popular music, the work comes in "double-fold album packages, with 500 pages of liner notes, bibliographies, discographies, and original American artwork on the covers," and offers "extensive information on the history and the music" (Davis, Elizabeth A., <u>Index to the New World Recorded Anthology of American Music</u> (New York: Norton, 1981), p. viii). Black music is fairly well represented in the first one hundred records produced; compositions by composers as diverse as Francis Johnson, Perry Bradford, Hale Smith, Alton Adams, J. Rosamund Johnson, Turner Layton, Sam Lucas, Charles Mingus, and George Russell are performed by an equally diverse group of performers that includes Duke Ellington, Dizzy Gillespie, Earl Hines, the Holiness Singers, Paul Robeson, Roland Hayes, Marian Anderson, the Soul Stirrers, Golden Gate Quartet, Bunk Johnson, Thelonius Monk, Clifford Brown, and others, including a large number of jazz sidemen.

## *FOLK*

319. Afro-American Blues and Game Songs. Washington, D.C.; Library of
Congress, Music Division Recording Laboratory. AFS L4. One disc.
Notes by Alan Lomax.

> Twenty game songs and four blues songs are the contents of this
> album.   They were field-recorded at locations in Mississippi,
> Arkansas, Texas, Alabama, and New York, and include "Shortnin'
> Bread," "Old Uncle Rabbit," "Two White Horses," and other songs.

320. The Great Jug Bands, 1926-1934.   Jersey City, N.J.:   Historical
Records. HLP-36. Produced by Arnold S. Caplin. One disc.

> Included here are recorded performances of Jed Davenport and His
> Beale Street Jug Band, Phillips' Louisville Jug Band, Cannon's Jug
> Stompers, Earl McDonald's Original Louisville Jug Band, and the
> Memphis Jug Band, performing sixteen blues, stomps, breakdowns,
> "shakedowns," and "cut offs," using jugs, guitars, kazoo, violin,
> mandolin, harmonica, and drums. Some cuts include vocals.

321. Negro Blues and Hollers. Washington, D.C.: Library of Congress, Music
Division Recording Laboratory. AFS L59. One disc. Notes by Marshall
W. Stearns.

> This album contains field-recorded camp hollers, cornfield hollers,
> religious songs, and blues songs.   Recorded at locations in
> Mississippi and Arkansas, they are performed by people who learned
> them in the folk tradition.

322. Negro Prison Camp Work Songs. Folkways Records. Ethnic Folkways
Library Album, no. FE 4475.   Moses Asch, production director.   One
disc. Notes.

> Ten Afro-American prison-camp work songs, recorded at two Texas
> prisons in 1951, are on this disc: "Let Your Hammer Ring," "Here
> Rattler Here," "Chopping in the New Ground," "Mighty Bright
> Light," "Go Down Old Hannah," "Grizzly Bear," "Lost John," "You
> Got to Hurry," "I Need More Power," and "We Need Another
> Witness."   The songs are accompanied by their printed texts and
> informative notes.

323. Negro Work Songs and Calls. Washington, D.C.: Library of Congress,
Music Division  Recording Laboratory. AAFS L8. One disc. Notes by
B. A. Botkin.

> Eighteen work songs and calls are recorded here.   Songs for
> "Unloading Rails," "Tamping Ties," and "Heaving the Lead Line"; for
> "Quitting Time," "Mealtime," and other work and related functions;
> "Sounding Calls" and "Cornfield Hollers"; and the others included in
> this collection were field-recorded at Mississippi, Texas, and
> Tennessee locations.   The Bahama Islands are represented by one
> song, "Roll 'Im on Down," described as a "Bahaman launching song."

324. Roots of Black Music in America. New York:   Folkways Records.
     FA2694. Two discs. Compiled and edited by Samuel Charters.

     Music from Africa, the Bahamas, and Mexico comprise the contents
     of this set. Dance music, vocal music, street band music, and drum
     music; work, wedding, gospel, and spiritual songs; banjo, harp, and
     xylophone instrumentals; brass band music; and jazz are presented.

## RELIGIOUS

325. Afro-American Spirituals, Work Songs, and Ballads. Washington, D.C.:
     Library of Congress, Music Division Recording Laboratory. AAFS L3.
     One disc. Notes by Alan Lomax.

     Seventeen songs representing Afro-American genres—spirituals,
     work songs, and ballads—here together form a handy source for
     listening to and comparing the variety of nineteenth-century black
     song. Three spirituals and one shout, several work songs and ballads
     were field-recorded at locations in Alabama, Virginia, Mississippi,
     Louisiana, Texas, Arkansas, Tennessee, and South Carolina.

326. Georgia Sea Island Songs. Recorded Anthology of American Music. New
     York: New World Records. NW 278. One disc. Notes by Alan Lomax.

     This collection of eighteen songs was field-recorded on St. Simons
     Island. The Sea Island Singers perform here spirituals and a wide
     variety of secular songs, including "Live Humble," "Beulah Land,"
     "The Buzzard Lope," "See Aunt Dinah," and "The Titanic."

327. The Gospel Sound. New York: Columbia Records. G 31086 and KG
     31595.  John Hammond, executive producer; Tony Heilbut, producer.
     Two albums, two discs each.

     This set contains fifty-three recorded gospel songs by sixteen
     individual and group artists. Spanning a period of forty-two years,
     these albums feature performances by Arizona Dranes, Eddie Head,
     Rev. J. M. Gates, The Golden Gate Jubilee Quartet, Blind Willie
     Johnson, Mitchell's Christian Singers, The Angelic Gospel Singers,
     Professor Alex Bradford, Dorothy Love Coats, The Dixie
     Hummingbirds, Bessie Griffin, Mahalia Jackson, The Staple Singers,
     Marion Williams, R. H. Harris, the Christland Singers, and the
     Pilgrim Travelers.

328. Negro Religious Music. America's Music Series. Berkeley, Calif.: LP
     Records. Notes by Pete Welding.

     Volume 1.  Sanctified Singers, Part One.  BC LP No. 17.  One disc.
     Volume 2.  Sanctified Singers, Part Two.  BC LP No. 18.  One disc.
     Volume 3.  Singing Preachers and Their Congregations. BC LP No. 19.
     One disc.

328.  Negro Religious Music (continued)

> Blind Joe and Emma Taggart, Blind Willie Johnson, Luther Magby,
> Arizona Dranes, Willie Mae Williams, Lightning Hopkins, and the
> Two Gospel Keys are among the more than twenty singers and
> groups featured on these albums. Rev. D. C. Rice, Elder Lightfoot
> Solomon Michaux, Rev. C. C. Chapman, Elder Otis Jones, and
> Deacon L. Shinault are among the eight preachers whose sermons
> were recorded in their home cities of Chicago, New York,
> Charlotte, N.C., Washington, Detroit, and Los Angeles.  On the
> records can be heard "long meter" hymn singing, responsorial
> renditions, blues- and jazz-inflected songs and sermons, and other
> Afro-American performance practices.  These performances are
> either typical or suggestive of those of the "core" black church.

## BLUES AND RHYTHM & BLUES

329.  The History of Rhythm and Blues.  New York:  Atlantic Recording
Corp. Atlantic SD8161-8209. Eight volumes, one disc each.

> This collection covers the development of rhythm & blues from 1947
> to 1967, its contents ranging from the genre's roots in the doo-wop
> groups of The Ravens, The Orioles, and other such "bird" groups to
> the artists of the Memphis sound such as Sam and Dave, Otis
> Redding, and Wilson Pickett. Ruth Brown, Joe Turner, the Drifters,
> Ivory Joe Hunter, Clyde McPhatter, Booker T. and the MGs, and
> approximately fifty others are recorded here at their best.

330.  Roots of the Blues.  Recorded Anthology of American Music.  New
York: New World Records.  NW 252.  One disc.  Notes by Alan Lomax.

> Based on the conclusion that "the Sudanese griot style is the
> progenitor of the blues, (p. 1), and that blues roots "may be traced"
> even further back" (p. 1), this collection contains work hollers, work
> songs, "original blues," religious parallels to the blues, and Delta
> blues 1900-1910 vintage.  The notes that accompany the record are
> copious and informative.  "Po' Boy Blues," "Church House Moan,"
> and "Rolled and Tumbled" are three of the eighteen titles on the
> record.

331.  The Story of the Blues.  New York: Columbia Records.  G 30008.  Two
discs.  Notes by Paul Oliver.

> The four sides of this collection are titled "The Origin of the Blues,"
> "Blues and Entertainment," "The Thirties, Urban and Rural Blues,"
> and "World War II and After."  Thirty-two blues by twenty single
> individuals, nine pairs of individuals, and four groups make up the
> contents of the set; among the performers included are Blind Lemon
> Jefferson, Leadbelly, the Mississippi Jook Band, Bessie Smith,
> Peetie Wheatstraw, Blind Boy Fuller and Sonny Terry, and Big Bill

331. Story of the Blues (continued)

>Broonzy. The jacket notes present an overview of the history of the blues and discuss the individual blues songs and singers featured in the collection.

## JAZZ

332. The Encyclopedia of Jazz in the Seventies on Records. New York: RCA Records. APL2-1984. Two discs. Notes by Leonard Feather.

>This collection contains at least one representative of the various styles of music that were a significant part of the jazz scene during the 1970s. Although it does not cover the entire spectrum, it does offer a unique possibility for exploring a variety of styles from the period. Lonnie Liston, Nina Simone, Blue Mitchell, Duke Ellington, Roland Hanna, Hank Jones, and Oliver Nelson are among those whose work is presented.

333. The History of Jazz. New York: Capitol Records, 1945, 1957. Four volumes, one disc each. Notes by Dave Dexter, Jr.

>The four albums in this set are titled: 1) "N'Orleans Origins," 2) "The Turbulent Twenties," 3) "Everybody Swings," and 4) "Enter the Cool." Running the gamut from pre-jazz to bebop, the set features the music of Blue Lu Barker, Barney Bigard, Leadbelly, Zutty Singleton, Sonny Greer, Ben Webster, Nat Cole, Harry Carney, Benny Carter, Coleman Hawkins, Eddie Heywood, Max Roach, Teddy Wilson, Miles Davis, Duke Ellington, Dizzy Gillespie, and Willie Smith.

334. History of Jazz Series. New York: Folkways Records. FJ2810-FJ2811. Eleven albums, one disc each.

>This essential and comprehensive set covers various aspects of jazz, including pre-jazz and pre-blues music. Its albums are titled: "The South," "The Blues," "New Orleans," "Jazz Singers," "Chicago," "New York: 1922-34," "Big Bands," "Piano," "Boogie Woogie," and "Addenda." More than 150 performances by nearly as many individuals and groups are included.

335. Introduction to Classic Jazz. New York: Riverside Records. SDP 11. Five discs. Notes by Charles Edward Smith.

>This collection traces the history of jazz from its backgrounds through the New York style. Included are cuts featuring African music, street cries, military music, ragtime, blues, Harlem piano and big band styles, Southside Chicago style, and boogie-woogie. The collection ends with a "revival" set featuring, among others, Kid Ory and Bunk Johnson with "Weary Blues" and "Make Me a Pallet on the Floor," respectively. Also represented are Louis

335. Classic Jazz (continued)

Armstrong, Meade Lux Lewis, Duke Ellington, Blind Lemon
Jefferson, Fats Waller, King Oliver, James Scott, Scott Joplin, Jelly
Roll Morton, Duke Ellington, and others. The booklet that
accompanies the records is an "Introduction to the Classic Jazz"
era; it includes "Discographical Notes" and an "Index of Musicians
and Selections."

336. The Smithsonian Collection of Classic Jazz.  Washington, D.C.:
Smithsonian Institution, 1973. Six discs. Notes by Martin Williams.

The selections in this collection represent original performances
ranging from Early Classic ragtime (Joplin playing his own "Maple
Leaf Rag" and Morton's rendition of the same piece) through the
free jazz of Ornette Coleman and the Neo-Be-Bop of John
Coltrane.   Performances by more than fifty individuals who
contributed to the evolution of jazz may be heard on the twelve
sides of the set; among them are Bessie Smith, King Oliver, Louis
Armstrong, Fats Waller, Billie Holiday, Charlie Parker, Duke
Ellington, Sarah Vaughn, Cecil Taylor, Ornette Coleman, and John
Coltrane. The discs are accompanied by a booklet which includes a
capsule description of the history of jazz, notes concerning use of
the recordings, annotations on the cuts, and a selected, annotated
bibliography. This set is an excellent survey of the history of jazz.

## CONCERT MUSIC

337. Anthology of Piano Music by Black Composers.  Ruth Norman, piano.
Greenville, Maine: Opus One (Number 39), 1977. One disc.

The fifteen works on this recording range from Ignatius Sancho's
"Ruffs and Rhees" (1779) to Margaret Bonds' "Troubled Waters"
(1967). The collection also includes works by James Hemmenway,
Francis Johnson, Thomas Greene Bethune, Samuel Coleridge-Taylor,
Morel Campos, William Grant Still, Wynn Boyd, and Ludovic
Lamothe.   Most of the pieces are of the social dance and
"characteristic" varieties (e.g., Johnson's "Johnson's Dream Waltz"
and Still's "Muted Laughter," respectively), although a composed
"African Dance" by Coleridge-Taylor and Bonds' spiritual-based
piece do represent aspects of the Afro-American experience.

338. Black Composers Series.  Paul Freeman, artistic director.  Columbia
Masterworks.   New York:   Columbia Records, 1974-1978.   Columbia
M-32781+. Nine discs. Notes by Dominique-René de Lerma.

The albums in this series contain recordings of twenty-four works
by fifteen composers whose birthdates range from 1737 to 1941, and
whose countries of birth span the Americas, Great Britain, and
Africa. The Chevalier de St. George, William Grant Still, Samuel
Coleridge-Taylor, Ulysses Kay, George Walker, Roque Cordero,
José Mauricio Nuñes Garcia, José Silvestre de los Dolores White,

338.  Black Composers (continued)

David N. Baker, Fela Sowande, Olly Wilson, T. J. Anderson, Talib Rasul Hakim, Adolphus Hailstork, and Hale Smith are all represented by at least one, and in one case, as many as four compositions.  The set's artistic activity, ranging from late classic to the most contemporary of styles, encompasses symphonies and other miscellaneous orchestral works, concertos, sonatas, vocal solos with orchestra, and a Mass, and are performed by the symphony orchestras of London, Helsinki, Baltimore, and Detroit; the Morgan State University Choir; violinists Miriam Fried, Jaime Laredo, Aaron Rosand, and Sanford Allen; trombonist Dennis Wick; pianists Natalie Hinderas and Richard Bunger; and singers Faye Robinson, William Brown, Doraline Davis, Betty Allen, and Matti Tuloisela.

# XVII

# Repositories and Archives

339. W. C. Handy Museum.

> Holdings. Sheet music: composed by Handy. Manuscripts.
> Hours: Tuesday through Saturday, 9-5.
> Contact: W. C. Handy Museum
> College Street
> Florence, AL 35630
> (205) 766-7410

340. Tuskegee Institute. The Tuskegee Institute Archives.

> Holdings. Sheet music: 97. Printed music: 59 volumes.
> Photographs: 200. Sound recordings: 215. Manuscripts and
> concert programs: 435.
> Collection(s) described in: Directory of Afro-American Resources
> by Walter Schatz.
> Logistical information: open stacks; collection open to all scholars;
> equipment available—cassette tape recorders and players,
> record players, microfilm and microfiche readers, filmstrip and
> slide projectors, photocopying service; materials not
> circulated; some materials available through interlibrary loan.
> Hours: Monday through Friday, 9-12 and 1-4.
> Assistance: in-house guides and indexes available.
> Staff: Archivist: Daniel T. Williams; Archives Assistant: Clara
> Heath.

340. Tuskegee Institute (continued)

    Contact:    The Tuskegee Institute Archives
                 Hollis Burke Frissell Library
                 Tuskegee Institute
                 Tuskegee Institute, AL  36088
                 (205) 727-8111

# ARKANSAS

341. The Arkansas Arts Center. John D. Reid Collection of Early American Jazz.

Holdings:  Sound recordings:  4,000 (most 78-rpms).  Books:  70. Periodicals and catalogues.  Primary source materials: memorabilia.
Publication:  Catalog of the John D. Reid Collection of Early American Jazz by Meredith McCoy and Barbara Parker.
Logistical information:  closed stacks; collection open to all scholars; equipment available for use—tape recorders and players, record players, slide projectors, photocopying service; materials neither circulated nor available through interlibrary loan.
Hours:  printed material available Monday through Friday, 9-5; records not available.
Assistance:  some in-house indexes or guides available.
Staff:  Senior Director:  Evelyn McCoy; Audio Visuals Librarian: Nancy DeLamar.
Contact:  The Arkansas Arts Center
         MacArthur Park
         P.O. Box 2137
         Little Rock, AR  72203
         (501) 372-4000

# CALIFORNIA

342. Los Angeles Public Library. Art, Music & Recreation Department.

Holdings.  Books:  25,000.  Printed music and scores:  46,810. Periodicals:  360.  Sheet music:  75,000.  Photographs:  3,000. Other:  Music Information and Biographical Indexes and Clippings; Song Index; Symphony Program Notes of Major American Orchestras.  Materials include information on a wide range of black American musical topics and composers; notable are the materials concerning William Grant Still.
Collection(s) described in: National Union Catalog.
Logistical information:  open stacks with closed reference stacks; collection open to all scholars; equipment available for use— microfilm and microfiche readers, slide projectors, photo-

342. Los Angeles (continued)

copying service; unrestricted circulation—reference materials
not circulated; materials available through interlibrary loan.
Hours: Monday through Thursday, 10-8; Friday and Saturday,
10-5:30.
Assistance: in-house guides and indexes available.
Staff: Department Manager and Principal Librarian: Katherine
Grant; 7 library staff members; 7 clerical and support staff.
Contact: Los Angeles Public Library
Art, Music & Recreation Department
630 W. Fifth Street
Los Angeles, CA 90071
(213) 626-7461

343. Los Angeles Public Library. Audio Visual Department.

Holdings. Sound recordings: collection includes many items of
black music.
Logistical information: collection open to all scholars and the
general public; equipment available—reel-to-reel and cassette
tape recorders and players, record players, microfilm and
microfiche readers, audio-visual projectors, photocopying
facilities; unrestricted circulation; materials available through
interlibrary loan.
Hours: Monday through Thursday, 10-8; Friday and Saturday, 10-
5:30.
Assistance: shelflist.
Staff: Manager: Richard Partlow; principal librarian; senior
librarian; support staff.
Contact: Los Angeles Public Library—Audio Visual Department
630 W. Fifth Street
Los Angeles, CA 90071
(213) 626-7555 ext. 267

344. University of California, Los Angeles Music Library. General
Collection, Ethnomusicology Archive, and Special Collections.

Holdings. Books: 33,000. Printed music: 47,000 volumes. Tapes
and sound recordings: 15,000; Ethnomusicology Archive
contains additional recordings—both field and commercial.
Other: numerous periodicals, theses and dissertations, music
manuscripts.
Collection described in: Dictionary Catalog of the University
Library, 1919-1962; "University of California, Los Angeles Music
Library" by Lester Brothers. Current Musicology 17 (1974), 36-
39; Subject Collections by Lee Ash; Reference Works in Music
and Music Literature in Five Libraries of Los Angeles County
by Helen W. Azhderian; and A Directory of Special Music
Collections in Southern California Libraries and in the
Libraries of the University of California and the California
State Universities and Colleges by Don L. Hixon, editor.

344.  UCLA Music Library (continued)

> Logistical information:  open stacks; collection open to all scholars;
> carrels available to UCLA students; open work space;
> equipment available for use—reel-to-reel and cassette tape
> players, cassette tape recorders, record players, microforms
> readers, photocopying services; in-house circulation only;
> materials available through interlibrary loan.
> Hours:  Monday through Thursday, 8-10; Friday, 8-5; Saturday, 9-5;
> Sunday, 1-9.
> Assistance: in-house guides and indexes available.
> Staff: Music Librarian: Stephen M. Fry; Associate Music Librarian
> for Public Services: Marsha Berman; Assistant Music Librarian
> for Technical and Audio Services:  Gordon Theil; Head of
> Circulation Services:  Shirley Thompson; Circulation
> Assistant: Amelia Triest; Technical Services Supervisor: Rhio
> Barnhart; Technical Processing Assistant: Darwin Scott; Audio
> Processing Assistant: Laura Horwitz; Microforms Acquisitions
> Assistant:  Egils Ozolins.  Ethnomusicology Archive Staff:
> Archivist: Ann Briegleb; Assistant Archivist: Nora Yeh.
> Contact:  Music Library
>           Schoenberg Hall
>           University of California
>           Los Angeles, CA  90024
>           Music Library (213) 825-4881
>           Ethnomusicology Archive (213) 825-1695.

## *CONNECTICUT*

345.  Beinecke Rare Book and Manuscript Library, Yale University.  James
Weldon Johnson Memorial Collection of Negro Arts and Letters.

> Holdings:  Printed music:  388 volumes.  Sound recordings: 1,200.
> Music manuscripts:  62.  Other:  books, photographs, and
> memorabilia.
> Logistical information:  closed stacks; collection open to all
> scholars; open work space available; equipment available for
> use—record players, microfilm readers, slide projectors,
> photocopying service;  materials neither circulated nor
> available through interlibrary loan.
> Hours: Monday through Friday, 8:30-5.
> Assistance: in-house indexes or guides available.
> Staff: Curator: David E. Schoonover.
> Contact:  Beinecke Rare Book and Manuscript Library
>           Yale University
>           Box 1603A Yale Station
>           New Haven, CT  06520
>           (203) 436-8438

346. Yale University Music Library. J. Rosamund Johnson Archives.

> Holdings. Personal papers. Music manuscripts. Memorabilia.
> Collection described in: National Union Catalog.
> Logistical Information: collection open to all scholars; open work
> space; equipment available for use—reel-to-reel and cassette
> tape players, record players, microfilm and microfiche readers,
> photocopying machine; materials neither circulated nor
> available through interlibrary loan.
> Hours: Monday through Friday, 8:30-5.
> Assistance: in-house guides or indexes available.
> Staff: Librarian: Harold E. Samuel; Assistant Librarian: Peggy
> Daub; Archivist: Adrienne Nesnow.
> Contact: Yale University Music Library
> 98 Wall Street
> New Haven, CT 06520
> (203) 436-8240

347. Yale University School of Music—Oral History, American Music. Duke
Ellington Oral History; Robert Neff and Anthony Connor Blues
Collection.

> Holdings. Ellington History: Interviews: more than 55 interviews
> of Ellington's colleagues. Neff and Connors Collection:
> Interviews: 60 interviews of blues performers.
> Collections described in: National Union Catalog and American
> Musical Resources Bibliography.
> Logistical information: open stacks; collection open to all scholars;
> work space available; equipment available for use—reel-to-reel
> and cassette tape players, photocopying service; in-house
> circulation, although Ellington materials are restricted.
> Hours: Monday through Friday, 9-5; by appointment.
> Assistance: in-house indexes and guides available.
> Staff: Director: Vivian Perlis; Assistant to the Director: Martha
> Oneppo; Staff: Jan Fournier and Mark Carrington;
> Interviewers: Valerie Archer and Jeremy Orgel.
> Contact: Yale University School of Music
> Oral History, American Music
> 96 Wall Street
> New Haven, CT 06520
> (203) 432-4169

## DISTRICT OF COLUMBIA

348. Library of Congress. Archive of Folk Song.

> Holdings. Sound recordings: 30,000 treating folksong, folk music,
> folk tales, oral history, and other types of folklore.
> Manuscripts: 225,000 sheets. Books and periodicals: 3,500
> treating folk music, folklore, and ethnomusicology. Other:
> magazines and newsletters.

348.  Archive of Folksong (continued)

>Collection(s) described in:  bibliographies published by the Archive
>and available upon request.
>Logistical information:  both closed and open stacks; collection
>open to the general public; open work space; appointment
>needed for listening; photocopying service available.
>Hours: Monday through Friday, 8:30-5.
>Assistance:  in-house guides and indexes available; staff assistance
>available for certain services.
>Staff: Head: Joseph C. Hickerson.
>Contact:    Archive of Folk Song
>            The Library of Congress
>            Washington, D.C.  20540
>            (202) 287-5510

349.  Library of Congress.  Music Division.

>Holdings:       Among  its  vast  holdings—in  its  Americana  and
>Composers' Holograph Collections, its Single Music Manuscripts
>Collection, and others—the Music Division preserves numerous
>books; hymnals and other song books; journals; libretti; sheet
>music  and  scores;  and  correspondence  of  many  black
>performers, musicians, and authors, e.g., William Grant Still,
>Leonard DePaur, Lillian Evanti, James P. Johnson, Bojangles
>Robinson, and others. (Note: The Copyright Office, not a part
>of the Music Division, holds copyright records and depository
>copies of musical compositions, unpublished music and musico-
>dramatic works, and film music.)
>Collection described in:  Resources in American Music History by
>D. Krummel et al.; National Union Catalog; and National Union
>Catalog of Manuscript Collections.
>Logistical information:   closed stacks; collection open to all
>scholars; open work space; equipment available for use—
>microforms readers and photocopying machine; materials not
>circulated; some materials available through interlibrary loan.
>Hours:    Monday through Saturday, 8:30-5 except for Federal
>holidays.
>Assistance: some in-house guides and indexes available.
>Contact:    Music Division
>            Library of Congress
>            Washington, D.C.  20540
>            (202) 287-5507

350.  Moorland-Spingarn  Research  Center.   Jesse E.  Moorland Collection;
Arthur  B.  Spingarn  Collection;  Glen  Carrington  Collection;  and
Washington Conservatory of Music Collection.

>Holdings. Books: 75. Sheet music: 3,200 pieces written by black
>composers. Sound recordings:  725 recordings of works by
>black composers. Other: letters, newspaper clippings, and
>photographs.

350. Moorland-Spingarn (continued)

Collection(s) described in:  Scholar's Guide to Washington, D.C.:
African Studies; Guide to Archives and Manuscripts in the
United States by Philip M. Hamer; Women's History Sources: A
Guide to Archives and Manuscript Collections in the United
States by Andrea Hinding; National Union Catalog of
Manuscript Collections; Directory of Archives and Manuscript
Repositories; Directory of Afro-American Resources by Walter
Schatz; A Researcher's Guide to Historical Institutions in
Washington, D.C. by Marc Ian Sherman.
Publications:  Dictionary Catalog of the Moorland-Spingarn
Collection; The Glen Carrington Collection: A Guide to the
Books, Manuscripts, Music and Recordings compiled by Karen
L. Jefferson; other guides, indexes, and dedication programs.
Logistical information:  closed stacks; collection open to all
scholars; microfilm readers available for use; photocopying
service available; materials neither circulated nor available
through interlibrary loan.
Hours:  collection available 9-1 and 2-4:30 by appointment only.
Scholars requesting services must have completed research in
available secondary sources. Briefcases, portfolios, coats, etc.,
not permitted in the research area.
Assistance: in-house guides and indexes available.
Staff: Music Librarian: Deborra A. Richardson.
Contact:  Moorland-Spingarn Research Center
Howard University
500 Howard Place, N.W.
Washington, D.C. 20059
(202) 636-7239

# GEORGIA

351. Georgia Historical Society.

Holdings. Sheet music: relating to Georgia.
Collection described in:  National Union Catalog.
Publications:  Georgia Historical Quarterly and Georgia Historical
Society Collections.
Logistical information:  closed stacks; collection open to all
scholars; equipment available for use—microfilm readers,
photocopying machine; materials neither circulated nor
available through interlibrary loan.
Hours: Monday through Friday, 10-6.
Assistance: in-house guides and indexes available.
Staff: Director: Anthony R. Dees; Assistant Director: Barbara
Bennett; Archival Assistant:  Karen E. Osvald; Archivist:
Susan F. Murphy.
Contact:  Georgia Historical Society
501 Whitaker Street
Savannah, GA 31499
(912) 944-2128

## ILLINOIS

352. Center for Research Libraries.

> Holdings. Sheet music: 25,000. Newspapers: on microfilm,
> including 20 black newspapers. Manuscripts: including the
> American Missionary Association Archives and the manuscript
> collection of the American Colonization Society. Periodicals:
> including 22 devoted to jazz or ragtime. Foreign doctoral
> dissertations.
> Collection(s) described in: National Union Catalog and Center for
> Research Libraries Catalog.
> Publications: Center for Research Libraries Catalog; a newsletter;
> handbook for the use of the collection.
> Logistical information:  closed stacks; collection open to all
> scholars; open work space available; equipment available for
> use—microforms readers and photocopying machine; materials
> may be used on the premises and are circulated among member
> libraries.
> Hours: Monday through Friday, 9-5.
> Assistance:  in-house guides and indexes available on a limited
> basis.
> Staff:  Collection Development Librarian:  Esther Smith; Head of
> Circulation: Emma Davis.
> Contact:   Center for Research Libraries
>                  5721 Cottage Grove Avenue
>                  Chicago, IL  60637
>                  (312) 955-4545

353. The Newberry Library.  J. Francis Driscoll Collection.

> Holdings: Sheet music: 80,000 to 83,000 pieces.
> Collection described in:  "Black Music in the Driscoll Collection,"
> by Samuel A. Floyd, Jr.  The Black Perspective in Music 2
> (1974), 158-171.
> Logistical information:   closed stacks; collection open to all
> scholars; some carrels available (arrangements made through
> the Main Reading Room desk) and open work space; materials
> may be kept on reserve; photocopying service available;
> materials available on microfilm through interlibrary loan.
> Hours: Tuesday through Saturday 9-5:40.
> Assistance:  in-house guides and indexes available; supplement to
> the Floyd article on file.
> Staff:  Curator of Modern Manuscripts:  Diana Haskell; Librarian,
> Main Reading Room:  Elizabeth Agaard; Technical Services
> Director: Bernard Wilson.
> Contact:   The Newberry Library
>                  60 West Walton
>                  Chicago, IL  60610
>                  (312) 943-9090

# INDIANA

354. Indiana University. Archives of Traditional Music.

Holdings. Sound Recordings: 6,000 wax cylinders, 35,000 discs, 100
wire spools, 15,000 original tape recordings; 8,000 duplicate
tape recordings. Other: books, periodicals, and memorabilia of
interest to enthnomusicologists, folklorists, and discographers;
film and microfilm collections.
Collection(s) described in: A Catalog of Phonorecordings of Music
and Oral Data Held by the Archives of Traditional Music;
African Music and Oral Data: A Catalog of Field Recordings,
1902-1975 compiled by Ruth M. Stone and Frank J. Gillis.
Publications: Folklore and Folk Music Archivist, 1958-1968; and
Ethnomusicological Series of scholarly phonorecords with
extensive notes.
Logistical information: collection open to all individuals; special
listening booths provided with writing tables and foot-operated
controls; photocopying service available; restricted circulation;
materials available through interlibrary loan.
Hours: Monday through Friday, 8-12 and 1-5.
Assistance: in-house guides and indexes available.
Staff: Director: Anthony Seeger; Assistant Director: Louise S.
Spear; Secretary: Marilyn B. Graf.
Contact: Archives of Traditional Music
Indiana University
Maxwell Hall 057
Bloomington, IN 47405
(812) 335-8632

355. Indiana University—School of Music. Black Music Collection.

Holdings. Books. Scores. Dissertations. Journals. Microfilms.
Reference materials. Sound recordings.
Publication: Annotations.
Logistical information: open stacks; collection available to all
scholars; equipment available for use—reel-to-reel and cassette
tape recorders and players, record players, microfilm and
microfiche readers, photocopying service; unrestricted
circulation (except records and tapes); materials available
through interlibrary loan.
Hours: Monday through Thursday, 8 A.M.-10:30 P.M.; Friday, 8-5;
Saturday, 10-5; Sunday, 2-10:30.
Assistance: catalogue with tracings providing several points of
access for each item.
Staff: five library faculty members and 8 support staff members.
Contact: Indiana University/School of Music
Sycamore 0009
Bloomington, IN 47405
(812) 332-0211

356. Indiana University.  Folklore Archives/Folklore Institute.

> Holdings: Field recording collections: 40,000. Periodicals: 7.
> Publications:  Guide to the Indiana University Folklore Archives,
>   and several periodicals.
> Logistical information:  open stacks; collection open to all scholars;
>   equipment  available  for  use—cassette  tape  recorders  and
>   players, slide previewer and sorter, photocopying service; in-
>   house  circulation  only;  materials  not  available  through
>   interlibrary loan.
> Hours:  Monday, 9-5; Tuesday, 2:30-5; Wednesday, ll-5; Thursday,
>   2:30-5; Friday, 8-5; other hours by appointment.
> Assistance: in-house guides and indexes available.
> Staff: Head Archivist: Timothy J. Kloberdanz; Archivists: Jeanne
>   Harrah and Eric Montenyohl.
> Contact:    Folklore Archives
>             504 N. Fess Street
>             Indiana University
>             Bloomington, IN  47401
>             (812) 337-3652

## KENTUCKY

357. Louisville Free Public Library.   Black Heritage Collection, Western
Branch.

> Holdings.     Books,   manuscripts,   photographs,   and   newspaper
>   clippings: 60,000.
> Collection described in: Subject Collections by Lee Ash.
> Logistical information:  open stacks; collection open to all scholars;
>   carrels or work space available; equipment available for use—
>   microfiche  readers,  photocopying  service;  circulating/non-
>   circulating  collection;  some  materials  available  through
>   interlibrary loan.
> Hours:     Monday  through  Wednesday,  2-8;  Thursday  through
>   Saturday, l0-5.
> Assistance: no in-house guides or indexes available.
> Staff: Coordinator, Adult Reference and Reader Services: Barbara
>   L. Pickett.
> Contact:    Louisville Free Public Library
>             Fourth and York Streets
>             Louisville, KY  40203
>             (502) 584-4154

358. Southern Baptist Theological Seminary.   James P. Boyce Centennial
Library.

> Holdings.   Books:  270,000.  Printed music:  120,000 volumes.
>   Pamphlets and minutes: 97,000 items. Microforms:  23,000.
>   Non-print material: 40,000 items. Periodicals: 1,300.
> Publication: Theological and Music Bibliography.

358.  Southern Baptist Theological (<u>continued</u>)

> <u>Logistical information</u>: open stacks; collection open to all scholars;
> carrels available for use only by graduate students; equipment
> available for use—reel-to-reel and cassette tape players and
> recorders, record players, microforms readers, audio-visual
> projectors, photocopying service; in-house circulation only;
> materials available through interlibrary loan.
> <u>Hours</u>: Monday through Friday, 7:45 A.M.-11:00 P.M.; Saturday, 8-5.
> <u>Assistance</u>: card catalogue available.
> <u>Staff</u>:     Music Librarian:     Martha C. Powell; Music Library
> Circulation Assistant; Music Library Cataloguer.
> <u>Contact</u>:   James P. Boyce Centennial Library
> Southern Baptist Theological Seminary
> 2825 Lexington Road
> Louisville, KY 40206
> (502) 897-4807

## *LOUISIANA*

359.  New Orleans Public Library.

> <u>Holdings</u>. <u>Books</u>. <u>Early sheet music</u>. <u>Sound recordings</u>: 20,000.
> <u>Collection described in</u>: National Union Catalog.
> <u>Publication</u>: book lists about black American topics.
> <u>Logistical information</u>:     open stacks; collection open to all
> interested persons; equipment available for use—cassette tape
> players, record players, microfilm and microfiche readers,
> photocopying machines; unrestricted circulation of all of the
> collection except reference records and books which are
> limited to in-house circulation; books available through
> interlibrary loan.
> <u>Hours</u>: Tuesday through Saturday, 10-6.
> <u>Assistance</u>: card catalogue available.
> <u>Staff</u>: Head: M. Wilkins.
> <u>Contact</u>:   New Orleans Public Library
> 219 Loyola Avenue
> New Orleans, LA 70140
> (504) 524-7382

360.  The Louisiana State Museum. New Orleans Jazz Club Collections of the
Louisiana State Museum (formerly New Orleans Jazz Museum).

> <u>Holdings</u>.   The collection is primarily devoted to traditional New
> Orleans jazz and contains the following materials.   <u>Sound
> recordings</u>: 7,000 (78-rpm, 45-rpm, and LPs). <u>Piano rolls</u>: 20.
> <u>Tapes</u>: 7 inch reel-to-reel—1,000. <u>Musical instruments</u>: 175.
> <u>Sheet music</u>: 1,000 items. <u>Visuals</u>: 10,000 photographs; also
> films.   <u>Other</u>:   books, periodicals, vertical files, paintings.
> Primary source material: posters and memorabilia.
> <u>Significant projects supported</u>. <u>Phonograph records</u>:   Time-Life
> Records—Jazz series; Smithsonian Records.

360. Louisiana State Museum (continued)

>Logistical information: at present, due to reorganization, the collection is available only to serious jazz scholars; closed stacks; equipment available for use—tape recorders and players (reel-to-reel and cassette), record players, photocopying service; no circulation.
>
>Hours: at present, due to reorganization, the collection is available only for very specialized research.
>
>Assistance: in-house indexes or guides in progress.
>
>Staff: Curator: Donald M. Marquis
>
>Contact:   New Orleans Jazz Club Collections of the Louisiana
>State Museum
>751 Chartres Street
>New Orleans, LA  70116
>(504) 568-6968 or
>(504) 529-5655

## *MARYLAND*

361. Prince George's County Memorial Library System.   Sojourner Truth Collection.

>Holdings. Books. Vertical file materials. Photographs. Early twentieth-century sheet music.
>
>Publication: a selective bibliography of government publications about black Americans.
>
>Logistical information: open stacks; collection open to all scholars; equipment available for use—microfilm and microfiche readers, photocopying machine; materials neither circulated nor available through interlibrary loan.
>
>Hours: Monday through Thursday, 9-9; Friday, 1-6; Saturday, 9-5.
>
>Assistance: in-house indexes and guides available.
>
>Staff: Curator: Cherie P. Barnett.
>
>Contact:   Sojourner Truth Collection
>Oxon Hill Branch Library
>6200 Oxon Hill Road
>Oxon Hill, MD  20021
>(301) 839-2400

## *MASSACHUSETTS*

362. Boston University—Mugar Memorial Library.   Cab Calloway and Ella Fitzgerald Collections.

>Holdings. Manuscripts. Musical scores. Photographs.
>
>Collections described in:  National Union Catalog of Manuscript Collections; Women's History Sources; American Literary Manuscripts.
>
>Publication: Special Collections at Boston University.

362. Boston University (continued)

> Logistical information: closed stacks; collection available to all scholars; equipment available—cassette tape recorders and players, photocopying service; materials not circulated; book materials available through interlibrary loan.
> Hours: Monday through Friday, 9-5.
> Assistance: in-house guides and indexes available.
> Staff: Assistant Director: Margaret Goostray; Manuscript Technicians: Douglas MacDonald, Charles Niles, and Charles Murphy; Administrative Assistant: Vita Widershein; Rare Book Selector: Kathy Cain; Exhibition Coordinator: Perry Barton; Secretaries: Rhona Swartz and Amy Sheperdson.
> Contact: Mugar Memorial Library
> Boston University
> 771 Commonwealth Avenue
> Boston, MA 02215
> (617) 353-3708

363. Harvard College Library. Harvard Theatre Collection.

> Holdings. Playbills and programs: 3 million. Photographs: 500,000. Engraved portraits and scenes: 250,000. Scenery and costume designs: 15,000. Promptbooks: 5,000. Manuscripts. Books. Journals. Newspaper clippings.
> Collection partially described in: The Catalogue of Engraved Dramatic Portraits in the Harvard Theatre Collection by Lillian A. Hall.
> Logistical information: closed stacks; collection open to all scholars; microfilm readers and limited photocopying service available; materials neither circulated nor available through interlibrary loan.
> Hours: Monday through Friday, 11-5.
> Assistance: some in-house guides and indexes available.
> Staff: Curator: Jeanne T. Newlin; Assistant Curator; Reading Room Supervisor; Staff Assistant.
> Contact: Harvard Theatre Collection
> Harvard College Library
> Cambridge, MA 02138
> (617) 495-2445

# MICHIGAN

364. Detroit Public Library. E. Azalia Hackley Memorial Collection of Negro Music, Drama and Dance.

> Holdings. Books: 900. Printed Music: 1,200 volumes. Sound recordings: 1,600. Sheet Music: 1,500. Photographs: 2,000. Other: manuscripts, scrapbooks, programs, playbills, letters, and memorabilia.

364. Detroit Public Library (continued)

> Collection described in: Catalog of the E. Azalia Hackley Memorial
>   Collection of Negro Music, Drama and Dance; Directory of
>   Afro-American Resources; and Writer's Resource Guide.
> Logistical information:   closed stacks; collection open to all
>   scholars and the general public; equipment available for use—
>   cassette tape recorders, record players, microfilm readers,
>   photocopying service/machine; materials neither circulated nor
>   available through interlibrary loan.
> Hours:    Tuesday, Thursday, Friday, and Saturday, 9:30-5:30;
>   Wednesday, 1-9.
> Assistance: in-house indexes or guides available for some items.
> Staff: Curator: Jean Currie Church.
> Contact:   E. Azalia Hackley Collection
>            Detroit Public Library
>            5201 Woodward Avenue
>            Detroit, MI  48202
>            (313) 833-1000

365. Arnold's Archives.

> Holdings. Out-of-print historical sound recordings: 200,000.
> Logistical information:   closed stacks; collection available to all
>   scholars; equipment available by appointment—reel-to-reel and
>   cassette   tape   recorders   and   players,   record   players,
>   photocopying service; materials available for purchase.
> Hours: by appointment; mail order purchase available.
> Assistance: catalogues available.
> Contact:   Arnold's Archives
>            1106 Eastwood, SE
>            East Grand Rapids, MI  49506
>            (616) 949-1398

## MISSOURI

366. Tichenor Ragtime Collection.

> Holdings. Sheet music and piano rolls.
> Significant projects supported:   Collected Works of Scott Joplin
>   published by the New York Public Library; Classic Rags,
>   Ragtime Rarities, and Ragtime Rediscoveries—reprints of rags,
>   published by Dover Press; Rags and Ragtime by Trebor
>   Tichenor and David Jasen; a Scott Joplin phonorecord
>   anthology; a study of the piano rolls by the Indiana Ragtime
>   Project directed by John Hasse; a dissertation by J. P. Scotti
>   treating Joe Lamb.
> Logistical information:   open stacks; this private collection is
>   available by appointment to all scholars; reel-to-reel or
>   cassette tape recordings and some photocopies of sheet music
>   can be procured from Tichenor.

366. Tichenor Ragtime Collection (continued)

>   Contact:  Trebor J. Tichenor
>             3801 Federer Place
>             St. Louis, MO 63116
>             (314) 351-1062

367. Washington University, Gaylord Music Library.    Ernst C. Krohn
Musicological Library, George C. Krich Collection for the Classical
Guitar, and others.

>   Holdings.   Sheet music:  50,000.   Printed music:  more than 500
>       volumes.  Photographs: more than 2 linear meters.  Other: the
>       Ernst C. Krohn Papers; musical programs; 14 vols. of
>       scrapbooks and clippings.
>   Collection described in:  Resources of American Music History.
>   Significant research supported:   articles and an anthology on
>       ragtime by John Hasse; A Century of the Symphony by Richard
>       E. Mueller; articles on J. W. Postlewaite by Samuel A. Floyd,
>       Jr.; an article and lecture-recital on music in Missouri in the
>       late 1880s by David C. Nichols; a dissertation on music printing
>       in the U.S. prior to 1860 by W. W. Scott; "Music Publishing in
>       St. Louis," a manuscript by Ernst Krohn to be published by
>       Detroit Information Coordinators; and others.
>   Logistical information:   Special Collections and Archival stacks
>       closed, remainder open; collection open to all scholars; open
>       work space only; equipment available for use—7 reel-to-reel
>       and 2 cassette tape player/recorders, 8 record players, 3
>       microfilm readers, a microfiche and a microcard reader, a slide
>       projector, a photocopying machine; materials not circulated;
>       Special Collections and Archival material not available through
>       interlibrary loan.
>   Hours: Monday through Friday, 8:30-5.
>   Assistance: in-house guides and indexes available.
>   Staff:   Music Librarian:   Elizabeth Krause; Assistant Music
>       Librarian: Susanne Bell; Head, Reader Services: Nathan Eakin;
>       Circulation/Reserve Head:  Mary Ann Weidinger; Score/Sound
>       Recording Cataloguer:   Thelda Bertram;   Acquisitions
>       Assistant:  Nada Vaughn; Technical Services Assistant:  Wes
>       Lundin; and Circulation Assistant: Virginia Britten.
>   Contact:  Gaylord Music Library
>             Washington University
>             6500 Forsythe Boulevard
>             St. Louis, MO 63105
>             (314) 889-5560

## NEW JERSEY

368. Newark Public Library.     Music Division of the Art and Music
     Department.

> Holdings.  Books, printed music, and phonorecords:  25,000 items.
> Periodicals:  100.  Vertical Files:  35 drawers, including many
> items  directly  related  to  black  music  both  locally  and
> nationally.
> Logistical  information:     open  stacks;  reference  stacks  closed;
> collection  open  to  all  scholars  and  interested  persons;
> equipment  available  for  use—cassette  tape  recorders  and
> players, record players, microfilm and microfiche readers, slide
> projectors,  photocopying  machine;  most  unrestricted
> circulation—reference  materials,  periodicals  and  vertical  file
> materials  do  not  circulate;  materials  available  through
> interlibrary loan.
> Hours:  Monday, Wednesday, and Thursday, 9-9; Tuesday and Friday,
>      9-6; Saturday, 9-5.
> Assistance:  in-house guides and indexes available.
> Staff:     Supervising  Librarian:     William  J.  Dane;  Principal  Art
>      Librarian:  Joan E. Burns; Senior Reference Librarian:  Charles
>      Miller.
> Contact:    Music Division
>             Newark Public Library
>             5 Washington Street
>             Newark, NJ  07102
>             (201) 733-7761

369. Rutgers University.  Institute of Jazz Studies.

> Holdings.  Sound recordings:  78-rpm—35,000; 45-rpm—1,550; LPs—
> 15,000;  transcriptions,  acetates,  and  test  pressings—2,500;
> cylinders—200;  reel-to-reel  tape  recordings—500;  numerous
> cassette tape recordings.  Piano rolls:  20.  Books:  more than
> 3,000.  Periodicals:  more than 100 subscriptions to U.S. and
> foreign  jazz  publications  from  the  1930s  to  the  present.
> Research files:  1) artists and personalities; 2) topics.  Visuals:
> photographs,  films,  and  videotapes.    Primary  source
> materials:  sheet music, memorabilia.
> Collection(s) described in:  Microform Review; OCLC Data Base;
>      Special Libraries Directory of Greater New York.
> Publications:  Annual Review of Jazz Studies (annual); the quarterly
>      IJS Jazz Register and Indexes (a microfiche register of the
>      Institute's catalogued entries).
> Significant projects supported.  Books:  a biography/discography of
>      Benny Carter by Morroe Berger and Ed Berger (forthcoming);
>      Bibliography of Jazz Discographies by Dan Allen (in progress);
>      and others.  Phonograph records:  Time-Life Records—Jazz
>      series; New World Records—Jazz issues.  Pedagogy:  jazz
>      instruction at Rutgers University, particularly at Livingstone

369. Institute of Jazz Studies (continued)

>College; graduate jazz seminars at Princeton University. Oral
>history: The Jazz Oral History Project—more than 95
>interviews.
>
>Logistical information: open stacks; collection open to all scholars;
>two listening rooms (available by appointment) and open work
>space; equipment available for use—tape recorders and players
>(reel-to-reel and cassette), record players, microfilm and
>microfiche readers, film projector, slide projector,
>photocopying service; materials not circulated (although
>certain materials can be loaned under special conditions); some
>materials available through interlibrary loan.
>
>Hours: Monday through Friday, 9-5; appointments required for non-
>routine visits.
>
>Assistance: in-house indexes and guides are available; staff
>assistance is available for certain levels of access.
>
>Staff: Director: Dan Morgenstern; Curator: Ed Berger;
>Librarian: Marie Griffin; Assistant Curators: Robert
>Kenselaar and Vincent Pelote; Oral History Project
>Coordinator: Ronald Welburn; Assistant Oral History Project
>Coordinator: Phil Schaap.
>
>Contact: Institute of Jazz Studies
>135 Bradley Hall
>Newark, NJ 07102
>(201) 648-5595

370. Edison National Historical Site. Audio Archives, Museum Collection, and Archives.

>Holdings. Sound recordings: of Edison manufacture made before
>1929. Phonographs. Documents. Record catalogues.
>Memorabilia.
>
>Publication: Edison Disc Recordings.
>
>Logistical information: collection open to all scholars upon written
>statement of intent and permission; photocopying service
>available; materials neither circulated nor available through
>interlibrary loan.
>
>Hours: Monday through Saturday, 9-3; by appointment only.
>
>Assistance: in-house guides and indexes available.
>
>Staff: Curator: Leah Burt.
>
>Contact: Edison National Historical Site
>Main Street and Lakeside Avenue
>West Orange, NJ 07052
>(201) 736-5050

# NEW YORK

371. Buffalo & Erie County Public Library. A Collection of Minstrel Songs.

>Holdings. Photocopied nineteenth-century minstrel songsters and
>song folios: 90 volumes; originals also available.

371.  Buffalo & Erie County (continued)

> Significant project supported:  Blacking Up by Robert C. Toll.
>
> Logistical information:   open stacks; collection is open to all
>   scholars; open work space; equipment available for use—tape
>   players (reel-to-reel and cassette) and tape recorders (reel-to-
>   reel), record players, microforms readers, photocopying
>   machine; in-house circulation only; photocopies available
>   through interlibrary loan.
>
> Hours:   Monday and Thursday, 10-9; Tuesday, Wednesday, Friday,
>   and Saturday, 10-5:30.
>
> Assistance:   The set is catalogued by book titles and compilers;
>   individual book contents are uncatalogued.
>
> Staff:   Head, Music Department:  Norma Jean Lamb; Librarian II:
>   Helen I. Khan; Librarian I:  Judith Lopez del Moral.
>
> Contact:   Buffalo & Erie County Public Library
>            Lafayette Square
>            Buffalo, NY  14203
>            (716) 856-7525

372.  David A. Jasen Private Collection.

> Holdings.  Ragtime sheet music.  Sound recordings.  Piano rolls.
>
> Significant research supported:   sound recordings on the Folkways,
>   Yazoo, Herwin, Biograph, and other labels; Jasen's Recorded
>   Ragtime; Rags and Ragtime by Jasen and Tichenor; anthologies
>   of ragtime music such as Ragtime Rarities and Ragtime
>   Rediscoveries; and other works treating ragtime published in
>   the last decade.
>
> Contact:   David A. Jasen
>            40-21 155th Street
>            Flushing, NY  11354
>            telephone non-published

373.  James J. Fuld Private Collection.

> Holdings.  First editions and autographs:  works by black composers
>   such as Scott Joplin, W. C. Handy, and others.
>
> Significant research supported:   "The Few Known Autographs of
>   Scott Joplin," forthcoming in American Music.
>
> Logistical information:   collection open to all scholars by
>   appointment only; no circulation.
>
> Contact:   James J. Fuld
>            1175 Park Avenue
>            New York, NY  10028
>            (212) 348-3961

374.  Hatch-Billops Collection.

> Holdings.  Books: 3,000.  Oral history tapes: 700.  Visuals: 10,000
>   35mm slides; 1,400 photographs.  Research files:  300 art
>   catalogues; 20,000 newspaper clippings.  Primary source
>   material:  posters and letters; memorabilia.

374. Hatch-Billops Collection (continued)

Collection described in:  Black Playwrights, 1823-1977 by Hatch and
   Abdullah.
Significant projects supported.  Books:  Black Theater U.S.A. by
   Hatch and Shine, eds.; Black Playwrights, 1823-1977 by Hatch
   and Abdullah, eds.; Harlem Book of the Dead by Van Der Zee,
   Dodson, and Billops.  Dissertations:  completed at New York
   University, Nouvelle Sourbonne, Indiana University, Ohio
   University, the University of Connecticut, University of
   Tennessee, and the University in Hamburg, West Germany.
Logistical information:  both open and closed stacks; collection
   open to all scholars; open work space; equipment available for
   use—reel-to-reel and cassette tape players and recorders,
   record players, film and slide projectors, some photocopying
   service; materials neither circulated nor available through
   interlibrary loan.
Hours: by appointment only.
Assistance: in-house guides and indexes available.
Staff: Executive Secretary: James V. Hatch.
Contact:  Hatch-Billops Collection, Inc.
          491 Broadway
          New York, NY 10012
          no telephone number available

375. The New York Historical Society Library.

Holdings.  Books and pamphlets:  500,000.  Newspapers:  large
   collection of newspapers from the late eighteenth century
   through the nineteenth century.  Periodicals:  nineteenth- and
   twentieth-century publications.    Manuscripts:    1,000,000
   pieces.  Visuals: photographs, maps, prints, etc.
Logistical information:  closed stacks; collection open to graduate
   students, professors, teachers, and other post-graduate
   scholars; equipment available for use—microfilm and microcard
   readers, photocopying service; materials not circulated; some
   materials available on microfilm through interlibrary loan.
Hours: Tuesday through Saturday, 10-5.  Fee for use: $1.00 daily for
   non-members.
Assistance: in-house guides and indexes available.
Staff: Curator of Manuscripts: Thomas J. Dunnings, Jr.
Contact:  The New York Historical Society
          170 Central Park West
          New York, NY 10024
          (212) 873-3400

376. The New York Public Library. The General Library and Museum of the
   Performing Arts.

Holdings. Sound recordings. Books. Printed music. Periodicals.
   and Vertical files.
Logistical information:  open and closed stacks; collection open to
   all scholars and the general public; no carrels; record players

376. New York Public Library (continued)

>and photocopying machines/services available; circulation varies according to material needed; material available through interlibrary loan.
>
>Hours: Monday, 10-8; Tuesday, 10-6; Wednesday, 10-8; Friday and Saturday, 12-6.
>
>Assistance: in-house guides and indexes available.
>
>Staff: Music Librarian: Florence Fanshel.
>
>Contact:  The New York Public Library
>The General Library and Museum of the Performing Arts
>111 Amsterdam Avenue
>New York, NY 10023
>(212) 870-1625

377. New York Public Library at Lincoln Center. Performing Arts Research Center, Music Division.

>Holdings.    Books.    Printed music.    Programs.    Clippings. Photographs. Prints.
>
>Collection described in:  Directory of Music Research Libraries by Rita Benton; Dictionary Catalog of the Music Collection, New York Public Library; Dictionary Catalog of The Research Libraries, of the New York Public Library; and others.
>
>Publication: Elliot Carter: Sketches and Scores in Manuscript (an exhibition catalogue).
>
>Logistical information:  stacks both open and closed; collection open to all scholars and the general public over 18; carrels available upon appointment with the Assistant Chief of the Performing  Arts Research Center; equipment available for use—microforms readers and photocopying machine/service; in-house circulation only.
>
>Hours: Monday and Thursday, 12-8; Tuesday, Wednesday, Friday and Saturday, 12-6.
>
>Assistance: in-house guides and indexes available.
>
>Staff: Head, Americana Collection:  Richard Jackson, 10 reference librarians, 9 full- and part-time clerical assistants, 8 part-time pages, and 1 full-time secretary.
>
>Contact:   The New York Public Library at Lincoln Center
>Performing Arts Research Center, Music Division
>111 Amsterdam Avenue
>New York, NY 10023
>(212) 870-1650

378. The New York Public Library. Schomburg Center for Research in Black Culture.

>Holdings. Books: 75,000. Microforms: 20,000 reels of microfilm, large collection of microfiche representing periodical articles relating to the black experience. Sound recordings: several musical recordings and oral history recordings.    Visuals: paintings, prints, drawings, and African artifacts; motion pictures and videotapes.

378. Schomburg Center (continued)

 Collection(s) described in: National Union Catalog of Manuscript
  Collections; Dictionary Catalog of the Research Libraries of
  The New York Public Library; and Catalog of the Schomburg
  Collection.
 Logistical information: closed stacks; collection open to all
  scholars and the general public over the age of 18; no carrels
  available; equipment available for use—microfilm and
  microfiche readers, photocopying service; in-house circulation
  only; materials available through Research Libraries Group
  interlibrary loan.
 Hours: Monday through Wednesday, 12-8; Thursday through
  Saturday, 10-6. Summer hours: Monday and Thursday, 12-8;
  Tuesday, Wednesday, and Friday, 10-6.
 Assistance: in-house guides and indexes available.
 Staff: approximately 40 full-time staff members.
 Contact: The New York Public Library
   Schomburg Center for Research in Black Culture
   515 Lenox Avenue
   New York, NY 10037
   (212) 862-4000

# NORTH CAROLINA

379. North Carolina Division of Archives and History. "Bull City Blues: A
 Study of the Black Musical Community that Existed in Durham, North
 Carolina, in the 1920s, 1930s and 1940s."

 Holdings. Tape recordings: 15 reels of interviews and musical
  performances by black musicians in Durham, NC.
 Collection described in: National Union Catalog.
 Publications: N.C. Historical Review; and others.
 Logistical information: closed stacks; collection open to all
  scholars; carrels available upon request and by approval of the
  head of the Archives branch of the Division; equipment
  available for use--reel-to-reel and cassette tape players and
  recorders, microfilm and microfiche readers, film and slide
  projectors, photocopying service; materials neither circulated
  nor available through interlibrary loan.
 Hours: Tuesday through Friday, 9-5:30, Saturday, 8:30-5:30.
 Assistance: in-house guides and indexes available.
 Staff: 8 reference staff members.
 Contact: North Carolina State Division of Archives and History
   109 East Jones Street
   Raleigh, NC 27611
   (919) 733-7305

## PENNSYLVANIA

380. Free Library of Philadelphia. Music Department.

Holdings. Books: about music and dance. Periodicals: for music and dance. Scores: for chamber music, instrumental works, orchestra, and the stage. Reference works. Monumental editions. Research files: vertical files containing pamphlets, programs, and newspaper clippings. Primary source materials: 130,000 uncatalogued pieces of sheet music.

Collection(s) described in: Bernice Larrabee, "The Music Department of the Free Library of Philadelphia." Library Trends, 8 (1960), 574-576.

Significant projects supported. Books: Musical Miscellany in Occasional Numbers.

Logistical information: open stacks with reference stacks closed; collection open to all adults; open work space available; equipment available for use—record players, microforms readers, photocopying service/machines; limited circulation; some materials available through interlibrary loan.

Hours: Monday through Wednesday, 9-9; Thursday and Friday, 9-6; Saturday, 9-5; Sunday, 1-5.

Assistance: in-house guide available.

Staff: Head, Music Department: Frederick J. Kent; Reference and Information Librarian for Sheet Music Collection: Connie Jessum; Reference and Information Librarian: Linda Wood; Librarian II: Shirley Horowitz; Librarian I: Dennis Mullen.

Contact: Free Library of Philadelphia
Logan Square
Philadelphia, PA 19103
(215) 686-5316

381. Library Company of Philadelphia. Afro-Americana Collection.

Holdings. Printed material: 15,000 items. Manuscripts: 5,000. Documents: 1,000,000 held jointly with the Historical Society of Pennsylvania.

Logistical information: closed stacks; collection open to all scholars and the general public; microcard readers available for use; photocopying service; materials neither circulated nor available through interlibrary loan.

Hours: Monday through Friday, 9-4:45.

Assistance: in-house guides and indexes available.

Staff: Chief of Reference Services: Phil Lapsansky.

Contact: Library Company of Philadelphia
1314 Locust Street
Philadelphia, PA 19107
(215) 546-3181

## RHODE ISLAND

382. John Hay Library, Brown University. Sheet Music Collection.

> Holdings. Sheet music: 5,000 pieces by or about black persons.
> Logistical information:   closed stacks; collection open to all
> scholars; carrels available on special request, and open work
> space; equipment available—reel-to-reel tape players and
> recorders, record players, microfilm readers, photocopying
> service; in-house circulation; materials not available through
> interlibrary loan.
> Hours: Monday through Friday, 9-4:30.
> Assistance: limited index available; Computer Output Microform
> Catalog being prepared.
> Staff: Special Collections Librarian: John H. Stanley.
> Contact:   John Hay Library
> Brown University
> Providence, RI 02912
> (401) 863-2146

## TENNESSEE

383. Memphis State University. Mississippi Valley Collection.

> Holdings. Books: 200. Photographs: 200. Sheet music: 1,000.
> Other:   100 items concerning Afro-American music and
> musicians in the Mississippi Valley south of St. Louis, primarily
> since 1840.
> Collection described in:   National Union Catalog of Manuscript
> Collections.
> Special research projects supported: a study of the development of
> the blues and its association with W. C. Handy and with Beale
> Street in Memphis; and a study of the music publishing industry
> in the lower Mississippi Valley.
> Logistical information:   closed stacks; open to all scholars;
> equipment available for use—reel-to-reel and cassette tape
> players and recorders, record players, microforms readers,
> audio-visual projectors, photocopying services; materials
> neither circulated nor available through interlibrary loan.
> Hours: Monday, 8 A.M.-9 P.M. when the University is in session,
> other times, 8-5; Tuesday through Thursday, 8-5.
> Assistance: in-house guides and indexes available.
> Staff: Curator: Eleanor McKay; two Assistant Curators.
> Contact:   Mississippi Valley Collection
> Memphis State University
> Memphis, TN 38152
> (901) 454-2210

384. Country Music Foundation Library and Media Center.

> Holdings. Sound recordings: 75,000 (includes 78-rpm; 45-rpm; LPs;
> 10", 12", and 16" radio transcriptions; and 7" EPs); 4,000 reel-to-

384. Country Music Foundation (continued)

> reel, cassette, and 8-track tapes. Books: 6,500 volumes plus 5,000 bound and unbound song books. Periodicals: 1,700 bound volumes and 300 current subscriptions. Research files: 1,200 subject files. Visuals: 7,500 photographs, 550 video tapes, 700 reels of film. Sheet music: 4,000. Pamphlets: 500.
>
> Significant projects supported. Books: most major studies of country music done in recent years; Country Music Discography, 1922-1942 by Tony Russell (forthcoming).
>
> Logistical information: closed stacks; open to all scholars, and to the general public by appointment; equipment available for use—reel-to-reel and cassette tape players, record players, microfilm readers, film and slide projectors, photocopying service; materials not circulated; photocopies of some materials available through interlibrary loan.
>
> Hours: Monday through Friday, 9-5.
>
> Assistance: some in-house indexes or guides available.
>
> Staff: Director of Library Operations: Danny R. Hatcher; Director of Non-Print Acquisitions: Bob Pinson; Administrative Assistant: Linda Chesnut; Reference Librarian: Ronnie Pugh; Audio Engineer: Alan Stoker; Technical Services Director: Robert K. Oermann; Non-Print Cataloguer: Terry Gordon; and Clerical Assistant: Donald Roy.
>
> Contact:    Country Music Foundation Library and Media Center
> 4 Music Square East
> Nashville, TN 37203
> (615) 256-7008

385. Fisk University Library. Special Collections: Manuscripts and Archives; Black Oral History; The Baldwin Collection of African Drawings; The Bookman-Cheney-Schwerner Collection of Black Books for Children; The George Gershwin Collection of Musical Literature; the Ludie Collins Collection on the Jubilee Singers; the John Wesley Work III Collections, the Eileen Southern Papers, and Oral History Interviews with Afro-American Musicians.

> Holdings. Books. Periodicals. Musical scores. Miscellaneous materials: pertinent to research in black American music.
>
> Collection described in: Dictionary Catalog of the Negro Collection of Fisk University Library, Nashville, Tennessee.
>
> Logistical information: closed stacks; collection open to all scholars; open work space; equipment available—reel-to-reel and cassette tape recorders and players, record players, microfilm readers, audio-visual projectors, photocopying service; materials neither circulated nor available through interlibrary loan.
>
> Hours: Monday through Friday, 8-5.
>
> Assistance: in-house guides and indexes available.
>
> Staff: Special Collections Librarian: Ann Shockley; Assistant Librarian: Beth House.

385. Fisk University (continued)

> Contact:  Special Collections
> Fisk University Library
> Fisk University
> Nashville, TN  37203
> (615) 329-8646

## TEXAS

386. Texas Southern University. The Heartman Collection.

> Holdings. Books. Pamphlets. Lithographs. Oil paintings. Musical
> scores.   Almanacs.   Diaries.   Texas slave narratives.
> Scrapbooks.
> Collection described in: Catalog, Heartman Negro Collection.
> Logistical information:   closed stacks; collection open to all
> scholars; equipment available for use—tape players, record
> players, microforms readers, film, filmstrip and slide
> projectors, and photocopying machine; in-house circulation;
> materials not available through interlibrary loan.
> Hours: Monday through Friday, 8 A.M.-11 P.M.
> Staff:  Head Librarian, Heartman Collection:  Dorothy Chapman;
> Library Assistant: Rebecca Richard.
> Contact:   The Heartman Collection
> Texas Southern University
> 3201 Wheeler
> Houston, TX  77004
> (713) 527-7149

## VIRGINIA

387. Hampton Institute. Hampton Institute Archives.

> Holdings.   Photographs:   40,000.   Primary source material
> concerning:   Hampton Institute Department of Music, the
> Hampton Institute Choir, the Hampton Institute Quartette,
> Dr. R. Nathaniel Dett, Natalie Curtis Burlin, and others.
> Manuscripts:   8, written between 1880-1979.   Theses and
> dissertations: 5.
> Collection described in: Directory of Afro-American Resources by
> Walter Schatz, and Directory of Archives and Manuscript
> Repositories.
> Publications:   Southern Workman, 1872-1939; Hampton and Its
> Students by M. F. Armstrong and H. W. Ludlow; Religious Folk
> Songs of the Negro As Sung at Hampton Institute by R. N.
> Dett; Religious Folk Songs of the Negro As Sung on the
> Plantation by Thomas P. Fenner; A Brief Biography of Dr.
> Robert Nathaniel Dett by Margueritte Pope; and 1,300 other
> items.

387.  Hampton Institute Archives (continued)

> Logistical information:   closed stacks;  collection open to all
> scholars; equipment available for use—reel-to-reel and cassette
> players and recorders, record players, microforms readers,
> film, filmstrip and slide projectors, photocopying service;
> materials neither circulated nor available through interlibrary
> loan.
> Hours: Monday through Friday, 8-5.
> Assistance:  in-house guides and indexes available.
> Staff: Archivist and Curator of Archives: Fritz J. Malval; Archives
> Assistant: Cynthia P. Chapman; Secretary: Cynthia G. Poston;
> Clerk Typist: Constance Y. Grant.
> Contact:   Hampton Institute
>            Hampton Institute Archives
>            Hampton, VA  23668
>            (804) 727-5374

388.  Hampton Institute.  Huntington Library—Peabody Collection.

> Holdings.  Newspaper clippings:  7 notebooks compiled in the early
> 1900s,  including information about R. N. Dett, Harry T.
> Burleigh, James Reese Europe, E. Azalia Hackley, Roland
> Hayes, and S. Coleridge-Taylor.  Periodical articles:  various
> contained in Southern Workman, published 1872-1939.
> Collection(s) described in:  Directory of Afro-American Resources
> by Walter Schatz.
> Logistical information:   closed stacks;  collection open to all
> scholars;  equipment  available  for  use—microfilm  and
> microfiche readers, slide projectors, photocopying service;
> materials neither circulated nor available through interlibrary
> loan.
> Hours:  Monday through Thursday, 9-12, 1-5, 6-10:45; Friday and
> Saturday, 9-12, 1-5; Sunday, 3-5, 6-10.
> Assistance:  no index or guide available.
> Staff:  Librarian:   Gaynell Drummond; Library Clerk:   Cynthia
> McGee; student assistants.
> Contact:   Huntington Library—Peabody Collection
>            Hampton Institute
>            Hampton, VA  23668
>            (804) 727-5371

# Appendix

# Appendix

Included here are sources of a general nature that are indispensable to basic research--writing and style manuals, finding sources, indexes, and other reference works useful to research in several different fields. Since such works are critical to certain aspects of research in black American music, but will be unfamiliar to novice researchers, we have provided here an annotated listing. These works should not be overlooked.

## *DIRECTORIES*

A1. McDonald, Donna, ed. and comp. Directory of Historical Societies and Agencies in the United States and Canada. Nashville, Tenn.: American Association for State and Local History, 1956-. each vol. approx. 375-475 pp. index. published biennially.

This is a compilation of more than five thousand organizations whose efforts are devoted to the preservation and dissemination of historical knowledge. The Directory is arranged alphabetically by state and Canadian province, with each listing including the name of the society or agency, its mailing address, telephone number, and other basic information; it does not include specific information on the institution's holdings. While it is a valuable reference source for scholars involved in general historical research, it is equally useful to scholars engaged in biographical and genealogical studies on black musicians, as well as those researching aspects of the history of black American music.
Reviews: American Reference Books Annual 10:207 '79; American Reference Books Annual 11:83-84 '80

A2. Young, Margaret Labash, and Harold Chester Young, eds. Directory of Special Libraries and Information Centers: A Guide to Special Libraries, Research Libraries, Information Centers, Archives, and Data Centers Maintained by Government Agencies, Business, Industry, Newspapers, Educational Institutions, Non-profit Organizations, and Societies in the Fields of Science, Technology, Medicine, Law, Art, Religion, History, Social Sciences, and Humanistic Studies. 2 vols. Detroit: Gale Research Co., 1981. xix, 1425; ix, 776 pp. appendix. indexes.

> The first volume of this work is an alphabetical listing of libraries that were designed to serve particular needs or interests. The name of each library is accompanied by its address and other contact data, as well as information about the size of its staff, special collection(s), services provided to visiting scholars, publications issued by the library, an estimate of the size of its holdings, and other pertinent data. The subject index contains references to libraries under the topics of "Music," "Jazz music," "Folk music," and others. The second volume of the work comprises a geographical index and a personnel index. In the former, references to the main body (first volume) of the work are arranged alphabetically by state and by city; the latter contains the names of the librarians and curators of the special libraries in alphabetical order.
>
> Reviews: Religious Studies Review 7:61 Ja '81

## *RESEARCH TOOLS*

A3. Guide to Reprints. 2 vols. Kent, Conn.: Guide to Reprints, 1981. xii, 974 pp.
Subject Guide to Reprints. 2 vols. Kent, Conn.: Guide to Reprints, 1981. xvii, 1052 pp.

> The Guide is an annual cumulative listing of books and periodicals printed by more than four hundred international publishing firms; the entries in this set are listed alphabetically by author. The Subject Guide is a companion volume, published biennially, with the same information organized into subject classifications. Both versions of the work list materials that were out-of-print and are now back in print. Each entry in the two sets gives the following information: name of author or editor, title, volume number or number of volumes, date of original publication, publisher's designation, and price. A quick and random perusal of the listings will reveal the presence of a number of books on black music, including Alain Locke, The Negro and His Music (1936); Edith Isaacs, The Negro in the American Theater (1947); J. W. and J. R. Johnson, The Books of American Negro Spirituals (1942); and John W. Work, Folk Song of the American Negro (1915).

A4. Modern Language Association. MLA Handbook: For Writers of Research Papers, Theses, and Dissertations. New York: Modern Language Association, 1977. [ix], 163 pp. illustrations. appendix. index. sample pages.

A4.  MLA (continued)

A valuable aid to the mechanics and proper documentation of any scholarly writing, this book treats all phases of the technical procedure of writing a research paper from methods for selecting a topic to typing the final draft.  The book is divided into six sections:   "Research and Writing," "Mechanics of Writing," "Preparing the Manuscript," "Documentation," "Bibliography," and "Abbreviations and Reference Works."  Nearly one-half of the book is devoted to the Documentation and Bibliography sections, which contain numerous examples of an accepted bibliographic format for citing various sources of information.  Among the other topics discussed in the text are rules for punctuation and capitalization, for the spacing of margins and text in the typescript, and for the handling of quotations in the text.  The appendix treats the differing requirements for preparation of theses and dissertations.
Reviews:    American Reference Books Annual 10:66 '79; Quarterly Journal of Speech 64:359 O '78

A5.  Rivers, William L.   Finding Facts:  Interviewing, Observing, Using Reference Sources.  Englewood Cliffs, N.J.:  Prentice-Hall, 1975.  xi, 226 pp. index.

This book represents an attempt to bring together and relate the experiences and insights of researchers who search out, uncover, and weigh facts of all kinds.  The chapter on "Central Sources" will be particularly useful since it identifies and provides abstracts for the more general sources that are not listed in the present volume— sources such as the New York Times Index, Book Review Index, What Happened When, Encyclopedia of American History, and other generalized and specialized dictionaries, encyclopedias, biographical dictionaries and indexes, yearbooks and almanacs, books of quotations, atlases, guides, and other such reference tools; also included are some of the important sources of various disciplines such as history, philosophy and religion, and sociology and anthropology.  The chapter on interviewing will be helpful to researchers who conduct interviews for both oral history documentation and for the writing of research reports; it discusses the roles of the interviewer and the interviewee, questioning procedures, establishing guidelines for interviews, conducting the interview, and some of the benefits and pitfalls of the interview process.
Reviews: Journalism Quarterly 53:758 Winter '76

A6.  University of Chicago Press.   The Chicago Manual of Style:  For Authors, Editors, and Copywriters.  13th ed., rev. and enl.  Chicago: University of Chicago Press, 1982.  iv, 738 pp.  drawings, photographs, tables, figures. glossary. bibliography. index.

A standard guide to the proper preparation of a manuscript, the volume consists of three sections:  "Bookmaking," "Style," and "Production and Printing."  The second section makes up the main part of the work and is perhaps of most immediate interest to authors; contained in this section are rules, with examples, for

A6. University of Chicago Press (continued)

handling such topics as punctuation, quotations, illustrations, spelling and word division, capitalization, notes and footnotes, bibliographies, abbreviations, and indexes.

## *METHODOLOGY*

A7. Everton, George B., Sr. The How Book for Genealogists. 7th ed. Logan, Utah: Everton Publishers, 1977. vi, 237 pp. charts. index.

Researchers who wish to track down information on deceased musicians about whom little or nothing is known will need some familiarity with genealogical techniques. This book explains how to get started with such research, and provides a practical guide to genealogical study. Geared to local research, the book presents information on the formation, history, and vital records of every county in the United States, and a brief history of each state that was a member of the Union at the time the book was first published. For novices, a "Dictionary of Genealogical Words, Terms and Abbreviations" is included.

A8. Greenwood, Val D. The Researcher's Guide to American Genealogy. Introduction by Milton Rubicam. Baltimore: Genealogical Publishing Co., 1973. xv, 535 pp. charts, maps, facsimiles. index.

This guide discusses the basic principles of genealogical research and examines the records that researchers will encounter when engaged in such work. Recognizing genealogy as a branch of history that demands an investigation based on the discovery and interpretation of facts, the author presents a detailed approach to research in the field, discussing such topics as: the nature of genealogical research, records and terminology, research tools, organization and evaluation, correspondence, newspapers, vital records, census returns, wills, deeds, probate records, and burial records. This is a thorough and basic background and reference work.
Reviews: AB Bookman's Weekly 75:660 Au 27 '73; Choice 10:1698 Ja '74; Kirkus Reviews 42:472 Ap 15 '74; Library Journal 99:1692 Ju 15 '74; Reference Services Review 2:27 Jy '74

## *DICTIONARY CATALOGUES AND RELATED SOURCES*

A9. Ash, Lee, comp. Subject Collections: A Guide to Special Book Collections and Subject Emphases As Reported by University, College, Public and Special Libraries and Museums in the United States and Canada. 5th ed. New York: R. R. Bowker Co., 1978. x, 1184 pp.

Collections in libraries and museums, as well as several personal holdings, are listed in this book. The entries are organized by

A9. Ash (<u>continued</u>)

subject with subheadings that refer to particular institutions. Contact data includes the name of the librarian or director and the address of the institution; the body of each subheading is a brief outline of the contents of the collection with which it is concerned. While this book is a general reference work, it does contain descriptions of collections that are important to the study of black American music.

Reviews: Catholic World Library 50:407 Ap '79; College and Research Libraries 40:378 Jy '79; Library Journal 104:1043 My 1 '79; Wilson Library Bulletin 53:587 Ap '79

A10. Library of Congress, Copyright Office. <u>Dramatic Compositions Copyrighted in the United States, 1870 to 1916.</u> 2 vols. Washington, D.C.: Government Printing Office, 1918. v, 3547 pp.

Titles of plays copyrighted between 1870 and 1916 are listed alphabetically in this two-volume book. Each entry in the book contains information concerning the title, author, copyright date, copyright owner, and copyright number. Access to a drama by a particular author may be obtained through the use of the index of authors, editors, and translators. Among the black authors whose works are listed in this set are Bob Cole, Will Marion Cook, and J. Rosamund Johnson.

Reviews: Library Journal 44:14 '19

A11. Library of Congress. <u>National Union Catalog</u>. Washington, D.C.: Library of Congress, 1942-. each vol. approx. 500-600 pp.

In several compilations, the catalogue appears with varying subtitles and has been published by three different firms: <u>Pre-1956 Imprints</u>. London: Mansell Publishers, 1968-1980. <u>1956 Through 1967</u>. Totowa, N.J.: Rowman and Littlefield, 1970-1972. <u>Author List, 1968-1972</u>. Ann Arbor, Mich.: J. W. Edwards Publishers, 1973. <u>Author List, 1973-1977</u>. Totowa, N.J.: Rowman and Littlefield, 1978. <u>Author List, 1978-</u>. Totowa, N.J.: Rowman and Littlefield, 1979-.

A compilation of photocopied catalogue cards which reflects the holdings in the U. S. Library of Congress, arranged alphabetically by author, entries in this catalogue provide bibliographic information, the Library of Congress and Dewey decimal system numbers, and an indication of other libraries in which the particular book may be found. This set is indispensable for researchers who wish to locate and acquire certain materials. For example, a user consulting <u>Pre-1956 Imprints</u> for works by W. C. Handy will find 21 different entries—four books, ten music collections, and seven pieces of sheet music—held variously by more than fifty libraries in the United States and Canada, all of which have interlibrary loan services.

A12. Library of Congress. <u>National Union Catalog of Manuscript Collections,</u> 1959-1976. Washington, D.C.: Library of Congress, 1962-. each vol. approx. 250 pp. indexes.

A12. NUC Manuscript Collections (<u>continued</u>)

> This series of books contains succinct descriptions of the contents of manuscript collections held by various American repositories. Each entry indicates the following information: 1) the number of items held, 2) the general contents, 3) the names of prominent or famous persons to whom collection materials are related, and 4) the original source or contributor. The collections are arranged in order of card identification number. It is necessary to use the general index or the repository index in order to find a desired subject. Cumulative indexes are published for the years 1959-1962, 1963-1966, 1967-1969, and 1970-1974.
>
>> Reviews: AB Bookman's Weekly 43:279 Ja 27 '69; American Archivist 32:273 Jy '69; American Archivist 33:334 Jy '70; American Historical Review 75:193 O '69; Bibliographical Society of America—Papers 66:81 Ja '72; RQ 13:359 Summer '74

A13. Library of Congress. <u>New Serial Titles: A Union List of Serials Commencing Publication After December 31, 1949.</u> 8 vols. New York: R. R. Bowker Co., 1973. 6712 pp. supplement [published by The Library of Congress].

> This book is an alphabetic list of the titles of new serials that were received by the Library of Congress and cooperating libraries during the time period indicated. Each entry consists of the serial's bibliographic information, its Library of Congress classification number, a list of libraries that hold the serial, and the particular volumes held in those libraries. This set will contain periodical titles that will not be found in the <u>Union List of Serials.</u>
>
>> Reviews: Booklist 71:253 O 15 '74; Choice 11:740 Jy '74; College and Research Libraries 35:245 Jy '74; Reference Services Review 2:21 Ap '74; Wilson Library Bulletin 48:765 My '74

A14. Titus, Edna Brown, ed. <u>Union List of Serials in Libraries of the United States and Canada.</u> 5 vols. 3rd ed. New York: H. W. Wilson Co., 1965. 4649 pp.

> These volumes comprise a list of serial titles held by libraries cooperating, under the sponsorship of the American Library Association, in the compilation of the five-volume set. Prepared under the sponsorship of the American Library Association's Joint Committee on the Union List of Serials with the cooperation of the Library of Congress, it includes serials held in libraries in all fifty states in the United States and eight provinces of Canada. Alphabetized by serial title, each entry provides bibliographic information and indicates libraries in which the serial is held and inclusive dates of publication. This set is indispensable for determining the locations of periodicals not readily available to researchers.
>
>> Reviews: College and Research Libraries 27:306 Jy '66; Wilson Library Bulletin 40:483 F '66

# BIBLIOGRAPHIES OF BIBLIOGRAPHIES

A15. Besterman, Theodore. A World Bibliography of Bibliographies, Digests, Indexes, and the Like. 5 vols. 4th ed., rev. and enl. Lausanne, Switzerland: Societas Bibliographica, 1965-1966. 8425 pp. index.

> This set contains standard bibliographic information about bibliographies that appear as individual publications in all languages. Entries are arranged in chronological order under alphabetical subject headings; some are accompanied by brief annotations. Bibliographies relevant to black music research may be found under topical headings (e.g., jazz), under "Music" (especially "Music, United States"), and under rubrics of a more general nature (e.g., "Negroes"). The final volume of the set is an author index.

A16. Case, Ann Massie, ed. Bibliographic Index: A Cumulative Bibliography of Bibliographies. Bronx, N.Y.: H. W. Wilson Co., 1937-. each vol. approx. 500-1800 pp.

> Each volume in this set consists of an alphabetical list of subject headings under which is listed information about bibliographies containing more than fifty entries and appearing in periodicals, books, and pamphlets published in the year(s) with which the volume is concerned. Entries pertinent to black music researchers are contained under headings of a specific nature (such as "Jazz," "Blues," and "Ragtime"), as well as under headings of a more general nature (such as "Negroes in the United States"). The Index is useful in the early stages of research as a tool for finding bibliographies to be consulted for sources of information about a particular research topic.
> Reviews: Booklist 35:243 Ap 1 '39; Pratt Institute Quarterly p3 Winter '40; Wilson Library Bulletin 35:138 Jy '39

A17. Sheehy, Eugene P. Guide to Reference Books. 9th ed. Chicago: American Library Association, 1976. xviii, 1015 pp. supplement. index.

Revised and expanded version of the 8th edition by C. M. Winchell.

> This volume contains annotated bibliographic entries for general reference works and for reference sources in the fields of the humanities, the social sciences, history, and the pure and applied sciences. Among the categories into which the humanities section is divided are "Fine Arts," "Theater Arts," and "Music." Under "Music," the following headings are pertinent to black music research: "Bibliography," "Indexes," "Musical Theater," "Songs," "Jazz," "Folk and Popular Music," "Recorded Music," and "Reviews." The entries under each heading are composed of standard bibliographic information and a brief annotation. The majority of the reference works cited in this volume were published before 1974. The supplement is arranged in a manner similar to that of the main volume with the addition of a category concerned with computer data bases available for use by the researcher.

A17. Sheehy (continued)

> Reviews:   American Reference Books Annual 8:3 '77;
> Antiquarian Bookman 16:45 N '77; Choice 14:516 Ju '77; College
> and Research Libraries 38:262 My '77; Journal of Academic
> Librarianship 3:37 Mr '77; Library Journal 101:2560 D 15 '76;
> Library Quarterly 48:60 Ja '78; Special Libraries 70:6 Ja '79;
> Wilson Library Bulletin 51:442 Ja '77

## INDEXES AND GUIDES
## TO PERIODICAL LITERATURE

A18. American Studies Program, George Washington University, Washington,
D.C. Analytical Guide and Indexes to "The Crisis," 1910-1960.  3 vols.
Rose Bibliography (Project).  Westport, Conn.:  Greenwood Press, 1975.
x, 373; 397; 333 pp.  indexes.

> This index is a guide to the articles that appeared in Crisis
> magazine during the period indicated.  Volumes 1 and 2 are a
> chronological index which presents detailed information on each
> article listed—publication date, literary type, special character-
> istics, special literary devices employed, readership (i.e., literary,
> technical, popular, or scholarly), etc.  Volume 3 contains author,
> title, and subject indexes, each presented alphabetically, keyed to
> the chronological guide.   The subject index lists 126 articles on
> music.

A19. Faxon, Frederick W., Mary E. Bates, and Anne C. Sutherland, eds.
Cumulated Magazine Subject Index, 1907-1949: A Cumulation of The
F. W. Faxon Company's Annual Magazine Subject Index.  Boston:  G. K.
Hall & Co., 1964. xvi, 951; x, 935 pp.

> This work indexes articles that appeared in 175 periodicals during
> the first half of the twentieth century.  The entries are organized
> under an alphabetical listing of subjects.  Information about black
> music may be found by searching subjects such as "Negro Music,"
> "Folk Songs," and "Jazz"; more general sociological information
> may be found under the headings "Negroes," and "Negroes in the
> United States."

A20. Marconi, Joseph V.   Indexed Periodicals:   A Guide to 170 Years of
Coverage in 33 Indexing Services.   Ann Arbor, Mich.:  Pierian Press,
1976. xxvi, 416 pp.

> This book consists of an alphabetical listing of "approximately
> 11,000 periodical and serial titles, title changes, and cross
> references" (p. xi).  In addition to the title, each entry contains
> information about the publication dates of the work and a listing of
> the source(s) in which it is indexed, together with the volume
> numbers in the source and the dates during which the item was
> indexed in the source.  Some listed periodicals of possible interest
> to a black music researcher are Journal of Negro History, Phylon,

A20.  Marconi (continued)

Southern Workman, Crisis, Black Scholar, and Black World.  The book treats the contents of thirty-three indexes over a period of 170 years from 1802 to 1973.

Reviews:  American Reference Books Annual 8:24 '77; Catholic Library Review 49:405 Ap '78; Choice 14:1626 F '78; College and Research Libraries 38:323 Jy '77; RQ 17:364 Summer '78; Serials Review 5:62 Jy '79; Wilson Library Bulletin 51:265 N '76

A21.  Reader's Guide to Periodical Literature:  An Author and Subject Index. 40 vols. New York: H. W. Wilson Co., 1944-. each vol. approx. 1750 pp.

This guide indexes more than two hundred periodicals "of general interest published in the United States" since 1890 (p. [vii]).  Authors and subjects are listed under one alphabet.  In this cumulated set, one will find citations for a variety of articles on music and for reviews of books, musicals, operas, and phonorecords that appear in such magazines as Ebony, Essence, Humanist, New York Review of Books, New Republic, Opera News, Rolling Stone, People, Down Beat, and High Fidelity and Musical America.  This a standard source for journal citations of articles published outside the scholarly community.

## DICTIONARIES AND ENCYCLOPEDIAS

A22.  Akey, Denise S., ed.  Encyclopedia of Associations.  2 vols. in 3.  17th ed.  Detroit: Gale Research Co., 1982.  1781; 993 pp.  indexes.

Among the large number of national and international associations listed here can be found the names, addresses, telephone numbers, executive directors, and the descriptions of numerous musical associations, among which are included the Afro-American Music Opportunities Association and the National Association of Negro Musicians.

A23.  Crowley, Ellen T., ed.  Acronyms, Initialisms & Abbreviations Dictionary.  3 vols. 7th ed.  Detroit: Gale Research Co., 1980.  each vol. approx. 1300 pp. supplement.

In the course of certain studies, researchers will encounter the acronyms of various organizations and agencies.  For example, the Association for the Advancement of Creative Musicians and the National Association of Negro Musicians have their identifying initials, respectively, as follows:  AACM, NANM.  Such acronyms can be identified by consulting this work.

# Indexes

# Index of Titles

(Roman numerals refer to pages in the front matter; Arabic numerals refer to entry numbers in the text; Arabic numerals preceded by the letter "A" refer to entry numbers in the Appendix.)

"Black Women in American Bands and Orchestras," 250
"Blacking Up," 174
"Blacks in America," 33
"Blacks in Blackface," 246
"Blacks in Classical Music," 247
"Blind Tom," xvi
"Blue Book of Hollywood Musicals, The," 242
"Blue Book of Tin Pan Alley," 227
"Blues/An Anthology," 315
"Blues and Gospel Records," 75,79
"Blues and the Poetic Spirit," 179
"Blues Harp Songbook," 314
"Blues Line, The," 187
"Bluesmen, The," 254
"Blues People," 136
"Blues Records, January 1943 to December 1966," 79
"Blues Who's Who," 129
"Book of Jazz, From Then Til Now, The," 197
"Book of Rock Lists, The," 236
"Book of the Blues, The," 316
"Book Review Digest," ix
"Book Review Index," ix
"Books of American Negro Spirituals, The," 306
"Brass Bands and New Orleans Jazz," 224
"Brown Sugar," 253


"Calhoun Plantation Songs," 290
"Catalog of Afro-American Music and Oral Data Holdings," 60
"Catalog of Copyright Entries: Music," 106
"Catalog of Copyright Entries: Sound Recordings," 58
"Catalog of Phonograph Records," 60
"Catalog of Published Concert Music by American Composers," 103
"Catalog of the E. Azalia Hackley Memorial Collection of Negro Music, Dance, and Drama," 14
"Catalog of the John D. Reid Collection of Early American Jazz," 70
"Check-List of Recorded Songs. . . ," 59
"Chicago Manual of Style, The," A6
"Choral Music of Afro-American Composers," 57
"Classic Piano Rags," 308
"Collected Works of Scott Joplin, The," 309
"Colored Sacred Harp, The," 305
"Combined Retrospective Index to Book Reviews in Scholarly Journals, 1886-1974," ix
"Complete Catalogue of Sheet Music and Musical Works, 1870," 99
"Complete Encyclopedia of Popular Music and Jazz, 1900-1950, The," 120
"Composing for the Jazz Orchestra," xvii
"Concert Music and Spirituals," 84
"Contemporary American Composers," 126
"Conversations with Jazz Musicians," 258
"Cumulated Magazine Subject Index, 1907-1949," A19
"Current Book Review Citations," ix

Index of Titles

"Fifteen Black Composers," 248, 249
"Fifty Years of Recorded Jazz, 1917-1967," 63
"Finding Facts," A5
"Finding List of Vocal Music," 104
"Folk and Traditional Music of the Western Continents," xvi
"Folk Music," 60
"Folk Music of the United States," 60
"Folk Music of the United States and Latin America," 60
"Folk Music Sourcebook, The," 161
"Folksingers and Folksongs in America," 158
"Folk Song of the American Negro," 164
"Folk Songs of the American Negro," 296
"Folksongs of Virginia, The," 56
"Four Lives in the Bebop Business," 256
"Free Jazz," 206


"Giants of Ragtime," 310
"Georgia Sea Island Songs," 326
"Golden Age of Jazz, The," 265
"Golden Oldies," 80
"Gospel Sound, The," 225
"Gospel Sound, The," (sound recording), 327
"Great Jug Bands, 1926-1934, The," 320
"Guide for Dating Early Music," 9
"Guide to Jazz," 212
"Guide to Reference Books," A17
"Guide to Reprints," A3


"Harvard Guide to Contemporary Literature," xvii
"History of Jazz, The," 333
"History of Jazz in America, A," 219
"History of Jazz Series," 334
"History of Military Music in America, A," xv
"History of Philadelphia, 1609-1885, A," xv
"History of Rhythm and Blues, The," 329
"Honkers and Shouters," 239
"How Book for Genealogists, The," A7


"Improvising Jazz," 273
"In Black and White," 34
"Indexed Periodicals," A20
"Index to Biographies of Contemporary Composers," 27
"Index to Black Poetry," xvii
"Index to Jazz," 62
"Index to Negro Spirituals," 100
"Index to Periodical Articles By and About Blacks," 87
"Index to Periodical Articles By and About Negroes," 87
"Index to Record and Tape Reviews," 94
"Index to Selected Periodicals Received in the Hallie Q. Brown Memorial Library," 87

215

"Index to the New World Recorded Anthology of American Music," 101
"Inside Be-Bop," 198
"International Bibliography of Discographies," 29
"International Index of Dissertations," xviii
"International Jazz Bibliography," 37
"Interpretation of the Jazz Language, The," 279
"Introduction to Classic Jazz, An," 335
"Inventory of the Bibliographies and Other Reference and Finding Aids. . .,
     An," 25


"Jazz," 73
"Jazz: A History," 280
"Jazz: A History of the New York Scene," 194
"Jazz: Hot & Hybrid," 213
"Jazz: An Introduction to Its Musical Basis," 275
"Jazz, New Orleans, 1885-1963," 257
"Jazz: A People's Music," 199
"Jazz: A Photo History," 263
"Jazz and the White Americans," 208
"Jazz Bibliography," 42
"Jazz Book, The," 189
"Jazz Dance," 217
"Jazz Improvisation," xvii
"Jazz Index, The," 96
"Jazz in the Movies," 210
"Jazz in the Sixties," 192
"Jazz Lexicon, A," 117
"Jazz Life, The," 204
"Jazz Masters in Transition, 1957-69," 220
"Jazz Masters of New Orleans," 221
"Jazz Masters of the Fifties," 201
"Jazz Masters of the Forties," 200
"Jazz Masters of the Thirties," 218
"Jazz Masters of the Twenties," 203
"Jazz Music in Print," 110
"Jazz on Record," 65
"Jazz on Record; A Critical Guide to the First Fifty Years," 69
"Jazz People," 260
"Jazz Photo Album," 267
"Jazz Publicity II," 47
"Jazz Records, 1897-1942," 67, 72
"Jazz Records, 1942-1969," 67, 72
"Jazz Reference and Research Materials," xvii, 49
"Jazz-Rock Fusion," 228
"Jazzshots," 269
"Jazz Solography Series, The," 64
"Jazz Street," 271
"Jazz Styles," 276
"Jazz Talk," 118
"Jazz Text, The," 277
"Jazz Tradition, The," 222
"Jubilee Singers and Their Campaign for Twenty Thousand Dollars, The," 170

Index of Titles

"Language of Twentieth Century Music, The," 111
"Lillian Roxon's Rock Encyclopedia," 122
"Listener's Guide to the Blues, The," 180
"Listening to Jazz," 274
"Literature of American Music in Books and Folk Collections, The," xi, 43
"Literature of Jazz, The," (Kennington and Read), 45
"Literature of Jazz, The," (Reisner), 53
"Lydian Chromatic Concept of Tonal Organization for Improvisation, The," xvii


"Making of Jazz, The," 195
"Ma Rainey and the Classic Blues Singers," 255
"Max Morath's Guide to Ragtime," 311
"Mellows: A Chronicle of Unknown Singers," 293
"Men of Mark," xvi
"MLA Handbook," A4
"Music: A Dissertation Bibliography," xviii
"Music and Phonorecords," 18, 22
"Music and Some Highly Musical People," 151
"Music Article Guide," 95
"Music, Books on Music and Sound Recordings," 18
"Music Index, The," ix, 93
"Music in Europe and the United States," xiv
"Music in Latin America," xv
"Music in New Orleans," xv
"Music in Philadelphia," xv
"Music in the Americas," xv
"Music in the 20th Century," xiv
"Music Library Association Catalog of Cards for Printed Music, 1953-1972," 22
"Music of Africa, The," xv
"Music of Black Americans, The," 149
"Music on My Mind," xvi
"Music Periodical Literature," 26
"Music, Printed and Manuscript, in the James Weldon Johnson Memorial Collection of Negro Arts and Letters," 13
"Music Reference and Research Materials," 39
"My Songs," 304


"Name List of Black Composers, A," 2
"National Union Catalog," A11
"National Union Catalog of Manuscript Collections, 1959-1976," A12
"Negro Almanac, The," 145
"Negro and His Folklore in Nineteenth Century Periodicals, The," 155
"Negro and His Music, The," 143
"Negro and His Songs, The," 159
"Negro Authors and Composers of the United States," 251
"Negro Blues and Hollers," 321
"Negro Folk Music, U.S.A.," 153
"Negro in the American Theatre, The," 244
"Negro Minstrels," 172

217

Index of Titles


"Researcher's Guide to American Genealogy, The," A8
"Resources in American Music History," xix
"Rhythm on Record," 81
"Right On," 235
"RILM Abstracts," 92
"Rock Is Rhythm and Blues (The Impact of Mass Media)," 238
"Rockmaster," 78
"Rock On," 121
"Rock Record," 78
"Rolling Along in Song," 292
"Roll, Jordan, Roll," xiv
"Roots of Black Music in America," 224
"Roots of the Blues," 330


"Saint Helena Island Spirituals," 299
"Savannah Syncopators," xv, 185
"Scandalize My Name," 230
"Select Bibliography of Music in Africa, A," xv
"Selected Bibliography of Published Choral Music by Black Composers," 57
"Seventy Negro Spirituals," 303
"Shining Trumpets," 190
"Sibley Music Library Catalog of Sound Recordings," 23
"Sinful Tunes and Spirituals," 154
"Singing Campaign for Ten Thousand Pounds, The," 171
"Singing Soldiers," 295
"Sketches of Noted Banjo Players," 252
"Slave Narratives," 152
"Slave Songs of the United States," 298
"Smithsonian Collection of Classic Jazz, The," 336
"Social Implications of Early Negro Music in the United States, The," 156
"Some Aspects of the Religious Music of the United States Negro," 226
"Songs from Hollywood Musical Comedies, 1927 to the Present," 124
"Songs in Collections," 102
"Songs of the American Theater," 55
"Songs of Zion," 301
"Sound of Soul, The," 233
"Source Book of African and Afro-American Materials for Music Educators," 283
"Spirituals and the Blues, The," 165
"Stomping the Blues," 182
"Story of the Blues, The," 186
"Story of the Blues, The," (sound recording), 331
"Story of the Jubilee Singers, The," 169
"Story of the Original Dixieland Jazz Band, The," 191
"Subject Collections," A9
"Subject Guide to Reprints," A3
"Sweet and Lowdown," 229
"Swing Out," 264


"Ten Modern Jazzmen," 205
"Theses and Dissertations on Black American Music," 50

# Index of Authors, Editors, and Compilers

(Roman numerals refer to pages in the front matter; Arabic numerals refer to entry numbers in the text; Arabic numerals preceded by the letter "A" refer to entry numbers in the Appendix.)

Abdul, Raoul, 247
Abrahams, Roger D., 35
Adkins, Cecil, xviii
Aebersold, Jamey, xvii
Akey, Denise S., A22
Allen, William Francis, 298
American Studies Program, George Washington University, A18
Anderson, Ruth E., 126
Ash, Lee, A9
Austin, William, xiv

Baker, David N., xvii, 248
Ballanta-(Taylor), Nicholas George Julius, 299
Banner, James M., Jr., 33
Baraka, Amiri, 136
Bardolph, Richard, 137
Bates, Mary E. A19
Béhague, Gerard, xv
Bell, Michael D., 33
Belt, Lida M., 248

Benford, Robert J., 51
Berendt, Joachim E., 189, 263
Berlin, Edward A., 175
Besterman, Theodore, A15
Biesenthal, Linda, 97, 98
Blackstone, Orin, 62
Blesh, Rudi, 176, 190, 308
Board of Music Trade of the United States of America, 99
Bodkin, B. A., 152
Boggs, Ralph, xvi
Bogle, Donald, 253
Bordman, Gerald, 241
Borenstein, Larry, 256
Borroff, Edith, xiv
Boston Public Library, 12
Botkin, B. A., 323
Breed, Paul F., 102
Briegleb, Ann, 1
Brook, Barry S., 92
Brown, Rae Linda, 13
Brown, William W., 300
Brunn, H. O., 191

Hady, Maureen E., 91
Hadlock, Richard, 203
Hallie Q. Brown Memorial Library, 87
Hallowell, Emily, 290
Handy, D. Antoinette, 250
Handy, W. C., xvi, 251, 315
Haralambos, Michael, 235
Hardy, Phil, 119
Hare, Maud Cuney, 141
Harris, Sheldon, 129
Harrison, Max, 69
Hatch, James V., 32
Haverly, Jack, 172
Havlice, Patricia Pate, 195
Hayes, Cedric J., 77
Hayes, Roland, 304
Haywood, Charles, 41
Hefele, Bernhard, 42
Heilbut, Tony, 225
Hentoff, Nat, 204
Holland, Laurence B., 33
Hood, Mantle, 8
Horn, David, xi, 43
Hounsome, Terry, 78
Howard, John Tasker, xv
Howard University Library, 16, 17
Hudson, Herman C., 248
Hughes, Langston, 266

Irvine, Demar, 7
Isaacs, Edith Rich, 244

Jablonski, Edward, 112
Jackson, Bruce, 155, 290
Jackson, George Pullen, 167
Jackson, Irene V., 44
Jackson, Judge, 305
Jackson, Richard, 24
Jacobs, Donald M., 88
James, Michael, 205
Janis, Harriet, 176
Jasen, David A., 66, 177
Jepsen, Jorgen, 67, 72
Johnson, Guy B., 159, 160
Johnson, J. Rosamund, 292, 306
Johnson, James Peter, x
Johnson, James Weldon, 306
Jones, John Paul, 223
Jones, Max, 267
Jost, Ekkehard, 206

Kaiser, Ernest, 145
Kane, Randall, 110
Katz, Bernard, 156
Keepnews, Orin, 268
Keil, Charles, 181
Kennedy, R. Emmett, 293
Kennington, Donald, 45
Kinkle, Roger D., 120
Kmen, Henry A., xv
Knauss, Zane, 258
Kofsky, Frank, 207
Korner, Alex, 65
Krehbiel, Henry Edward, 157
Kretzschmar, Florence, 93
Krummel, D. W., xix, 9
Kunstadt, Leonard, 194

LaBrew, Arthur, 142
LaBrie, Henry G., 89
Laing, Dave, 119
Landeck, Beatrice, 294
Lawless, Ray M., 158
Lawrence, Vera Brodsky, 309
Lawrenz, Marguerite Martha, 46
Layne, Maude Wanzer, 261
Leadbitter, Mike, 79
Leonard, Neil, 208
Levine, Lawrence, xiv
Lewine, Richard, 55
Library of Congress, 90, A10, A11, A12, A13
Library of Congress, Archive of Folk Song, 25
Library of Congress, Copyright Office, 58, 106, A10
Library of Congress, Music Division, 59, 60, 107, 108
List, George, xv
Locke, Alain, 143
Lomax, Alan, 319, 325, 326, 330
Lovell, John, 168
Lovinggood, Penman, 262
Lyons, Len, 68

McCarthy, Albert, 69, 209
McCoy, Meredith, 70
McDonald, Donna, A1
McIlhenny, E. A., 307
McPherson, James M., 33
Maleady, Antoinette O., 94
Mapp, Edward, 4
Marconi, Joseph V., A20
Markewich, Reese, 47, 48

Southern, Eileen, xvi, 132, 149, 150, 287
Spalding, Henry D., 134
Spellman, A. B., 259
Spitzer, David D., 270
Spradling, Mary Mace, 34
Stagg, Tom, 73
Stambler, Irwin, 123
Standifer, James A., 283
Stearns, Jean, 217
Stearns, Marshall, 217, 321
Stein, Kevin, 236
Stewart, Rex, 218
Stewart, S. S., 252
Stewart-Baxter, Derrick, 255
Stock, Dennis, 271
Strache, Neil E., 91
Sutherland, Anne C., A19
Szwed, John F., xiv, 35

Terry, Clark, 379
Tichenor, Trebor Jay, 177, 313
Tirro, Frank, 280
Tischler, Alice, 248, 250
Titon, Jeff Todd, 188
Titus, Edna Brown, A14
Toll, Robert C., 174
Trotter, James M., 151
Tudor, Dean, 74, 82, 97, 98
Tudor, Nancy, 74, 82
Turner, Patricia, 86

Ulanov, Barry, 219
University of Chicago Press, A6
University of Rochester, Eastman School of Music, 23

Voigt, John, 110

Ware, Charles Pickard, 298
Waschsmann, K. P., xv
Weiss, Nancy J., 33
Weissman, Dick, 161
Welding, Pete, 328
Welsch, Erwin K., 91
Wentworth, Harold, 135
Wescott, Thompson, xv
West, Earle H., 36
Whitburn, Joel, 83

White, Evelyn Davidson, 57
White, Newman I., 163
White, William Carter, xv
Whitten, Norman E., xiv
Williams, Martin, 220, 221, 222, 336
Wilmer, Valerie, 260, 272
Winchell, C. M., A17
Wiskerchen, George, 281
Woll, Allen L., 124
Wood, Graham, 125
Work, Frederick J., 296
Work, John Wesley, 164, 297
Work, Monroe N., xiv

Yenser, Thomas, xvi
Young, Harold Chester, A2
Young, Margaret Labash, A2

# Index of Subjects

(Roman numerals refer to pages in the front matter; Arabic numerals refer to entry numbers in the text; Arabic numerals preceded by the letter "A" refer to entry numbers in the Appendix.)

chain-gang, 160; characteristics of, 164; check-list of recorded, 59; Creole, 157, 294; of Cuba, 294; for dance, 162; dialect in, 298; discographies of, 158; discussions of, 157, 163; of the Georgia Sea Islands, 299; of Haiti, 294; himes, 293; jail-house, 292; jubilees, 292; lists of, 158; of love, 292; lullabyes, 162; about man-woman relationships, 160; mellows, 293; melodic characteristics of, 160; of Mexico, 294; miscellaneous, 163, 297; origin of, 298; of Panama, 294; performance practice and, 298; plantation, 296; prison, 291; of Puerto Rico, 293; railroad, 162; religious, 160; ring shouts, 292; "seamy" songs, 163; shouts, 294, 298, 306; social, 297; sociological study of texts of, 159, 160; spirituals, 292-294, 297; texts, 159; transmigration and transmission of, 164; of Trinidad, 294; of Venezuela, 294; white spirituals, 163; about women, 163; work, 160, 163, 291, 293, 294, 297, 306
Free Library of Philadelphia, 380
Fuld, James J., Private Collection, 373

Genealogy: burial records, A8; census returns, A8; deeds, A8; guide to, 11; local research, A7; probate records, A8; societies and agencies, A1; vital records, A7, A8; wills, A8
Georgia Historical Society, 351
Gospel music: bibliographies of, 44, 50; development of, 225; discographies of, 77; recordings of, 61, 70, 82; songs, 301

Hackley, E. Azalia, Collection, 364
Hampton Institute: Archives, 387; Peabody Collection, 388
Handy, W. C., Museum, 339
Harlem Renaissance: holdings, 13; music of the, 143
Harvard College Library: Harvard Theatre Collection, 363
Hatch-Billops Collection, 374

Indiana University: Archives of Traditional Music, 354; Black Music Collection, 355; Folklore Archives/Folklore Institute, 356
Institute of Jazz Studies, 369
Instruments: literature on, 92; their roles in jazz, 197
Interviewing: guide to, A5
Interviews: with musicians, 248, 258, 260, 284, 287

Jasen, David A., Private Collection, 372
Jazz: and aesthetic values, 208; African survivals in, 190; analysis, 45, 195, 211, 214, 284; anthologies of printed music, 13, 45, 110; appreciation, criteria for, 274; arrangements, 110; articulation, 279; and atonal techniques, 192; and aural perception, 215; bebop, 198; big bands, 209, 216; biographical studies, 284; and black nationalism, 207; and black revolution, 207; and the black underground, 215; blindfold test, 116; censorship and, 208; and the classics, 51; the Clef Club, 196; Clef Club orchestras, 209; clubs, 207; commercial, 208; compositions, bibliographies of, 48, 110; criticism, 51, 205, 207, 208, 222; critics, names and addresses of, 47; dance, 217; dance band techniques, 281; definitions, 189, 274, 275; development of, 219; discographical studies,

319; gospel songs, 327; Harlem piano style, 335; harp instrumentals, 324; hollers, 321, 323, 330; jug bands, 320; long-meter hymn singing, 328; military music, 335; miscellaneous folk songs, 326; miscellaneous piano pieces, 337; music for chorus and orchestra, 338; orchestral music, 338; "original blues," 330; ragtime music, 335; "religious parallels to the blues," 330; religious songs, 321; sanctified singing, 328; Sea Island spirituals, 326; sermons and sermons-with-singing, 328; shake-downs, 320; shouts, 325; social dance music, 337; spirituals, 325; stomps, 320; street bands, 324; street cries, 335; symphonic music, 338; vocal music with orchestra, 338; work songs, 322, 323, 325, 330; xylophone instrumentals, 324

Recordings, listings of: American music, 101; ballads, 60; blues, 13, 60, 61, 70, 82, 180; bootlegs, 76, 80; children's songs, 61; game and rhyme songs, 41, 60; jazz, 68; jazz/rock fusion, 78; jokes, 62; lieder, 13; lyric songs, 41; operas, 13; piano and organ solos, 70; private releases, 76; race records, 139; ragtime, 66, 176; reggae, 78, 82; religious music, 73; rhythm & blues, 61, 82; "rhythm" orchestras, 81; sermons and services, 61; shouts, 61; soul music, 82; soundtracks of musicals, 124; spirituals, 60, 61, 70, 84; unissued, 73, 76; washboard bands, 61; work songs, 60, 61

Religious: denominations, 145; liturgy, 92; organizations, 145

Religious music: African survivals in, 226; gospel, 301; jubilee songs, 226; origins and development of, 226; sacred-harp songs, 305; spirituals, 301

Reprints of books: guide to, A3

Reviews of: books, 284, 285, 287, A21; compositions, 287; dissertations, 287; musicians, 247; operas, A21; periodicals, 287; recordings, 94, 97, 98, 284, 285, 287, A21

Revues: bibliographies of, 32

Rhythm & blues: bibliographies of, 50; business aspects of, 239; discographies of, 63; doo-wop groups, 233; economic aspects of, 239; musicians in films, 125; rock and, 238; singers, 240; survey of, 239

Rutgers University: Institute of Jazz Studies, 369


Schomburg Center for Research in Black Culture, 378

Scores: listed in dictionary catalogues, 12, 13, 20, 22

Sheet music: black images in, 230; copyright, 9; copyright registration, 9; covers, 178, 308; dating, design, editions, 9; indexes of, 99; listed in dictionary catalogues, 12, 13, 16, A11, A12; lists of ragtime, 176; plate numbers, printing practice, publishers addresses, 9; social dance, 99

Singers: biographies of folk, 158; classic blues, 240, 255; jazz and popular, 240; phonophotography of folk, 160; recordings of, 86

Singing: dialect in, 10; doo-wop groups, 233, 234; falsetto in, 10; literature on, 92; ornamentation in, 10; sanctified, 161; voice patterns in, 10

Slang: black American, 117, 118, 135, 193, 208; onomatopoeia and pig latin, 135

Slaves: interviews with, 152

Social dance music: See Recordings

Societies: historical, A1

Sojourner Truth Collection, 361

Song books: lists of, 104, 105, 107

Songs: Afro-American, 164; art, 102, 317; carry-me-backs, 230; children's, 41, 290; of the civil rights movement, 288; comic, 230; composers of, 55, 251; coon, 230, 243; Creole, 41, 161; of derision, 230; of emancipation,

300; in films, 227, 242; of freedom, 288; gospel, 301; hit, 83, 120, 121, 122, 126; from Hollywood musicals, 55, 124; in the military, 295; minstrel, 292, 294; from movie musicals, 242; from musicals, 55, 227, 229; plantation, 290; popular, discussions of, 227, 230; popular, indexes and lists of, 104, 105, 109, 227, 229, 232; of protest, 288, 289; pseudo-spirituals, 230; religious, 226; sacred harp, 305; sentimental, 230; slave, 157; social, 41; work, 41; writers, 229
Soul: history of, 233
Soul music: and the blues, 235; discography of, 240
Southern Baptist Theological Seminary, 358
Spirituals: African origins of, 168; Afro-American history in, 166; analysis of, 303; arrangers of, 251; bibliographies of, 33, 41, 57, 303; collections of, 169, 170, 171, 302; country, 161; dialect in, 306; discographies of, 41, 63; discussions of, 153; the Fisk Jubilee Singers and, 169, 170, 171; historical significance of, 306; indexes of, 107; interpretation of, 165, 304; lists of, 100; in literary fiction and literary meaning in, 168; in radio, motion pictures, and stage works, 168; origins of, 166, 306; performance practice, 304; pseudo-, 230; in slave life, 166; and southern white mythology of slavery, 307; transformation in, 168; white-origins theory and, 163, 167; white-origins theory attacked, 168; writings about, 156
Symbols: in dance band charts, 281
Symphonic music: bibliography of blacks in, 33


Teaching: See Curriculum
Terminology: black music, 112; contemporary musical, 111; dance band, 281; See also Slang
Texas Southern University: The Heartman Collection, 386
Textbooks: black music discussed in, 138
Theses and dissertations: bibliographies of, 36, 40, 50
Tichenor Ragtime Collection, 366
Tuskegee Institute Archives, 340


University of California, Los Angeles Music Library, 344


Vital records: for genealogical and biographical research, A7


Washington University, Gaylord Music Library: Ernst C. Krohn Musicological Library, George C. Krich Collection for the Classical Guitar, 367
Women: in bands and orchestras, 250; composers, 251; in entertainment, 253; in jazz, 250
Writing: research papers and theses, style in, 7


Yale University Library: Beinecke Rare Book and Manuscript Library, 345; J. Rosamund Johnson Archives, 346; School of Music, Duke Ellington Oral History, Robert Neff and Anthony Conner Blues Collection, 347